EVANGELISM RENEWED

Evangelism Renewed

~

The Theological Revisioning of Evangelism

HENRY H. KNIGHT III

CASCADE *Books* · Eugene, Oregon

EVANGELISM RENEWED
The Theological Revisioning of Evangelism

Copyright © 2025 Henry H. Knight III. All rights reserved. Except for brief quotations in critical publications or reviews, no part of this book may be reproduced in any manner without prior written permission from the publisher. Write: Permissions, Wipf and Stock Publishers, 199 W. 8th Ave., Suite 3, Eugene, OR 97401.

Cascade Books
An Imprint of Wipf and Stock Publishers
199 W. 8th Ave., Suite 3
Eugene, OR 97401

www.wipfandstock.com

PAPERBACK ISBN: 979-8-3852-1534-8
HARDCOVER ISBN: 979-8-3852-1535-5
EBOOK ISBN: 979-8-3852-1536-2

Cataloguing-in-Publication data:

Names: Knight, Henry H., III, author.

Title: Evangelism renewed : the theological revisioning of evangelism / Henry H. Knight III.

Description: Eugene, OR: Cascade Books, 2025 | Includes bibliographical references.

Identifiers: ISBN 979-8-3852-1534-8 (paperback) | ISBN 979-8-3852-1535-5 (hardcover) | ISBN 979-8-3852-1536-2 (ebook)

Subjects: LCSH: Evangelistic work—Philosophy | Theology

Classification: BV3790 K35 2025 (paperback) | BV3790 (ebook)

VERSION NUMBER 04/07/25

Scriptures taken from the New Revised Standard Version Bible, copyright © 1989 the Division of Christian Education of the National Council of the Churches of Christ in the United States of America. Used by permission. All rights reserved.

This book is dedicated to *The Foundation for Evangelism*, created in 1949 by Harry Denman to enable Methodists to "diffuse the blessings of the gospel of the Lord Jesus Christ," and to three persons in particular:

Paul Ervin, whose vision and tireless work established evangelism professorships in Methodist seminaries in America and across the world,

Stephen Gunter, who has graciously shared his wisdom as a mentor to so many of those professors, and

Jane Boatwright Wood, who has led the foundation into the future as it supports local churches and leaders in evangelism throughout the Wesleyan family.

Contents

Acknowledgments ix
Introduction 1

PART ONE: THEOLOGICAL FOUNDATIONS
1. The Nature of Evangelism 9
2. Mission and Evangelism 20

PART TWO: ANNOUNCING GOOD NEWS
3. The Message Proclaimed 33
4. Sharing the Faith 44

PART THREE: BRINGING GOOD NEWS
5. Word and Deed 63
6. Evangelism with Power 83

PART FOUR: KINGDOM AND COMMUNITY
7. Evangelistic Community 101
8. Evangelism as Initiation 124

PART FIVE: LEARNING FROM TRADITION
9. A Cloud of Witnesses 143
10. Heirs of the Protestant Reformation 163
11. Wesleyan Ways of Evangelism 175
12. Evangelism in a Religiously Pluralistic World 194

Conclusion 205
Bibliography 209

Acknowledgments

THANKS FIRST GOES TO three decades of students in my evangelism classes. The hesitation of some about the practice of evangelism as they understood it underscores the continued need to make known the sorts of theologies and practices advocated by the authors discussed in this book. The warm reception and glad appropriation for their own ministries of these theologically informed evangelism texts indicates their value. The many conversations I have had with students over these years have enabled me to understand and analyze these theologies of evangelism with greater depth and insight.

I give special thanks to Suzanne Werthmann for typing the bulk of this manuscript from my handwritten notes. Her diligence and dedication have enabled this project to be completed much faster than my poor typing skills would have.

I am grateful to Wipf and Stock for agreeing to publish this book and for their always careful editorial work.

Finally, I celebrate the authors I have surveyed in this book for all they have done for the gospel of Jesus Christ. I hope what I have written here will make more persons aware of their work so they can read it in its entirety and draw upon it to share the good news with integrity and passion.

Introduction

> O for a thousand tongues to sing
> My dear Redeemer's praise!
> The glories of my God and King,
> The triumphs of his grace!
>
> —CHARLES WESLEY[1]

EVANGELISM IS BEING RE-ENVISIONED. An array of new forms of evangelism has emerged in recent decades that are less individualistic and more communal, less formulaic and more relational, not just conveying information about God but promising transformation by God. Most importantly these newer approaches understand the heart of the good news to be about the love of God in Jesus Christ and the promise of new life in the present as well as the age to come.

What is fueling this evangelism renaissance is theological reflection. To think prayerfully and deeply about evangelism in relation to the triune God, church, mission, and the kingdom of God reframes and transforms it. It allows the story of God to decisively shape evangelistic theory and practice.

I call this an evangelism renaissance because these new forms of evangelism are as much retrievals of past wisdom as proposals for innovation. Either explicitly or implicitly they draw from past spiritualities and religious awakenings while at the same time utilizing contemporary insights and addressing an increasingly postmodern context.

---

1. Wesley, *Collection of Hymns*, 79.

Introduction

This book is a celebration of these theologies of evangelism. It presents over two dozen and highlights their contributions, providing comparative analysis as well. As we will see, they are not all alike and differ among themselves over what constitutes evangelism. I see this as a strength, not a weakness. In my teaching theologies of evangelism for three decades I have invited my students not just to assess strengths and weaknesses but to also see the various theologies as angles of vision, each telling us something essential about the nature and practice of evangelism. That is what I invite you to do as well.

I have termed these newer proposals theologies of evangelism, and most are explicitly that. But in some cases, I will be discussing approaches to evangelism in which the theological influences have been kept largely in the background. For these I will try to make theologically explicit what is implicit. My use of the term *theologies of evangelism* will at times be stretched to include these as well.

While I will be discussing a diverse array of theologies of evangelism there are some limitations that should be noted. The exemplars have all come from the Protestant branch of the Christian family, so the significant Roman Catholic and distinctive Eastern Orthodox contributions are not considered. Also, the book has a Western, even American focus, with only a couple of representatives from the Majority World where arguably the most vigorous evangelistic ministries are occurring. That said, there is a great variety of both approaches and proponents in these chapters.

This is not the only comparative study of evangelism. Frances S. Adeney compares seven contemporary theologies of evangelism in her book *Graceful Evangelism*.[2] Priscilla Pope-Levison provides an invaluable survey of eight models of evangelism in her book by that title.[3] My approach is quite different from theirs, and the specific theologies of evangelism I discuss at most overlap those they present. I see this book as distinctive from and complementary to what they have written.

A Matter of Terminology

Readers of the literature on evangelism in the English language will consistently encounter two terms: *evangelism* itself, and *evangelization*. David Barrett argues that the two "are not exact synonyms." Evangelism, he says,

2. Adeney, *Graceful Evangelism*.
3. Pope-Levison, *Models*.

Introduction

has to do with "human evangelistic activity" while evangelization is broader, referring to both human and divine activity "as well as the overall situation and status produced by such activities."[4] Yet Barrett's proposal does not reflect actual usage. Rather than utilizing both terms in different ways, major segments of the Christian world seem to choose one or the other as their preferred way to speak of evangelism.

The ecumenical movement, dominated by mainline Protestants, uses the term *evangelism* in documents of the World Council of Churches when it appears at all. More common are words like *witness* and *mission* which point to a holistic evangelism of word and deed that addresses both persons and sociopolitical structures.[5]

Since the publication of *Evangelii Nuntiandi* ("On Evangelization in the Modern World") by Pope Paul VI in 1975 the term *evangelization* has become pervasive in Roman Catholic writings in English. The processive connotations and Latin rootage of the word are possible reasons for choosing it over *evangelism*, which is associated in popular Protestantism with revivals and decisions. Evangelization is understood holistically to include not only verbal proclamation but the "witness of life," and its goal is "the renewal of humanity in all its aspects, both individual and collective."[6]

Protestant evangelicals use both *evangelism* and *evangelization* in their ecumenical statements. While frequently synonymous, evangelization does take on the connotation of both the process of spreading the gospel throughout the world and the name for that process. This is reflected in the name of the Lausanne Committee for World Evangelization, which is the chief cooperative missional arm of global evangelicalism. Yet within the Lausanne Covenant the term *evangelism* is continually used to describe the practice of spreading good news.[7]

As we will see, the persons surveyed in this volume differ on which term they prefer. I will try to represent their preference in my discussion of their work. As for myself, I will normally use the term *evangelism*, saving *evangelization* for specific reference to a process of evangelism.

---

4. Barrett, *Evangelize!*, 78.
5. Pope-Levison, "Evangelism in the WCC," 127–28.
6. Schreiter, "Changes in Roman Catholic Attitudes," 122.
7. "Lausanne Covenant," 235–39.

Introduction

A Note on the Great Commission

Many advocates of world evangelization find their basic motivation in the Great Commission given by the risen Jesus to his disciples at the end of Matthew's Gospel. Some of the authors we will examine do the same. While it is often assumed that this passage has always been the impetus for evangelism, it in fact did not come into prominence in Christian thinking until the nineteenth century.

The reason is that for most of church history the passage was interpreted as applying only to the apostles in the early church. As James Logan has noted, the major Protestant "reformers did not view it as binding, claiming that it had been delivered to the Apostles and fulfilled by them."[8] It was the Anabaptist wing of the Reformation that first emphasized the Great Commission as binding on all Christians, and William Carey who in 1792 refuted the traditional interpretation and made the Great Commission the foundation for the missionary movement.[9] That the appeal to the Great Commission is a relatively late occurrence does not mean it is not applicable to us today—I believe that it is. What it does mean is that it is not the only motive for evangelism.

The eighteenth-century awakening was one of the most significant evangelistic events in church history, but none of the leaders cited the Great Commission as the basis of their work. For example, as James Logan has shown, John and Charles Wesley believed there was an imperative to share the good news, but for them it was rooted in the "trinitarian action of the Father sending Christ and the Spirit," that is, "in the very being of God."[10]

What then is the motivation? If the Great Commission is the ground for evangelism, then the motivation is obedience to Christ's command. While not appealing to the Great Commission, eighteenth-century awakening leaders like the Wesleys were aware of other biblical commands to share the gospel, as well as the example of Jesus and the apostles who did so. But I believe their root motive was not obedience but love—God's love for us in Jesus Christ, and our love for God and neighbor in return. One can obey even if one does not want to do something (or not obey and live with the guilt). But the early apostles and the Wesleys and their colleagues were passionate about sharing the good news, even to the point of risking

---

8. Logan, "Evangelical Imperative," 21.
9. Logan, "Evangelical Imperative," 21.
10. Logan, "Evangelical Imperative," 22–23.

their lives. That can only come from encountering a divine love that was wonderful beyond measure.

One further note: there is not simply one commissioning statement in the New Testament but four: Matt 18:18–20, Luke 24:44–49, John 20:21–23, and Acts 1:8. In addition, both the shorter and longer endings of Mark, though not part of the original text, have commissioning statements.

Mortimer Arias and Alan Johnson have analyzed each commission statement in the four Gospels in light of the entire gospel itself. In doing so, they implicitly show the intrinsic connection between proclamation and a wide array of actions both within and outside the church. For example, in the Great Commission in Matthew, Jesus tells the disciples to teach new disciples "to obey everything I have commanded you." To find out what this "everything" is one must examine the Gospel as a whole. What they discover is the obedience to Jesus' teachings about the kingdom of heaven "entails justice—in persons, communities, and nations."[11] It is to take up one's cross and follow Jesus, and to serve Jesus in and through "the least of these" (Matt 25:40). To obey the Great Commission is to proclaim the gospel of the kingdom, "a kingdom that comes to us in Jesus Christ, that takes the face of our neighbor and the form of love and justice."[12]

What Lies Ahead

Terms like *evangelism, evangelization,* and even *the Great Commission* take on different definitions according to the theology and practice of their proponents. We shall see this in the chapters that lie ahead.

We begin in part 1 with some theological foundations. In chapter 1 we examine the nature of evangelism. We will also take a brief, initial look at some of the definitions of evangelism we will encounter in later chapters. Chapter 2 explores the nature of God's mission in the world and the relationship between evangelism and mission.

Part 2 begins the presentation of particular theologies of evangelism by focusing on those who understand it as announcing the good news. Chapter 3 looks at evangelism as proclamation, while chapter 4 focuses on personal evangelism, or faith sharing.

Part 3 includes those who insist that evangelism not only consists of words but also actions. Chapter 5 includes advocates of evangelism

---

11. Arias and Johnson, *Great Commission*, 25.
12. Arias and Johnson, *Great Commission*, 27.

Introduction

including social action, while chapter 6 considers persons who argue it also includes signs and wonders.

Part 4 examines those who broaden evangelism to include a strong communal aspect. The approaches in chapter 7 understand in varied ways that the community is itself an evangelistic witness. Those in chapter 8 see evangelism as a form of initiation into the community, or into the kingdom of God by way of the community.

Part 5 covers highly diverse understandings of evangelism recovered from the Christian tradition. Those in chapter 9 draw more broadly from the tradition; in chapter 10, from the Reformation heritage as found in Lutheran and Reformed traditions; and chapter 11, from Wesleyanism. Chapter 12 examines the issue of evangelism and other religions, revisiting some of the authors presented in earlier chapters.

The conclusion summarizes themes throughout the book that demonstrate that this evangelism renaissance does indeed proclaim good news to all.

PART ONE
Theological Foundations

CHAPTER 1

The Nature of Evangelism

> Preaching... signals to society that a new order has come. It is eschatological in nature. It is powerful in its effect.... The Gospel is not good news unless it can be seen to create a new humanity in the earth.
>
> —WILLIAM PANNELL[1]

FROM THE BEGINNING CHRISTIANS have understood themselves to be the recipients of good news. At the heart of the good news is the victory of God over evil, sin, and death through Jesus Christ. The proclamation that the crucified Jesus is now risen and alive offered hearers forgiveness of sins and a new life through the power of the Holy Spirit. But more than this, it announced the beginning of a new age—in which the reign of God had broken into history and new communities were formed by the Spirit—and the promise that creation itself would ultimately be renewed by the love of God.

Is it any wonder the earliest Christians found themselves compelled to share this good news with others?

The New Testament itself is filled with language about sharing the good news. Chief among the terms used are those from which we derive the English word *evangelism*: the noun *euangelion* (meaning good news, or the "gospel") and the verb *euangelizo* (to proclaim or announce the good news). According to David Barrett, *euangelion* occurs seventy-six times in

---

1. Pannell, *Evangelism from the Bottom Up*, 98, 100.

Part One: Theological Foundations

seventeen of the twenty-seven books of the New Testament and *euangelizo* fifty-six times in twelve books. In addition, the noun *euangelistes* (evangelist) occurs three times, in Acts 21:8, Eph 4:11, and 2 Tim 4:5.[2]

Generally speaking, the noun *euangelion* is used by Matthew and Mark, who frequently link it with *keruso* (to preach), while Luke almost always uses the verb form. Paul uses both, while neither is found in the Johannine literature—there the preferred terms are *marturein* (to bear witness) and *marturia* (witness). In addition, Barrett's study shows there are a multitude of other terms used in the New Testament as synonyms for evangelism, the most frequent of which is *lalein* (to speak).[3]

Yet if the early church was passionate about sharing this good news, as the New Testament indicates, that can hardly be said of many local churches in America today. The reasons are no doubt complex. Some might point to changes in Western culture, both modern and postmodern, but the early church was in a culture that was arguably more resistant to their message. I believe the fundamental problem lies in Western Christianity itself and is twofold: we have settled for an impoverished understanding of salvation and a diminished understanding of God. To put it differently, our problem is theological, and weak theology has in turn undermined evangelism.

An Impoverished Salvation

Let's begin with the first. We have an impoverished understanding of salvation when we reduce it to something far less than what is promised in the New Testament. If we say that at a minimum salvation means receiving a transformed heart and life through Jesus Christ, then there are many in churches who have neither experienced nor expect or even desire such a new life. This is not a new problem—it has plagued the church throughout its history. Monastics, reformers, and pietists have called again and again for the renewal of the church or have created alternative communities in which they could live out a more authentic Christian life. Left unrenewed, it is understandable that persons and churches would lack a desire to share the good news of Jesus Christ, for their own experience and life seems neither as good nor as newsy as it does in the New Testament.

There are, I believe, two common misunderstandings within the church that keep us from the fullness of life that God promises. The first

2. Barrett, *Evangelize!*, 11.
3. Barrett, *Evangelize!*, 15.

is the belief that most of us are basically good enough that a loving and merciful God will let us into heaven. The idea that we have to be good to go to heaven is pervasive in our culture. It is a common assumption in music and movies, among Christians and non-Christians alike. Moreover, most people in American culture think being good enough is fairly easy. If one is a mass murderer, many believe the case is hopeless—God would never forgive such a person. But most of us are not mass murderers. We may not be perfect, but we are good enough to make the cut.

The form this often takes is "Moralistic Therapeutic Deism," a term coined by Christian Smith and Melinda Denton. Its guiding beliefs, as outlined by Kenda Creasy Dean, are these:

1. A god exists who created and orders the world and watches over life on earth.
2. God wants people to be good, nice, and fair to each other, as taught in the Bible and by most world religions.
3. The central goal of life is to be happy and to feel good about oneself.
4. God is not involved in my life except when I need God to resolve a problem.
5. Good people go to heaven when they die.[4]

One can contrast this with, say, the Apostles' or Nicene Creed to see how far this has veered from basic Christianity. Smith, Denton, and Dean believe that "Moralistic Therapeutic Deism is supplanting Christianity as the dominant religion in the United States."[5]

The second misunderstanding is often portrayed as the opposite of this moralism lite approach. Dallas Willard has called this a "bar-code faith." The analogy is with how the scanner in checkout lines reads the barcodes on products. If you put the barcode for ice cream on a sack of dog food, the scanner will read "ice cream"—the actual content of the package is irrelevant.

A "barcode faith" operates much the same way. We take some action— we have faith, get baptized—and that gives us a new barcode. God then pays no attention to our actual sinful content. When we are scanned, it reads "Christ's righteousness." We remain the same, only now we are forgiven

---

4. Dean, *Almost Christian*, 14.
5. Dean, *Almost Christian*, 14.

and going to heaven. As Willard says, our present life "has no necessary connection with being a Christian as long as the 'bar code' does its job."[6]

Although they seem to be opposites, these two misunderstandings share common assumptions. The first is they believe salvation is largely about a happy afterlife. They affect only minimally life in the present, requiring us to do just enough to qualify for heaven. Anything more is experienced as an unnecessary burden, an imposition that stands in the way of living what our culture deems a normal and fulfilling life. In their own focus on going to heaven they entirely miss the emphasis on salvation as receiving a new life in Christ in the present. Their requirement to do just enough to get into heaven undercuts growth in the Christian life and makes sanctification and discipleship something additional rather than the content of salvation.

A second common assumption is that salvation is only about individuals. This misses the emphasis on community throughout the New Testament. God's salvific goal is to form persons into communities that, in their life together, witness to the reality of the new creation begun with the resurrection of Jesus to be brought into fullness at his return.

And all this leads, finally, to their missing God's ultimate goal to renew the entire creation. Salvation not only happens *in* the world, it happens *to* the world. The world matters to God in a way that is hard to recognize when salvation is seen as primarily about leaving this world behind.

These two misunderstandings are not totally new—they have been around in one form or another through much of church history. John Wesley faced versions of both in the eighteenth century.

Wesley found the first, which he called formalism, to be common in his own Church of England. He described what many understood to be the characteristics of a good Christian in this way:

> By a religious man is commonly meant, one that is honest, just and fair in his dealings; that is constantly at church and sacrament; and that gives much alms, or (as it is usually termed) does much good.[7]

Those persons, then, who were honest, attended church regularly, and gave to the church had done enough to go to heaven when they died.

---

6. Willard, *Divine Conspiracy*, 37.
7. Wesley, *Journals*, Nov. 25, 1739, 123.

The second misunderstanding was called antinomianism, which claimed that because those who are justified are clothed in the righteousness of Christ, they no longer need to be righteous themselves. Those in the religious awakening who preached this offered forgiveness without new life. Wesley said, let a preacher "bawl out something about Christ, or his blood, or justification by faith, and his hearers cry out, 'what a fine Gospel sermon!' Surely the Methodists have not so learned Christ! We know no gospel without salvation from sin."[8]

Speaking about formalism but applicable to antinomianism as well, Wesley proclaims

> that there is a better religion to be attained, a religion worthy of God that gave it. And this we conceived to be no other than love: the love of God and all mankind; the loving God with all our heart and soul and strength, as having first loved us, as the fountain of all the good we have received, and of all we ever hope to enjoy; and the loving every soul which God hath made . . . as our own soul.[9]

"Wherever this is," Wesley says, "virtue and happiness" go "hand and hand." This religion has its seat "in the heart" but shows itself "by its fruits, continually springing forth," not only in doing no harm but in doing good to all.[10] In other writings Wesley extends this vision of love as the heart of salvation to the renewed church and to renewed creation. To miss this promise of renewal in love is to miss salvation itself.

A Diminished God

The second fundamental problem is a diminished understanding of God. We can see this at work in both moralistic therapeutic deism and the barcode faith. The first has a vague and distant God, the second depends on a single divine action in the past that allows us to escape an unhappy eternity with minimal alterations in our lives. What is so striking about both is that the focus is resolutely on us—on our eternal destiny. God is only involved minimally, just enough to provide us a good afterlife.

---

8. Wesley, "Letter to Miss Bishop," Oct. 18, 1778, in *Works*, ed. Jackson, 13:36.

9. Wesley, "An Earnest Appeal to Men of Reason and Religion," in *Appeals to Men*, 45–46.

10. Wesley, "An Earnest Appeal to Men of Reason and Religion," in *Appeals to Men*, 45–46.

Part One: Theological Foundations

The focus of Scripture is on God. There is the larger story of God's work from creation to new creation, and from Israel to the church. At the heart of that story is Jesus Christ. As N. T. Wright says, the ultimate goal of God is for all of creation to be filled with the glory of God. But the way to that goal "is through the outpouring of his love in Jesus and in the Spirit." What Jesus reveals is "the good news that the one true God is the God of utter, self-giving love."[11] The reign of God, which has already begun but is yet to come in fullness, consists in the renewal of humanity and all of creation in that love.

We can say, then, that the good news has both a soteriological and doxological dimension. Soteriologically it is about salvation, the announcement that human hearts and lives can be renewed in love, that relationships can be healed, and communities formed that both witness to this love in their life together and reach out to share this love through words and actions with others. Doxologically the good news evokes praise and thanksgiving to God for who God is and what God has done.

If the good news is centered on the victory of God's love then it is clear many twentieth-century forms of evangelism have been deficient at best. They have been too individualistic, too formulaic, too focused only on the life to come, too focused on us. There was an urgent need for evangelism with theological depth. Until recently one would have to go back to the eighteenth century—to John Wesley and Jonathan Edwards—to find robust theological reflection on evangelism (although neither called it by that name). Theologians since that time have largely ignored evangelism.

William Abraham, writing in 1989, said that "one of the undeniable features of modern theology is the scant attention it has given to the topic of evangelism. It is virtually impossible to find a critical, in-depth study of the subject by a major theologian."[12] Instead evangelism is seen "as a minor motif within practical theology," a field "construed as a rag-bag of bits and pieces on how to minister in the church."[13]

Abraham notes a number of reasons for this neglect.[14] Among these is the historic dominance of Christianity in the West (thus making evangelism seemingly unnecessary); that evangelism is seen by the scholarly community "as a sectarian issue that requires the kind of prior faith commitments

---

11. Wright, *Simply Good News*, 139.
12. Abraham, *Logic of Evangelism*, 1.
13. Abraham, *Logic of Evangelism*, 5.
14. Abraham, *Logic of Evangelism*, 2–10.

The Nature of Evangelism

that are out of place in a serious academic environment";[15] that other issues, from social action to the intellectual viability of any theological claim in the modern world, have seemed more crucial; and the poor image of mass evangelists in contemporary culture. Many evangelists, for their part, have been impatient with theological reflection and anxious to get on with the work of evangelism.

Likewise, Orlando Costas, writing before his untimely death in 1987, saw as "unfortunate that these two complementary ministries"—theology and evangelization—"have been viewed as adversaries rather than partners." While "theologians say relatively little about evangelization," and "evangelists have a hard time seeing the relevance of theology for their task," the two are actually interrelated. "Without theology the church" is "unable to understand itself or its message and mission in the world. . . . Without evangelization, theology is reduced to an academic, abstract, and exclusive intellectual exercise of little service to a faith that is inherently open and oriented to the world."[16]

The books by Abraham and Costas were among the first that sought to remedy this situation. They are full-scale theologies of evangelism. There were, to be sure, earlier attempts at theologies of evangelism by Julian N. Hartt, Edwin Lewis, and Albert C. Outler.[17] But these were limited both in the issues addressed and (with possible exception of Outler) their impact on the church.

What we now have is an abundance of theologies of evangelism brimming with analysis and insight that enables the practice of evangelism to have integrity and faithfulness at a deep level. They seek to answer questions about the nature of evangelism and why we do it, as well as address a range of issues around contextualization, pluralism, postmodernism, and the like. Above all they seek to deepen our understanding of the promise of salvation and to focus our attention on God. While we can't cover them all, examining a significant number of these theologies of evangelism is at the heart of this book.

---

15. Abraham, *Logic of Evangelism*, 5.
16. Costas, *Liberating News*, 1–2.
17. Hartt, *Toward a Theology of Evangelism*; Lewis, *Theology and Evangelism*; Outler, *Evangelism and Theology*.

Part One: Theological Foundations

What Constitutes Evangelism?

We have seen that the noun *euangelion* is often linked to the word *preach* in the New Testament. Likewise, the verb *euangelizo* is seldom translated "evangelize" but by a range of other words, the most common being "preach," "bring," "tell," "proclaim," "announce," and "declare" good news.[18] It would seem from these and other terms used to describe evangelism that it is essentially the activity of proclaiming the gospel, especially to those who have never heard it. This is certainly the consensus of most who write about evangelism.

Yet evangelism is a contested term. Competing definitions have been offered throughout the twentieth century, and over that time they have only grown more diverse. The result has been three broad approaches to defining evangelism: (1) Definitions that nuance proclamation in terms of its effectiveness in leading to genuine conversion; (2) Definitions that make evangelism more holistic by attending to the content of the proclamation or adding deeds and signs to proclamation; and (3) Definitions that decenter proclamation and define evangelism in terms of initiation or the church.

The question of effectiveness was the earliest source of debate, centered initially on the relation of evangelism and conversion. Barrett's 1987 survey showed there were two ways of construing the relationship. Biblical dictionaries consistently defined evangelism as announcing or proclaiming good news, while English language dictionaries since 1850 have included a second definition: "to win or convert persons to the Christian faith."[19]

The impetus to define evangelism as winning converts was considerably strengthened by the highly influential "classic" definition published by the Church of England in 1918.

> To evangelize is so to present Christ Jesus in the power of the Holy Spirit, that men shall come to put their trust in God through Him, to accept Him as their Saviour, and serve Him as their King in the fellowship of His Church.[20]

While adopted as a model definition by many, some altered it by replacing "shall" with "may," indicating faithful evangelism does not always produce conversions.

---

18. Barrett, *Evangelize!*, 18.
19. Barrett, *Evangelize!*, 77.
20. Barrett, *Evangelize!*, 37.

The Nature of Evangelism

Significant issues were at stake for proponents of both understandings. Those defending the "may" position insisted that conversion is solely a work of the Holy Spirit—we do not convert anyone. Reformed theologian J. I. Packer argues that while evangelism is our work, "the giving of faith is God's." "Evangelism," he says, "is just preaching the gospel," hence "we ought not define evangelism in terms of achieved results."[21]

Likewise, Wesleyans H. Eddie Fox and George E. Morris insist "evangelizing is not something we do *to* people but something we do *with* the gospel." The results of our evangelism, no matter how carefully and prayerfully planned, remains in "God's hands."[22] They cite Luke's report that it was "the Lord," who "added to their number those who were being saved" (Acts 2:47). On this point they could also cite John Wesley and Jonathan Edwards.

To define evangelism this way places the emphasis on faithfulness in sharing the gospel rather than in the number of converts. It removes the temptation to manipulate hearers in order to produce converts, and respects both the freedom of hearers and the freedom of God.

Yet the decoupling of evangelism and conversion leaves many uneasy. Darius Salter wonders how the effectiveness of evangelism can be evaluated if it is understood apart from its results. Effective evangelism should evoke a positive response, and if no one responds it raises questions about whether the proclaimer is sufficiently open to God or insensitive to the hearer's context.[23]

One way to define evangelism to invite evaluation of its effectiveness is to see it as persuasive proclamation. Persuasion has biblical roots: Peter on the day of Pentecost "testified with many other arguments and exhorted them" (Acts 2:40) and Paul "argued persuasively about the kingdom of God" in the synagogue in Ephesus (Acts 19:8). Thus, Donald A. McGavran and Winfield C. Arn say that evangelism is "to proclaim Jesus Christ as God and Savior; to persuade people to become his disciples and responsible members of his church."[24]

Of course, a major question underlying this entire debate is the meaning of conversion. We have seen earlier in this chapter the various ways the gospel can be domesticated, and persons can in effect be Christians in

---

21. Packer, *Evangelism and the Sovereignty of God*, 40–41.
22. Fox and Morris, *Faith-Sharing*, 54.
23. Salter, *American Evangelism*, 23–24.
24. McGavran and Arn, *Ten Steps*, 51.

name only. Evangelism only has integrity if it envisions conversion in terms such as new life in Christ, regeneration, sanctification, discipleship, or as entering into a new way of life, new community, or the kingdom of God. It is this concern that drives many of the newer theologies of evangelism.

A second issue is whether proclamation alone is a sufficient definition of evangelism. Should good news also be demonstrated as well as announced? We see the linkage between proclamation and action in the passage read by Jesus to the synagogue in Nazareth: "The Spirit of the Lord is upon me, because he has anointed me to bring good news to the poor. He has sent me to proclaim release to the captives, and recovery of sight to the blind, to let the oppressed go free, to proclaim the year of the Lord's favor" (Luke 4:18–19). Jesus' ministry was indeed one of both "proclaiming and bringing the good news of the kingdom of God" (Luke 8:1), involving preaching, teaching, healing, casting out demons, confronting injustice, forgiving sins, and caring for the poor and marginalized.

These same actions marked the evangelistic activity of the early church as depicted in Acts. It is also found in Paul's description of his own ministry to the gentiles, "by word and deed, by the power of signs and wonders, by the power of the Spirit of God so that from Jerusalem and as far as Illyricum I have fully proclaimed the good news of Christ" (Rom 15:18–19).

This leads David Watson to argue "that the proclamation of good news was linked directly with a *demonstration* of that good news. Jesus was sent by his Father to the world not merely to conduct a preaching tour, but to show the reality of the living God in a way that powerfully met the personal needs of people."[25] Jesus did this through many diverse acts of compassion, including miraculous signs and wonders. In light of this Watson insists that "unless there is a demonstration of the power of the Spirit, the proclamation of the gospel will be in vain. It will not be evangelism."[26]

Similarly, Fox and Morris define evangelization as "the process of spreading the gospel of the kingdom of God by *word, deed, and sign* in various contexts, through the power of the Holy Spirit, and then waiting in respectful humility and working with expectant hope."[27] Word interprets the deed, and the enacted deed shows the integrity of the word. Hence, proclamation "must run concurrently with ministries of healing, serving,

---

25. Watson, *I Believe*, 27.
26. Watson, *I Believe*, 30.
27. Fox and Morris, *Faith-Sharing*, 55.

nurturing, liberating, reforming, and empowering."[28] Signs are also essential to evangelism, including art, sacramental signs, and "signs and wonders" such as healing.

A third issue is whether something other than proclamation should define evangelism. Proponents of definitions centered on proclamation tend to see discipling and Christian formation as occurring subsequent to evangelism itself. Advocates of more expansive definitions that decenter proclamation fear that seeing formation as subsequent leads all too often to the anomaly of undiscipled Christians, the nominal Christians discussed in this chapter. Thus, they seek to build into evangelism itself the practices that enable Christian growth.

One approach is to define evangelism as initiation into discipleship, the church, or the kingdom of God. For example, William Abraham proposes that "we should construe evangelism as primary initiation into the kingdom of God,"[29] and describes six practices into which a new Christian must be initiated before evangelism has been completed. Note that Abraham and other proponents of evangelism as initiation are not equating evangelism with Christian formation, just insisting that evangelism introduce persons to formational practices.

A second approach is to define evangelism as the witness of the Christian community in its life and ministry. Bryan Stone argues that "the most evangelistic thing the church can do today is to be the church—to be formed imaginatively by the Holy Spirit through core practices such as worship, forgiveness, hospitality, and economic sharing into a distinct people in the world, a new social option, the body of Christ." Thus, "the church does not really need an evangelistic strategy. The church *is* the evangelistic strategy."[30]

In the chapters ahead we will examine these varied approaches to evangelism in more detail. But even now, it is fair to say that those who seek a single, clear definition of evangelism will be disappointed. I see the different proposals for defining evangelism as a strength, not a weakness, because each proponent in presenting their understanding of evangelism is raising issues we dare not ignore, and lifting up insights we don't want to miss. What we have, I believe, is not a cacophony of voices but an abundance of riches.

---

28. Fox and Morris, *Faith-Sharing*, 55.
29. Abraham, *Logic of Evangelism*, 13.
30. Stone, *Evangelism After Christendom*, 15.

CHAPTER 2

Mission and Evangelism

> Both evangelism and social responsibility can be understood only in light of the fact that in Jesus Christ the Kingdom of God has invaded history and is now both a present reality and a future hope.
>
> —RENE PADILLA[1]

"Mission," says James Scherer, "occurs when the church reaches out beyond its inner life and bears witness to the gospel in the world." The "heart of mission is always making the gospel known where it would not be known without a special costly act of boundary-crossing witness."[2] If this is a fair definition, it is no wonder that mission and evangelism have historically been considered synonyms.

The great Western missionary movement of the late nineteenth and early twentieth centuries understood mission more precisely as evangelism directed to the non-Christian world. Perhaps nothing captures this so well as the watchword of the Student Volunteer Movement: "The evangelization of the world in this generation."[3]

While this missionary movement fell short of its goal, its accomplishment was nonetheless impressive. Christianity has become a truly global phenomenon. The movement has been praised for its idealism, sacrifice,

---

1. Padilla, *Mission Between the Times*, 197.
2. Scherer, *Gospel, Church and Kingdom*, 37.
3. Scherer, *Gospel, Church and Kingdom*, 13.

Mission and Evangelism

and compassion, and condemned for cultural insensitivity and complicity with Western colonialism. Here it is enough to note that it always assumed mission to be the evangelization of the world. Its concern was how to complete this task and to mobilize the resources to do it.

The last half of the twentieth century brought an end to that era of mission. Colonialism had collapsed, and the newer churches were beginning to assume leadership not only in their own cultures but within global Christianity. The majority of Christians were no longer found in Europe and North America but in the global South. The West itself was no longer seen as a Christian culture but as a mission field. Thus, there are no longer Christian and non-Christian nations, or sending and receiving continents. Churches across the globe are now partners in mission, and each continent both sends and receives missionaries.

With this came a new focus on developing a theology of mission. Unlike evangelism, which, as we saw in chapter 1, suffered theological neglect, the content and definition of mission, as well as its relation to God, church, and world, has been the subject of global theological discussion for much of the twentieth century. It became clear to almost all participants in those discussions that mission involves a number of things, of which evangelism is only one. Mission included social concern, care for the environment, dialogue with non-Christian religions, and working for peace in the world. It is only when the definition of evangelism is expanded so broadly as to encompass all or most of these areas, or mission is narrowed only to sharing the gospel with others, that mission and evangelism are still treated as synonyms.

There is disagreement between such bodies as the Roman Catholic Church, World Council of Churches, the Lausanne Committee on World Evangelization, and the World Evangelical Fellowship over the relative priority of these elements and their exact meaning for ministry. That is to be expected. What is astonishing is the degree of convergence. This is itself a remarkable theological achievement and bodes well for mission in the twenty-first century.

The Mission of God[4]

At no point is this theological convergence more significant than understanding mission as the mission of God (*missio Dei*). Previously, mission

---

4. The discussion in this section is drawn in part from Bosch, *Transforming Mission*.

was seen as the mission of the church and defined as saving souls or planting new churches. To see it as the *missio Dei* is to move the focus from church to God and to let God's purposes in the world entirely govern those of the church.

Rather than mission being a facet of ecclesiology, it finds its theological home in the doctrine of the Trinity. The triune God is a sending God. The Father sends the Son, who is incarnate in Jesus of Nazareth. Through what he teaches and does, Jesus embodies the reign of God on earth. Through his death and resurrection, he conquers death and makes available forgiveness of sins and a new life of love, enabling all persons to participate in that reign both in this age and in the age to come.

The Holy Spirit is sent following the ascension of Jesus to be God's presence and power at work in the world. It is the Spirit that creates, guides, and empowers the church. While the work of the Spirit is not limited to the church, the church is the most distinctive and visible result of that work.

Thus, empowered and guided by the Spirit, the church is sent into mission. "As the Father has sent me, so I send you," the risen Jesus tells his disciples in John 20:21 before breathing on them so they can receive the Spirit. In Acts 1:8 he promises, "You will receive power when the Holy Spirit has come upon you; and you will be my witnesses in Jerusalem, in all Judea and Samaria, and to the ends of the earth." In carrying out this mission the church both witnesses to what God has done in Jesus Christ for salvation and continues to say and do those things that characterized the ministry of Jesus.

While the original intent in placing the focus on the mission of God was to keep mission centered on God, by the 1960s, the term was proving to be quite elastic in meaning, especially in the World Council of Churches. If the mission was God's and God was at work in the world, then it seemed to some that the task of the church was simply to point others to what God is doing. For example, if part of God's mission is to liberate the oppressed, then the church would identify those movements or activities working for liberation and both endorse and join their efforts.

Recent decades have seen a decisive move back to the church as central to God's mission. Thus, mission is more than a program or emphasis, or commitment of the church. Just as God is missional, the church is essentially missional. This also means that mission is not only to other cultures but occurs in one's own, within the neighborhood of the local church.

A Mission of Love

Love is the motivation, content, and goal of God's mission in the world. God is love (1 John 4:8) and love motivates all that God does in creation and redemption. Thus, as David Bosch says, "Mission has its origin in the heart of God. God is a fountain of sending love. This is the deepest source of mission. It is impossible to penetrate deeper still; there is mission because God loves people."[5] To this may be added, God loves the entire creation as well.

Likewise, Darrell Guder argues that "the compassion of God is the motivating power of God's mission." Drawing on Bosch, Guder says, "God's act of creation and God's determination to heal his rebellious creation are the compelling reason for the salvation history which unfolds from Abraham onward."[6] This culminates with the sending of Jesus, whose own "mission was God's mission" and "was characterized by the same compassion that had been the central theme of Israel's experience and testimony through the preceding centuries of salvation history."[7]

This love, then, is not an empty word waiting to be filled by cultural definition. It takes its meaning from the life and actions of God, from creation to new creation, from the prophets to the apostles, from exodus to Easter. It is, above all, revealed in the life and death of Jesus Christ.

Love is not only motive for God's mission but also its goal. God seeks a world in which love governs and fills all that is. Humanity was created in God's image, and for humanity to be redeemed is for persons and communities to love God, one another, and the creation in the same way God loves us, as revealed in Jesus Christ.

This means that mission must be understood eschatologically. The culmination of God's mission is the new creation, in which both heaven and earth are renewed in love. But while God's reign will be fully realized in the age to come, there are real anticipations of it in the present age. To know what that means, we look to Jesus, whose own teachings and actions embodied what it would mean for God's will to be done on earth as it is in heaven. Our present participation in the coming kingdom of God through the power of the Holy Spirit enables us to see the world with new eyes, identifying those aspects of personal, social, and institutional life that are

---

5. Bosch, *Transforming Mission*, 392.
6. Guder, *Continuing Conversion*, 32.
7. Guder, *Continuing Conversion*, 34.

Part One: Theological Foundations

not in accord with God's purposes, and, empowered by the Spirit, to join God's work of transformation.

The Church in Mission

If the church participates in the mission of God, what form does that participation take? Darrell Guder suggests that it is to serve as a witness. He notes,

> The concept of witness provides a common missional thread through all the New Testament language that expounds the church's mission. It serves as an overarching term drawing together proclamation (*kerygma*), community (*koinonia*), and service (*diakonia*). These are all essential dimensions of the Spirit-enabled witness for which the Christian church is called and sent.[8]

It is, therefore, much more than proclamation alone. "It is," he says, "the demonstration in the life and activity of God's people of the tangible fact that God's rule is breaking in among the disciples of Jesus Christ."[9]

Although Guder speaks of the mission of the church, he is abundantly clear that the mission is God's. "The essence of witness," he argues, "is the gracious action of God that produces such witnesses and their testimony." Our calling "comes from outside ourselves" and "is the result of God's initiation of God's mission."[10]

Jason Vickers sees the mission of the church as twofold. "Beginning at Pentecost and continuing across the centuries to the present day," he says, "we can observe the Holy Spirit enabling and empowering the church to do two things." First, "the Holy Spirit is ever at work in the church, enabling her to worship God." Second, "the Holy Spirit is ever at work in the church, enabling her to bear witness to the life, death, and resurrection of Jesus Christ."[11]

While Vickers distinguishes worship and witness, Guder includes worship as an aspect of missional witness.[12] For both, worship is foundational to witness. Guder says that in public worship, the community "claims, affirms, and celebrates the promised real presence of Jesus Christ as

---

8. Guder, *Continuing Conversion*, 53.
9. Guder, *Continuing Conversion*, 62.
10. Guder, *Continuing Conversion*, 60.
11. Vickers, *Minding*, 53.
12. Guder, *Continuing Conversion*, 207.

Savior and Lord in its midst." As persons "encounter the risen Lord in word, sacrament, and fellowship . . . they are sent back out for their continuing ministry of witness as light, leaven, and salt."[13] Worship evangelizes again and again the community.[14]

By distinguishing worship from witness, Vickers gives even greater emphasis to this formational impact of worship. Worship, he says, is (or should be) explicitly Trinitarian "because in worship, the Holy Spirit attunes our minds and hearts to the presence of our resurrected Lord and,[15] incorporating us into his body, makes us one with each other even as the Spirit and the Son are one with God the Father (John 17)." Such worship bears witness to Jesus Christ and is thereby the basis and impetus of the second aspect of mission. Because "witnessing to the life, death, and resurrection of Jesus in word and deed is inherent in the church's worship," the church then

> extends her witness to Jesus Christ in word and deed in a variety of ways, including evangelistic and missionary activities, catechesis and spiritual formation, works of mercy and love, hospitality to strangers, care for widows and orphans, support for the diseased and dying, care for the creation, and advocacy for social justice throughout the world.[16]

Vickers is writing about renewing the church and argues that the goal of church renewal is "perfect ministry and perfect love." By this, he does not mean flawless community but "the goal toward which the church strains."[17] While he does not explicitly connect this to his earlier discussion of mission, the linkage is not hard to see. It is the church that strives for this goal that is most faithful in its worship and witness. At the same time, worship and witness is used by the Holy Spirit to renew the church in this way.

The locus of renewal is in what Vickers calls the sacramental life of the church, by which he means more than the sacrament of baptism and Eucharist. Through "means of grace, including prayer, repentance, confession, fasting, worship, reading the Scriptures, the sacraments, and the like, the Holy Spirit creates divine graces in the people of God that they would not otherwise enjoy and for which they would not otherwise have a capacity."[18]

13. Guder, *Continuing Conversion*, 153.
14. Guder, *Continuing Conversion*, 163.
15. Vickers, *Minding*, 60.
16. Vickers, *Minding*, 64.
17. Vickers, *Minding*, 96–97.
18. Vickers, *Minding*, 97.

Part One: Theological Foundations

While mission of the church and means of grace seem to be overlapping categories for Vickers at the point of worship, for David Whitworth they are identical. "The church and persons participate in the *missio Dei*," he says, "by participating in the means of grace."[19] They are enabled to do so by the triune God and are shaped by "the grand narrative" of the mission of God in Scripture.[20] Whitworth draws upon John Wesley's typology of means of grace as works of piety and works of mercy, similar but not identical to Vickers's twofold mission of worship and witness. Works of piety are means of grace such as prayer, Scripture, worship, and sacraments and are directed to God; works of mercy are directed to persons.

Corresponding to works of piety and mercy are two ways of participation in these means of grace, waiting and sending. Whitworth argues that a missiological emphasis on sending overlooks the equally important need for active waiting on God through works of piety. These "personal and communal activities are, from a Wesleyan perspective of waiting, to be considered participation in the *missio Dei* as much as the engaged activities that are toward a neighbor."[21]

This is a theology of participation. Whitworth identifies "three participants: Trinity, person, and neighbor." Participation in mission is through "a tri-directional rhythm: God to person, person to God, and person to person." All of these "mutually fulfilling relationships" embody "the love shared between the triune God and the triune God with persons, even while God reaches out and enters into the life of others, and they in turn participate in the life of God and our lives as well."[22]

What both Vickers and Whitworth highlight is that through the means of grace the Holy Spirit forms and shapes a missional people even, as Whitworth insists, our participation in them is our participation in the mission of God. For John Wesley, both works of piety and works of mercy were means of grace to form Christian lives in love; they were also the ways Christians live out that love within the church and in the world.

---

19. Whitworth, *Missio Dei*, 117.
20. Whitworth, *Missio Dei*, 35.
21. Whitworth, *Missio Dei*, 111.
22. Whitworth, *Missio Dei*, 109.

Evangelism as the Heart of Mission

The consensus understanding is that evangelism is part of God's mission but not the whole of it. This still leaves the question of exactly how evangelism is related to mission.

Darrell Guder gives a twofold answer. On one hand a "theology of evangelistic ministry must be rooted in a biblical theology of mission and, above all, dominated and shaped by the gospel it seeks to proclaim."[23] Evangelism is not a stand-alone activity, but its very nature is determined by mission and the gospel of which it is a witness. Yet Guder can also say, "The center or core of the *missio Dei* is evangelization: the communication of the gospel . . . across all borders and into the world." This being sent—this bringing the "joyful message" of salvation "to all the world"—is both evangelism and the impetus that governs the entire mission of God.[24] Pentecost is "the divine event which turned the people of God into a missionary people."[25]

For Guder this implies an expansive understanding of evangelism. Defining mission as witness, Guder argues that while witness in Scripture is mostly "oral communication, there is ample reason to understand witness in a much more comprehensive sense, as defining the entire Christian life, both individually and corporately." As the core of mission, evangelization must also be more comprehensive than proclamation alone.[26] It is incarnational. Therefore,

> evangelism, carried out as incarnational witness, is the heart of the church's mission and ministry. All that the Body of Christ is and does must be linked to that of the heart just as every part of the human body must be linked to the human heart.[27]

The metaphor of evangelism as the heart of mission was first introduced by David Bosch in a 1991 lecture.[28] Guder is developing the metaphor further. But the most extensive exploration of Bosch's metaphor was by Dana Robert, writing a few years prior to Guder.

---

23. Guder, *Continuing Conversion*, 28.
24. Guder, *Continuing Conversion*, 49.
25. Guder, *Continuing Conversion*, 50.
26. Guder, *Continuing Conversion*, 55–56.
27. Guder, *Continuing Conversion*, 207.
28. Robert, *Evangelism*, 4.

Part One: Theological Foundations

For Robert, evangelism is to share the good news Jesus told Nicodemus in John 3:16, "For God so loved the world that he gave his only Son, so that everyone who believes in him may not perish but have eternal life." Jesus not only manifested the reign of God in his life and ministry but was the way for others to enter into that reign.[29]

Evangelism is the heart; mission is the body. The good news is the life force of mission. Thus, "with the heart pumping away, the life force travels around the body and enlivens it. The work of the heart builds up the body. Yet the body does not live for itself.... The body lives to continue Jesus' own mission of announcing and demonstrating the reign of God."[30] Evangelism provides the "emotional fervor, the love affair with the gospel," that keeps mission alive. "To take evangelism out of mission is to cut the heart out of it."[31]

A major advantage of this metaphor is it permits "contextualization while remaining faithful to God's self-revelation through Jesus Christ."[32] This is a central issue for both mission and evangelism. For Robert, understanding evangelism as the heart of mission creates "a flexible, contextual model of mission that resists an easy separation of gospel and culture." It allows mission to take many forms appropriate to different contexts while at the same time keeping "God's self-revelation through Jesus Christ" at the center of mission. In this way, it echoes the "paradox of the incarnation" itself.[33]

That evangelism is the heart of mission is an appealing metaphor, especially as Dana Robert has presented it. But there is an ambiguity over the meaning of evangelism that runs through Robert's discussion and is most clearly evident in her conclusion. There she presents two criteria for authentic mission.

> First of all, I believe authentic mission is characterized by having life at its center, specifically life in Jesus Christ. It may be possible to be in mission without reference to Jesus Christ, but it is not Christian mission unless Jesus Christ is at the heart of all that we do. The Good News of Jesus Christ is the life force of our mission. ... Secondly, I believe that authentic mission can be judged by whether it moves toward or away from the kingdom of God.[34]

29. Robert, *Evangelism*, 5.
30. Robert, *Evangelism*, 30.
31. Robert, *Evangelism*, 4.
32. Robert, *Evangelism*, 5.
33. Robert, *Evangelism*, 6.
34. Robert, *Evangelism*, 12.

Mission and Evangelism

These are sound criteria. Darrell Guder echoes these concerns when he speaks of God's justice revealed on the cross being reduced "to a humanly managed program of social change" or "recasting the gospel as a program of social justice, without the lordship of Christ and the future tense of the kingdom."[35] Both Guder and Robert resist mission divorced from Jesus Christ and the reign of God.

The ambiguity is found in the first criterion, where Robert speaks of Jesus Christ as "the heart" and "the life force" of mission. Is the heart of mission evangelism, or is it Christ?

While evangelism and Christ are clearly related, they are not the same thing. Yet Robert seems to use them interchangeably.

This ambiguity has been noticed by Mark Teasdale. Appreciating the great strengths of Robert's approach, he has sought to clarify and extend the metaphor in ways that both strengthen it further and bring it up to date. Teasdale argues Robert "implicitly suggested that evangelism is defined by how Christians relate to the gospel rather than by specific practices of sharing the gospel." It is the body, after all, not the heart, "that enacts the gospel in the world." Yet although scholars of evangelism do not agree on which practices, they are largely in agreement "that evangelism is best defined in terms of practice."[36] This raises questions about the usefulness of the metaphor.

Teasdale's solution is "to add a mouth to the body. Since all evangelism scholars agree that evangelism at least entails a verbal proclamation of the gospel, the mouth would be dedicated to the work of evangelism." This would move evangelism out of the heart and into the body, with proclamation having a distinct role within mission. However, it would not "resolve whether any non-verbal practice of the body was missional or evangelistic."[37]

This blurring of nonverbal evangelism and mission is not a defect for Teasdale but an advantage, as they are not clearly distinguishable in ministry. This has been the case historically as it is in the present. Thus, the "word witnesses by demonstrating what a world patterned according to the reign of God looks like." Both, says Teasdale, "invite people to participate in the

---

35. Guder, *Continuing Conversion*, 124.
36. Teasdale, "Extending the Metaphor," 53.
37. Teasdale, "Extending the Metaphor," 55.

abundant life God offers by believing the gospel and becoming disciples of Jesus Christ."[38]

Leaving open the difference between evangelism and mission has yet another advantage for Teasdale as it resists the limiting of evangelism to a prescribed set of practices. It recognizes the interplay of a wide range of practices that actually reach persons as well as the need for flexibility in different contexts. In this way, the Robert metaphor, as extended by Teasdale, helpfully counters the tendency of most to define evangelism only as a set of practices.[39]

The metaphor, as amended, now envisions the "mouth, hands, and feet" all engaged in a common mission, enlivened by the heart, which is the gospel itself. But the gospel here is more than a propositional statement: "It is a passionate heart that clings to the gospel joyfully as the ultimate message of hope and life for all creation."[40] If evangelism is defined "as our belief and passion for the gospel message,"[41] then we can still say that evangelism is the heart of mission.

This leads Teasdale to one further extension of the metaphor. Just as the lungs bring oxygen to the heart, so "the Holy Spirit, the Breath of God," is what makes possible the passion for the gospel, as well as aligning our other passions with the gospel. "The Spirit then moves with that passion both to empower our body to act missionally and to direct our words and deeds to be as good as the gospel we proclaim."[42]

What we can now call the Robert-Teasdale metaphor has much to commend it. It places the passion for the gospel—the passion for evangelism—at the center of mission. Its emphasis on the Holy Spirit as the source of that passion recognizes the divine initiative and that the mission is God's. It organically combines proclamation in words and demonstration in deeds. And it maintains contextual flexibility without compromising the gospel. It provides a rich and dynamic visual image of the relation of God, evangelism, and mission.

---

38. Teasdale, "Extending the Metaphor," 56.
39. Teasdale, "Extending the Metaphor," 57.
40. Teasdale, "Extending the Metaphor," 57.
41. Teasdale, "Extending the Metaphor," 59.
42. Teasdale, "Extending the Metaphor," 59–60.

PART TWO

Announcing Good News

CHAPTER 3

The Message Proclaimed

> I mean by "preaching the gospel," preaching the love of God to sinners, preaching the life, death, resurrection, and intercession of Christ, with all the blessings which in consequence thereof are freely given to true believers.
>
> —JOHN WESLEY[1]

AS WE HAVE SEEN, the most common conception of evangelism is that of proclaiming or announcing the gospel. But what is this "good news" that is being proclaimed? For many it was something like this: Jesus died for your sins, and if you believe in Jesus, you will be saved, in that when you die you will go to heaven. Even when this was not the full content of the message—some would speak of a present new birth, for example—the focus of the message was on avoiding judgement and attaining a happy afterlife.

To say this is inadequate to the message of Scripture is to put it mildly. Scripture is filled with the language of kingdom of God, new creation, new birth, new life in Christ, forgiveness, repentance, eternal life in the present, as well as love for one another, community, healing, caring for the poor, and so much more. The promise of the gospel has to do with a transformation of the heart, a new way of life, entering the kingdom, entering a new community, following Christ, and being baptized in the Spirit.

The writers discussed in this book all want to have a theologically richer understanding of the good news than the "be saved and go to heaven"

---

1. Wesley, *Letters II*, 482.

Part Two: Announcing Good News

version that had become so common. The three that will be presented in this chapter are focused on this. They all understand evangelism as proclamation and want the message that is proclaimed to be genuine good news.

Mortimer Arias: Announcing the Reign of God

Writing in the 1980s, Mortimer Arias believed, despite the thousands of books produced every year on it, that evangelization was in crisis. The crisis was multiform involving its credibility as a practice, its proper motivation, its definition, and its methodology.[2] The problem as he diagnosed it was that the kingdom of God, which was central to the message of Jesus, had disappeared from the evangelistic message. Instead, that message had been reduced to personal salvation or individual conversion. Jesus had proclaimed a kingdom of God that "is multidimensional and all-encompassing," involving persons, communities, societies, and creation itself.[3] The recovery of the reign of God as the central theme of evangelism is the way out of the crisis.

Arias looks to the message of Jesus to guide contemporary proclamation. There he finds three essential elements. First, it "is an announcement of something that God is doing right here and now."[4] The kingdom *has* come. The kingdom, then, "is not a human construction or a human program" but "God's gift of grace."[5] We experience the kingdom through forgiveness of sins, the entry into the fullness of life, and the restoration of community, such that sinners become welcome at Jesus' table fellowship.[6]

Second, the kingdom is also "not yet"—it is coming in fullness, it is imminent. The kingdom *will* come. We not only experience the kingdom but await it. This does not make us a people of fear but of hope: because the future belongs to God we can live in the present as a people of hope.[7]

Third, the kingdom is in-breaking, "the center of a tremendous struggle of cosmic proportions that calls for a confrontation." The kingdom

---

2. Arias, *Announcing*, xii.
3. Arias, *Announcing*, xv.
4. Arias, *Announcing*, 15.
5. Arias, *Announcing*, 16.
6. Arias, *Announcing*, 20–25.
7. Arias, *Announcing*, 27–39.

is coming, and its arrival "produces a crisis."[8] It is God's new order that subverts all existing human orders.[9] It

> takes the shape of prophetic denunciation of personal and public sin; of confrontation of powers and institutions; of unmasking ideologies and traditions; of challenge to unbelief, prejudice, and hostility; of a challenge also to triumphalistic belief. Finally, it takes the form of repentance, conversion, and radical discipleship.[10]

Such a message Jesus both practiced and embodied. It produced a violent reaction from the forces of evil, who ultimately nailed Jesus to the cross.[11]

The death of Jesus, says Arias, was "the eclipse of the kingdom," the seeming "collapse of all hopes around the announced kingdom." But with the resurrection of Jesus from the dead hope was restored, and the cross becomes the power of God—"the Lord of the universe ruling from a cross."[12]

Then came Pentecost, and the coming of the Holy Spirit, creating a church and empowering it for mission. The early church saw itself as an "eschatological community . . . living 'in the last days,' between Pentecost and the Parousia."[13] At the heart of the apostolic witness was Jesus Christ, crucified and risen, savior and lord.

Thus, while "Jesus proclaimed the coming kingdom, . . . the early church proclaimed Jesus the Christ."[14] Arias does not see this as the abandonment of Jesus' message of the kingdom for a very different message about Jesus. Rather, because Jesus is risen, to proclaim Jesus as lord is to proclaim the kingdom, because Jesus himself embodies the reign of God.

For Arias the problem is that contemporary proclamation has reduced the message of the kingdom to a transcendent heaven outside of history, an institutional church, an apocalyptic end of the world, an inner experience, or a political program. The church has lost "any reference to Christ's lordship over the totality of life." But the "subversive memory of Jesus" remains in the Scriptures to confront and challenge us, and the Holy Spirit is present to help us remember the message of Jesus. Together, Scripture and the Holy Spirit—"the two great subverters of history and the church—are

8. Arias, *Announcing*, 42.
9. Arias, *Announcing*, 43.
10. Arias, *Announcing*, 53.
11. Arias, *Announcing*, 43.
12. Arias, *Announcing*, 61.
13. Arias, *Announcing*, 61–62.
14. Arias, *Announcing*, 56.

Part Two: Announcing Good News

calling us to recover the fullness of the biblical gospel of the kingdom to be announced to our generation."[15]

How, then, should we undertake evangelization today? Drawing on the three elements of Jesus' proclamation, Arias believes we should announce the kingdom as gift, hope, and challenge.

As gift, the kingdom is a present experience. Because it now "has a face and a name: Jesus Christ"[16] we announce the graciousness of the kingdom through telling the story of Jesus. We announce forgiveness, which removes the barrier of sin which separates us from "God, from neighbor, from nature, from oneself, and from life itself."[17] We speak and work in defense of life in a world of suffering and death. We offer compassion to those who have been sinned against. And we maintain an open eucharistic table, offering hospitality to all, including the outcasts and marginalized.[18]

As we hope, we live in expectation of the coming kingdom. Evangelism is a ministry of annunciation, announcing an undefeatable "future in which every present takes meaning from, and in which any past is redeemed."[19] Evangelism is also a ministry of denunciation, opposing "anything, any power, any program, any trend which opposes God's purpose for humanity."[20] This prophetic ministry is costly, and often leads to *martyria*, in which one witnesses to the gospel by putting one's life on the line.[21] Evangelism is also a ministry of consolation, bringing comfort and hope to the brokenhearted.[22]

As challenge, the in-breaking kingdom calls us to radical discipleship. "Jesus' call was to turn to *God* and *kingdom*, present in *him*. It was an invitation to enter into a community and a movement."[23] To be converted to Christ is to be converted to one's neighbor. Conversion involves radical decision and turning, but it is also an ongoing process. We learn from

---

15. Arias, *Announcing*, 67.
16. Arias, *Announcing*, 69.
17. Arias, *Announcing*, 72.
18. Arias, *Announcing*, 75–81.
19. Arias, *Announcing*, 89.
20. Arias, *Announcing*, 92.
21. Arias, *Announcing*, 97.
22. Arias, *Announcing*, 98.
23. Arias, *Announcing*, 112.

the neighbor and especially the poor even as we evangelize them. Thus the "conversion of the evangelizer continues in the process of evangelizing!"[24]

Arias believes the eclipse of the kingdom in our day is passing, and the fullness of the gospel is beginning to shine in all its radiance and hope. The "two subverters of history"—"the subversive memory of Jesus in the Scriptures and the subversive ... work of the Holy Spirit in the Christian community"—continue their mission of establishing God's rule in the world.[25]

Stephen K. Pickard: Praise-Centered Evangelism

"At its heart," writes Stephen Pickard, "the church is called to be a community of the evangel bearing the glad tidings of God in the world."[26] This is both "a task and a joy,"[27] yet the church has largely abdicated its calling to evangelize. Part of the problem may be in the perception of what evangelism is. Pickard wants to liberate evangelism "from false and restrictive notions," enabling persons to "discover joy and confidence in the gospel" and delight "in the inmost being ... that the evangel truly liberates."[28]

Pickard believes the root of the problem lies in two broken relationships: between theology and evangelism, and the church and evangelism. Due to the former, "Evangelism has been deprived of a critical stimulus, and theology has forgotten that its impulse and source is nothing less than 'the truth that is in Jesus' (Eph 4:21)."[29] The effect of the latter has led to "an introverted church life and the relegation of evangelism to the outskirts of the Christian community."[30] Pickard seeks a theology of evangelism that will aid in repairing these two relationships.

To do this he builds on the definition of evangelism proposed by Daniel Hardy and David Ford: "The content of praise repeated and explained to others so that they may join the community of Jesus Christ."[31] Pickard argues that

---

24. Arias, *Announcing*, 114.
25. Arias, *Announcing*, 121.
26. Pickard, *Liberating*, 3.
27. Pickard, *Liberating*, 2.
28. Pickard, *Liberating*, 2.
29. Pickard, *Liberating*, 4.
30. Pickard, *Liberating*, 5.
31. Pickard, *Liberating* 83; citing Hardy and Ford, *Jubilate*, 19.

the Christian tradition has identified the twin coordinates for this praise: the life, death, and resurrection of Jesus of Nazareth and the ongoing presence and action of God's Holy Spirit. As evangelism takes its cue from a community of people formed in relation to such a God, it will be truly liberating in the world and in turn will be liberated from its own false and distorted forms.[32]

He then addresses the first of his two fundamental issues, the relation of evangelism and theology. To do so he identifies three features essential for communicating the gospel evangelistically and theologically.

The first feature is simplicity. Sacrificing neither depth nor profundity, the task of the evangelist is to offer a brief but "compelling snapshot of the faith," "a rich compression of the truth." The evangelistic message is a "word in season," somewhat akin to poetic expression.[33] The ability to do this rests not in particular methods but in openness to God who gives the evangelist the words to speak. Theology, in contrast, is a much more extensive discussion of the gospel. There is a reciprocal movement between evangelism and theology, compression and extension, making the two forms of gospel communication "catalysts for each other."[34]

The second feature is repetition. "Good evangelism evidences certain recurring patterns or references to God's ways with this world and human life."[35] The challenge for both evangelism and theology is to say the same thing in newly creative and insightful ways, "freshness through sameness."[36]

The third feature is the presence of wisdom, the content of the gospel message. This wisdom is those two coordinates of praise cited earlier, the work of the triune God in the world through Christ and the Spirit, which is "experienced and praised in the Christian community" and "repeated in rich simplicity in evangelism."[37]

The goal of gospel communication, whether through evangelism or theology, is the transformation of human life and all creation. It is as God is praised in evangelism and theology that God's love is experienced, and human lives are taken up into and reoriented by this loving presence of God.[38]

32. Pickard, *Liberating*, 5.
33. Pickard, *Liberating*, 42.
34. Pickard, *Liberating*, 43–44.
35. Pickard, *Liberating*, 44.
36. Pickard, *Liberating*, 51.
37. Pickard, *Liberating*, 54.
38. Pickard, *Liberating*, 55–56.

In addressing the second issue, the relation of evangelism to the church, Pickard defines the church as "a community for the praise of God."[39] Evangelism, he argues, is essentially ecclesial, and is not only one means to praise God, but is itself motivated, directed, and shaped by praise. Again drawing on Hardy and Ford, Pickard describes evangelism "as the 'horizontal dimension' of our praise," while worship and prayer are "the vertical dimension."[40] Hardy and Ford identify two elements of praise which Pickard applies to evangelism.

The first is the penitential aspect of praise. It is only one who acknowledges that one is a sinner who is able to praise God for forgiveness and freedom from sin. Evangelistic preaching that makes grace conditional on what we do is not praise-centered; that which tells what God has done and what that enables us to do is praise-centered.[41]

The second is the celebratory aspect of praise. There is an overflow of our delight in God which we share with others. Our praise of God draws others in, and at the same time intensifies our desire to invite others to share in our joy.[42]

The gospel, then, "is not about half-alive people or those with only a flicker of life being restored." It is "that God creates new people and communities out of nothing—a wholly unsurprising statement given that the main character of the gospel is Jesus Christ, the crucified Lord of glory (1 Cor 2:8)."[43] This "is praise that is focused on Christ and buoyed along in the same Spirit that raised Jesus from the dead."[44]

James O. Stallings: Telling the Story

Writing in the late 1980s, James Stallings describes Black America—"both the urban black poor and the upwardly mobile middle-class black professional"—as in an identity crisis. Black Americans (like Americans in general) seek "a definition of reality and self-understanding from" television, "a medium that is inherently steeped in preserving the status quo and stereotypical views of minorities." The result, he says, is a life oriented

---

39. Pickard, *Liberating*, 60.
40. Pickard, *Liberating*, 83; citing Hardy and Ford, *Jubilate*, 19.
41. Pickard, *Liberating*, 87–88.
42. Pickard, *Liberating*, 88.
43. Pickard, *Liberating*, 97–98.
44. Pickard, *Liberating*, 98.

toward "conspicuous consumption," in which the urban poor view "material possession as a declaration of somebodiness" and the black middle class spend money on possessions that still do not gain them entry as equals into white society.[45]

Over three decades later, with the emergence of the internet, the situation Stallings describes is not appreciably different. Consumerism is the dominant way of life for most Americans, and, despite some progress, minorities remain disadvantaged and marginalized. What Stallings presents has lost none of its relevance in the twenty-first century. Evangelism entails confronting the story of the dominant culture with the story of God.

Stallings defines evangelism in black churches as including "all activities and methods . . . through which God's saving grace and liberating activity in Jesus Christ among men and women was communicated; calling them into community with other Christians for wholeness, growth, and freedom."[46] Central to all of this evangelistic activity is story. In black churches, evangelism "has always been the telling of the story, the story of Jesus, the story of people, the personal story of individuals. In its finest moments, these stories have been shared to transform communities and lives."[47] It is when these stories are supplanted by other stories that black churches face a crisis of identity.

Story is intrinsic to black life and culture, shaping all forms of communication. "The black American community is" itself "a story-shaped community" in that it's "self-understanding, language, beliefs, attitudes, and ideals are passed from one generation to another through story."[48] Story belongs to a community. "While there are personal stories," Stallings notes,

> they are personal only to the extent that the individual who lives out his or her experience in a community is shaped by that community while at the same time the individual participates in the shaping of the community.[49]

This gives priority to the communal story while keeping it open to fresh insight and retellings.

---

45. Stallings, *Telling the Story*, 113.
46. Stallings, *Telling the Story*, 21.
47. Stallings, *Telling the Story*, 122.
48. Stallings, *Telling the Story*, 16.
49. Stallings, *Telling the Story*, 15.

Story is more than a sequence of events—"it is an imaginative way of ordering our experience."[50] So as much as it is interpretive, it provides not only memory but meaning. The distinctive story of black Christianity in America is just that: "an attempt to help a particular community recall its own history with God; to remember those times when God's deliverance was sure and God's providential care was self-sustaining."[51] Thus slaves did not accept the Christianity of whites but "fashioned it to suit their own needs." As a result, they created a powerful means of evangelism: "a Christ-centered community that almost unconsciously reaches out to others automatically, bringing them into God's church."[52]

Community and story are at the core of the black evangelistic lifestyle. This is the heritage from evangelism among the slaves, in which, often in the absence of a slave preacher, "the Christian community as a whole assumed the responsibility of spreading the faith to the sinner."[53] This is not to say preachers were unimportant, only that there was a wide range of public and personal modes of evangelism. Stallings sums up these methods in this way:

> In the area of public evangelism, there were testimonies, preaching, public worship, prayer meetings, experience meetings, and regular Sunday worship as well as conversion stories. Personal evangelism was primarily done through mutual storytelling and mutual listening. All of this was done in the context of a caring, nurturing community.[54]

For Stallings a "critical issue is how can I be sure my story meets and joins the Christian story, or, how to use the issues of truthfulness in story so as to avoid self-deception."[55] The Christian story is the story of God throughout history, culminating in Jesus Christ.

A prime example of how the story of God can imaginatively and truthfully shape the communal story is the spirituals. "The spirituals were communal songs that engaged its singers in a ritual."[56] They were improvisational, such that an experience or event could be expressed in

---

50. Stallings, *Telling the Story*, 15.
51. Stallings, *Telling the Story*, 17.
52. Stallings, *Telling the Story*, 61.
53. Stallings, *Telling the Story*, 54.
54. Stallings, *Telling the Story*, 89.
55. Stallings, *Telling the Story*, 93.
56. Stallings, *Telling the Story*, 94.

light of the biblical story. The spiritual drew upon scriptural imagery and figures, like Moses and Daniel; indeed, these biblical characters who had faced their own trials and tribulations were considered members of the community.[57] They "told of a God whose activity in the community was immediate and intense."[58]

In addition to calling sinners to conversion, the spirituals told stories of oppression and divine deliverance and affirmed the truth that enslaved persons were not property but a chosen people, sons and daughters of God.[59] It was the liberation from spiritual bondage that led black Christians to seek political liberation. Rather than an otherworldly focus, personal salvation and freedom from sin were seen as intrinsically connected to freedom from slavery and racial discrimination.[60]

In order for the story of God to provide meaning and hope as it shapes communal and personal stories, it must be an open story. A story becomes closed when our response to it is rational, seeking explanation, "once for all times engraved in stone." But God's story is inherently relational and should evoke a transrational or intuitive response. As an open story it "remains imaginative, always developing, capable of making the pilgrimage with us, providing exhortation and nurture." It is a story that remains unfinished, lives "with uncertainty and ambiguity," and finds its resolution in God.[61]

Stallings argues that the evangelistic challenge facing the black church is to do in the present context what the slaves did in theirs. Living in a hostile environment, they used "spirituals and conversion stories . . . to pass on a world view, values, and beliefs to each succeeding generation." Slavery could "not destroy their self-transcendence." They passed on "a tradition that provided clarity of identity and a purposefulness of mission."[62]

To do this they can draw upon the story of a caring God, and on the good news that "what God has done in the past, God will do again even if it is under changing circumstances."[63] The tragedy for Stallings is he suspects this story has not been heard by many because it has not been communicated.

---

57. Stallings, *Telling the Story*, 95.
58. Stallings, *Telling the Story*, 97.
59. Stallings, *Telling the Story*, 99–100.
60. Stallings, *Telling the Story*, 59.
61. Stallings, *Telling the Story*, 100–101.
62. Stallings, *Telling the Story*, 122.
63. Stallings, *Telling the Story*, 114.

The hope is the story continues as it always has to offer "the healing, liberating, transforming word from the gospel."[64]

The Fullness of Good News

In different ways each of these three authors reminds us that the good news is about God. By focusing on what God has done in Jesus Christ and the Holy Spirit, they provide a message that encompasses and yet transcends personal salvation, that speaks of the reign of God's love, the creation of communities that witness to that love, and the renewal of creation. The promise of the gospel remains centered on the transformation of human hearts and lives. But the expansive vision of God's redeeming work provides a rich portrayal of the content of the new life in Christ, in which our motivations and desires are governed by love and a passion for God's will to be done on earth as it is in heaven.

---

64. Stallings, *Telling the Story*, 114.

CHAPTER 4

Sharing the Faith

> Christianity is one beggar telling another beggar where he found bread.
> —D. T. NILES[1]

PERSONAL EVANGELISM, THE SHARING of the gospel from one person to another or within small groups, is considered to be the responsibility of all Christians. Yet most contemporary Christians in America seem at best to feel inadequate to the task, and at worst oblivious or resistant to the call to share their faith with others. To remedy this a massive amount of books and other resources have been produced to encourage and train persons in personal evangelism.

The best of these books are written as well to protest against forms of evangelism that are insensitive, formulaic, or manipulative. They instead advocate more relational forms of evangelism rooted in compassion and respect for others, and dependent on the Holy Spirit. Because these books are written to wide audiences, their theology is often in the background. But there is sound theological reflection present, and we will in this chapter seek to bring it to the foreground.

---

1. Niles, *That They May Have Life*, 96.

Rebecca Manley Pippert: Christ-Shaped Evangelism

"Evangelism," says Rebecca Manley Pippert, "in its simplest form is introducing our friends to Jesus."[2] For a more extensive definition she turns to Michael Green, who defines it as "a presentation of Jesus Christ in the power of the Holy Spirit so that people will put their trust in God through him, accept him as their Savior, and serve him as their king in the fellowship of his church."[3] Both of these definitions are foundational to her approach to evangelism.

Pippert believes that fear—of rejection, of showing our lack of knowledge, of our beliefs being challenged—"is the real enemy of evangelism."[4] Much of her writing is designed to allay these fears, not by assuring the reader that they are misplaced but by relativizing them through a comprehensive presentation of how to do effective evangelism. But her primary source of assurance is not from training persons. It is the recognition that it is not all up to us and we are not alone: "it is God who takes the initiative to pursue seekers; it is his Spirit that converts; it is his gospel that saves. Evangelism is God's business from start to finish."[5]

God not only takes the initiative but provides three ways for us to do evangelism. The first is to proclaim the good news, which is "done primarily through the telling of the gospel" but also "when we tell our story of salvation, for our conversion story illustrates the power of the gospel."[6] The second is "when we demonstrate Christ's compassion through our words and compassionate service."[7] The third is bearing witness "by walking in and pointing to the power of God's Spirit." The Spirit "will give us just what we need in the moment we need it" and transforms the lives of those who trust in Christ.[8] These three ways to witness are mutually reinforcing and they structure Pippert's discussion of specific evangelistic practices in the second half of her book.

What grounds all of this theologically is found in the first half, where she points to Jesus as both the model and motivation for evangelism. The

---

2. Pippert, *Out of the Saltshaker*, 133.

3. Green, *Evangelism Through the Local Church*, 8–9, 11; cited in Pippert, *Out of the Saltshaker*, 133.

4. Pippert, *Out of the Saltshaker*, 9.

5. Pippert, *Out of the Saltshaker*, 11.

6. Pippert, *Out of the Saltshaker*, 135.

7. Pippert, *Out of the Saltshaker*, 134.

8. Pippert, *Out of the Saltshaker*, 136.

approach is incarnational: the humanity of Jesus models what it means for us to be authentic in sharing our faith, and the divinity of Jesus—his being Lord—calls for our obedience. Pippert calls for Christians to look "more deeply at the life of Jesus." She promises that "if you live by the same values and priorities he had, you will find evangelism happening naturally. It will become a lifestyle and not a project."[9]

There are three aspects of Jesus' life and ministry that Pippert lifts up for Christians to emulate. The first is the love which led Jesus to be radically identified with the world. "Jesus was wholly concerned with God and wholly concerned with people." It was a life "of loving God, our neighbors and ourselves" that celebrated "the supreme value, dignity and preciousness of human life."[10] "His life demonstrated the love of God for all."[11]

The second was holiness, which led Jesus to be radically different from the world. Holiness has to do with how we treat others, and that means we are called to think and behave in ways distinct from what is the cultural norm. God's people are to be set apart, a holy people.[12]

How, then, do we both identify with the world yet stand apart from it? "Christ," Pippert says, "both was merciful and made judgments.... Indeed, it was his love that prompted his judgment." With love, she says, "we accept our neighbor unconditionally and with open arms and at the same time desire God's very best for their lives." Only the Holy Spirit convicts persons of sin, she cautions, not us.[13] Sometimes though, we are called to speak painful truths to our friends.[14] What is crucial to our witness is our knowledge that we, too, are sinners; we also have struggles and go through difficulties. It is "our honesty before others," our "sharing our weaknesses," that can shatter "the stereotype that all Christians are judgmental and critical people."[15]

The third aspect is obedience. "Jesus had a theology of obedience," the object of which "was a living person—not a historical norm, not a code of laws, but himself."[16] The motive for this obedience is "our love and devo-

---

9. Pippert, *Out of the Saltshaker*, 55.
10. Pippert, *Out of the Saltshaker*, 56.
11. Pippert, *Out of the Saltshaker*, 57–58.
12. Pippert, *Out of the Saltshaker*, 75–76.
13. Pippert, *Out of the Saltshaker*, 78.
14. Pippert, *Out of the Saltshaker*, 79.
15. Pippert, *Out of the Saltshaker*, 80.
16. Pippert, *Out of the Saltshaker*, 86.

tion to him."[17] Pippert fears too many people stop "at the door that leads to conversion"—they have said a prayer or made a decision—and do not enter into new life. A true disciple "does what Jesus does—obeys the will of God."[18]

Living our lives by Jesus' values leads to evangelism flowing naturally, but without divine assistance we are not able to do it. The good news is that we are not alone. Christ is with us in three distinct ways.[19]

First, "Jesus is with us, and by the power of the Holy Spirit, he calls, equips, and motivates us for ministry."[20] The Holy Spirit is an "absolute requisite" for evangelism; hence, "We must pray, first, for a renewal of the Holy Spirit in our lives as we seek to minister, and then for his activity in the lives of the people we are seeking." Prayer, then, "is another absolute requisite for evangelizing."[21]

Second, Christ's presence "brings us his power and ability to use our limited resources in his limitless ways."[22] Through the power of the Holy Spirit, even the simplest act of kindness and hospitality can become an occasion for persons to encounter, knowingly or unknowingly, the love of God.

Third, the presence of Jesus not only indwells us but is also in others. Pippert cites Mother Teresa, who said that "Jesus comes to us as the sick and the homeless, he comes in the distressing disguise of the poor."[23] We are called to practice compassion (which enables us to grow in compassion), "to look outward" to others in obedience to Christ, and to remember all persons are created in the image of God.[24]

Most of Pippert's examples are of one person sharing their faith with another person, which is the central purpose of her book. But she does not neglect the witness of the Christian community. Because God is the Trinity, "it is the community of God's people who will represent him more fully and completely."[25] One way the church can do this is to "offer the world a model of unity amid great diversity," consisting of persons from different generations,

17. Pippert, *Out of the Saltshaker*, 85.
18. Pippert, *Out of the Saltshaker*, 88.
19. Pippert, *Out of the Saltshaker*, 94.
20. Pippert, *Out of the Saltshaker*, 94.
21. Pippert, *Out of the Saltshaker*, 95.
22. Pippert, *Out of the Saltshaker*, 94.
23. Pippert, *Out of the Saltshaker*, 99.
24. Pippert, *Out of the Saltshaker*, 99.
25. Pippert, *Out of the Saltshaker*, 233.

races, occupations, interests, and more.[26] Persons need to see the gospel being lived out in human relationships. The demonstration of the love of Jesus through us "is especially powerful in a community of believers."[27]

It is when our lives and our churches reflect the love, holiness, and obedience of Jesus, living "in his power and with his presence," that "seekers will be drawn to us." Sharing the gospel will cease to be a chore, and instead "will become a true delight and evangelism will become a lifestyle."[28]

H. Eddie Fox and George E. Morris: Relational Evangelism

Fox and Morris believe the time has come "for the church to put primary emphasis upon verbal witnessing to the gospel of Jesus Christ."[29] While they firmly believe the gospel is "both visible and verbal," they also recognize that for many Christians and churches, it often is "easier to do the deed of the gospel than to name the name of Jesus Christ." The reason, they suspect, is to put "the deepest thoughts, commitments, and desires of life" into words makes persons vulnerable.[30] They seek to reverse that by enabling people to share their faith through preaching and testimony.

Faith sharing, they argue, originates with God. We worship "a seeking God whose nature is shown in creation and in the divine intention to recreate a new humanity after people turned away in disobedience and sin."[31] Faith sharing is therefore theologically grounded. Although we often use language "about the church's evangelistic task" and the like, the mission is God's, and "the church is called to participate in" it.[32] Given that humanity has turned away from God, and the tragic consequences of sin for our lives, relationships, and the world, we are in dire need for the restoration of our relationship with God and the new life God provides through Jesus Christ.[33]

Indeed, our primary motivation for faith sharing is God's love. God is not only a seeking God but a sending God. We encounter the love of God

---

26. Pippert, *Out of the Saltshaker*, 238.
27. Pippert, *Out of the Saltshaker*, 240.
28. Pippert, *Out of the Saltshaker*, 93.
29. Fox and Morris, *Redeemed*, xv.
30. Fox and Morris, *Redeemed*, xvi.
31. Fox and Morris, *Faith-Sharing*, 13.
32. Fox and Morris, *Faith-Sharing*, 28.
33. Fox and Morris, *Faith-Sharing*, 16.

in Christ and then are sent to share that love with others.[34] In addition, faith sharing fulfills the Great Commission of Matt 28:19–20, but only if love motivates that fulfillment.[35] Love also undergirds our motivation to share the gospel in order to address "deep personal and social needs."[36]

Having shown how evangelism is grounded in and motivated by God's love, Fox and Morris offer this definition:

> Evangelization is the process of spreading the gospel of the kingdom of God by word, deed, and sign in various contexts, through the power of the Holy Spirit, and then waiting and watching in respectful humility and working with expectant hope.[37]

This is a carefully constructed and theologically rich definition. We will examine it one phrase at a time.

First, evangelism "is the process of spreading the gospel," that is, "an ongoing process of communication" concerning this good news.[38] Evangelism is not, they emphasize, our converting others—only the Holy Spirit converts. "Evangelizing is not something we do to people but something we do with the gospel."[39] This means that faith sharing is necessarily relational and entails fundamental respect for the dignity of persons. Evangelism is not a sales technique designed to entice a decision but creates "an atmosphere or an occasion of freedom in which people can respond authentically to the leadership of the Holy Spirit."[40] Nor is it a one-way communication of information aimed at eliciting mental assent.[41] The communicator should "always be honest, clear, and non-exploitative."[42]

The relationality of evangelism not only applies to the evangelizer and the recipient of the good news. The invitation to believe this good news "is given on behalf of Christ and the community of faith" and therefore invites persons into relationship with Christ and the community. God's intent is

---

34. Fox and Morris, *Faith-Sharing*, 25–27.
35. Fox and Morris, *Faith-Sharing*, 29.
36. Fox and Morris, *Faith-Sharing*, 30.
37. Fox and Morris, *Faith-Sharing*, 55.
38. Fox and Morris, *Faith-Sharing*, 53.
39. Fox and Morris, *Faith-Sharing*, 54.
40. Fox and Morris, *Redeemed*, 115; see also *Faith-Sharing*, 90.
41. Fox and Morris, *Redeemed*, 114; see *Faith-Sharing*, 90.
42. Fox and Morris, *Redeemed*, 116; see *Faith-Sharing*, 89.

not only for us to have our relationship with God restored but also to bring us together as a people of God.[43]

Second, what is spread is "the gospel of the kingdom of God." To turn the gospel into a "psychological panacea" degrades it into "a consumer product" that "fosters self-centeredness whose chief aim is personal fulfillment."[44] Rather,

> the gospel is indeed the good news of the kingdom, and since the kingdom is the detailed expression of God's caring reign over the whole of life, and since the goal of testimony and preaching is that of initiating people into the kingdom of God, then we are to proclaim a message about God whose nature is to uphold justice, mercy, and equity; to watch over the circumstances of strangers, widows, and orphans; to help the sick; to liberate the poor and the prisoners.[45]

While their earlier work *Faith-Sharing* focused on personal evangelism, their sequel *Let the Redeemed of the Lord Say So!* discussed verbal witnessing—preaching and testifying—more broadly. There, they offer a definition of preaching and testifying that is also carefully constructed and I believe is complementary to the one we are examining here:

> To proclaim the biography of the deeds of God in terms of one's autobiography with the hope that persons, enabled by the power of the Holy Spirit, respond to God's act of forgiveness in Jesus Christ, in repentance and faith, and live out the new life in faithfulness to the kingdom of God.[46]

The emphasis on the kingdom of God remains prominent in this definition. It makes clearer the relation between the story of God and our story, in that the latter is to point to the former.

Third, the good news is spread by word, deed, and sign. This anticipates understandings of evangelism we will examine in the next two chapters. Here, Fox and Morris argue that, as in the ministry of Jesus and the early church, the "gospel must be made both visible and verbal." With

---

43. Fox and Morris, *Redeemed*, 117.
44. Fox and Morris, *Redeemed*, 31.
45. Fox and Morris, *Redeemed*, 32–33.
46. Fox and Morris, *Redeemed*, 13.

regard to deed, proclamation "must run concurrently with ministries of healing, serving, nurturing, liberating, reforming and empowering."[47]

By signs they mean "visible tokens of invisible realities that are spiritually significant," which includes art, signs and wonders such as divine healing, and sacraments.[48] Their emphasis on verbal witnessing is not intended to reduce the importance of deed and sign but to correct the de-emphasis on evangelistic preaching and testimony they have found in many churches.

Fourth, the gospel is shared in various contexts. Faith sharing is incarnational. As God has entered our world in Jesus Christ, so are we to enter the worlds of others. "We are called to empathize with people," that is, "to attempt to feel and see the world from the other person's perspective."[49] We are "to enter into the sufferings of people and allow ourselves to become vulnerable," standing alongside others in their struggles. The incarnational principle follows the self-emptying of Christ in Phil 2, ruling out any stance of superiority, condescension, or pity toward others.[50] Consistent with this, Fox and Morris insist that an essential element of evangelism is listening: "honest, perceptive, non-judgmental, relational listening which conveys trust and acceptance of the other."[51]

Fifth, evangelism occurs through the power of the Holy Spirit. It is the Holy Spirit who gives us "a passion to witness," enables us to become more like Jesus, and guides our living out the new life in Christ and witnessing to Christ.[52] The Holy Spirit gives us a living faith and motivates us to share it with others.[53] The Holy Spirit is also "active in the lives of all people" through prevenient grace, enabling them to hear and respond to the good news. "It is the Holy Spirit who fills the faith-sharer with compassion for other persons, and it is the Spirit who draws people to Christ."[54]

Finally, after sharing the gospel, we wait in humility while we work with expectant hope. We wait in humility because without the power of the Holy Spirit, we can do nothing.[55]

---

47. Fox and Morris, *Faith-Sharing*, 55.
48. Fox and Morris, *Faith-Sharing*, 57–58.
49. Fox and Morris, *Faith-Sharing*, 72.
50. Fox and Morris, *Redeemed*, 122.
51. Fox and Morris, *Faith-Sharing*, 94.
52. Fox and Morris, *Faith-Sharing*, 132–33.
53. Fox and Morris, *Faith-Sharing*, 134.
54. Fox and Morris, *Faith-Sharing*, 135, 74.
55. Fox and Morris, *Faith-Sharing*, 58.

This drives us to prayer. We work in expectant hope because of God's "victory of life over death, love over hate, reconciliation over alienation" and that "the risen Christ is available to everyone." We know that God's word "will accomplish that for which God sent it."[56]

Brenda Salter McNeil: Being a Credible Witness

For Brenda Salter McNeil, the promise of the gospel is a reconciled community. In Christ we are reconciled both to God and one another; salvation enters us into not only a new life but a new community. "Our unity in the midst of our diversity," she says, "is one of the most powerful ways we reveal the reality of what Jesus accomplished on the cross."[57]

In light of this, evangelism must be redefined. It "is more than getting people into heaven. It is calling people into a new community."[58] It is more than a change in lifestyle—it is an invitation "to join God's family and join forces with what God is doing in the world."[59] She rejects an individualistic approach for one that sees "people as individuals in community," that takes their culture and context seriously. Evangelism must be more than verbal—it must include "how we live and interact with people" as we invite them to join God's community.[60]

Such a holistic evangelism has everything "to do with social justice and racial and ethnic reconciliation." Jesus himself is the model. His was "a startling kind of evangelism that loves people deeply, crosses religious, ethnic, and sociopolitical barriers, builds relationships of mutuality, and calls us into profound, far-reaching transformation."[61] What he began will be fulfilled in the age to come when people from all tribes and nations will gather before God; the church in which such reconciliation is already a reality is a beacon of hope and present witness to that future reality.[62]

To provide a description of the elements of such an evangelism, McNeil uses the story of Jesus' encounter with the Samaritan woman at Jacob's well in John 4. Brevity requires our forgoing a full discussion of her

56. Fox and Morris, *Faith-Sharing*, 59.
57. McNeil, *Credible Witness*, 16.
58. McNeil, *Credible Witness*, 17.
59. McNeil, *Credible Witness*, 21.
60. McNeil, *Credible Witness*, 20.
61. McNeil, *Credible Witness*, 18.
62. McNeil, *Credible Witness*, 133–34.

Sharing the Faith

interpretation of the passage. We will instead identify the major points of her approach to evangelism.

The first is that we are called to go where people are different from us. Jesus, she says, *had* to go through Samaria, whose people the Jews despised and whose territory they avoided.[63] This same divine mandate is given to us: we are compelled by God's love for us and all people "to cross gender lines, racial barriers, denominational divides, political affiliations, age separations, and class distinctions." Through listening to God, we discern our particular calling in our own context[64] in order to "engage in intentional interaction" with those different from us.[65] "This is," she says, "more than a method for doing cross cultural evangelism. It is about being in the right place at the right time and learning to be open and obedient to God's leading and direction."[66]

The second major point has to do with the nature of our interaction with others: we need to "relinquish power and embrace need."[67] Jesus models this in-depth in his conversation with the Samaritan woman, beginning with his asking her for a drink of water. Instead of taking a position of superiority where we assume we know something the other person does not, it was "Jesus' initial acknowledgment of his real need for a person who his society said had nothing of value to offer" that initiates the conversation.[68]

If we are to acknowledge our own need to receive from the "unique perspectives and expertise" of others "we will need to relinquish the power and control that keeps us from being challenged or influenced by them."[69] There "is something of God in every person and every culture"; in order to learn from them we will need to "become the helped instead of always being the helper."[70] Humility, she says, "is one of the most important characteristics in the ministry of reconciliation."[71]

Third, if we are to practice an evangelism that crosses barriers, we will have to be countercultural. "There will be times Jesus calls us to go against

---

63. McNeil, *Credible Witness*, 39–40.
64. McNeil, *Credible Witness*, 43.
65. McNeil, *Credible Witness*, 49.
66. McNeil, *Credible Witness*, 56.
67. McNeil, *Credible Witness*, 57.
68. McNeil, *Credible Witness*, 61.
69. McNeil, *Credible Witness*, 64.
70. McNeil, *Credible Witness*, 69.
71. McNeil, *Credible Witness*, 72.

the status quo,"⁷² as Jesus himself did when he conversed with the Samaritan woman. In doing this Jesus "broke religious rules, cultural norms, and social standards."⁷³ Likewise, "we must be willing to break unjust laws and take action that is counter to the culture around us"—"to go where we are not supposed to go and do what we're not supposed to do"—if we are to be credible witnesses.⁷⁴

Connecting with others who are different entails a double risk: "rejection from those they have extended themselves to and the possibility of alienation from their own group." But our taking this risk to share the gospel also attests "to our credibility and authenticity" because it demonstrates our respect for their differences and culture.⁷⁵

To do this kind of evangelism requires a "power beyond our own skills and abilities"—the power of the Holy Spirit. At Pentecost, the disciples were "empowered to be effective and bold witnesses of the kingdom," resulting in the birth of "a new multilingual, multiethnic and multinational movement." From the beginning, "the church was intended to be a global movement that brings together people from every tribe, language group, and nation."⁷⁶ This same Spirit will empower us to engage in an evangelism that reconciles.

McNeil published *A Credible Witness* in 2008. Events since that time have challenged the credibility of the church, and McNeil herself. There is the massive rise of violence and hatred: "Black people worshipping in churches and Jewish people in synagogues are massacred. Young people march through college campuses carrying torches and spewing racism. Brown children are mercilessly ripped from the arms of their parents and kept in cages." In response to this, "the church remains largely silent."⁷⁷

That silence has not gone unnoticed by a younger generation concerned about injustice. With many of them, the church has lost credibility. And while McNeil believed that a concern for justice was intrinsic to her teaching, younger hearers did not see her addressing it at all.⁷⁸

McNeil had begun her work believing that if she "could convince evangelical Christians that reconciliation was not some politically motivated

72. McNeil, *Credible Witness*, 116.
73. McNeil, *Credible Witness*, 114.
74. McNeil, *Credible Witness*, 116.
75. McNeil, *Credible Witness*, 126.
76. McNeil, *Credible Witness*, 132.
77. McNeil, *Becoming Brave*, 19.
78. McNeil, *Becoming Brave*, 17–18.

agenda but a biblical calling rooted in Scripture, they would pursue racial justice." But she has come to see her approach "was not effecting the type of change I knew in my heart needed to take place." What she concluded was that "I had to start preaching a more honest and direct message about how we, the church, must work to repair broken systems, alongside those affected by them, in order to engage in reconciliation."[79]

So, in her 2020 book *Becoming Brave*, she uses the story of Esther to share how we are to go about it. She now defines reconciliation as "an ongoing spiritual process involving forgiveness, repentance, and justice; its goal is to transform broken relationships and systems so that they better reflect God's original intention for all creation to flourish."[80]

I don't believe her newer call for a more brave and forthright approach to injustice is a repudiation of her earlier book on evangelism, but it is a significant modification. It means that issues of social justice cannot be bracketed even temporarily in order to build multicultural bridges—true reconciliation cannot exist without justice.

What links the two books is her desire for the church to be a credible witness. Moreover, the church has something to offer that no one else can. McNeil says,

> I've come to the conclusion that we do need the church, rag-tag army though we may be, because we've been entrusted with the transcendent narrative of faith that offers us hope and the possibility of transformation. That's why the church cannot abandon its leadership in the work of reconciliation. The message of the gospel, the story we must tell, infuses the work of reconciliation with *hope*![81]

Martha Grace Reese: Unbinding the Good News

Martha Grace Reese wants to reverse the aversion to evangelism in mainline Protestant churches—to "break the curse," which holds them captive.[82] The large majority of pastors and laity she describes as "evangelism-cautious,"

---

79. McNeil, *Becoming Brave*, 22.
80. McNeil, *Becoming Brave*, 23.
81. McNeil, *Becoming Brave*, 191.
82. Reese, *Unbinding the Gospel*, 3.

as often "living with fears of coercive misuses of evangelism."[83] She seeks to show them why we should do evangelism, and how do it faithfully and well.

Reese was a participant in the Mainline Evangelism Project which examined hundreds of congregations in order to find which churches were doing evangelism well and why. Her writing on evangelism was shaped by what the study discovered.[84]

By evangelism, Reese means faith sharing. More precisely, it "is anything you do to help another person move closer to a relationship with God, or into a Christian community."[85] The most important finding of the Mainline Evangelism Project was "that a vivid relationship with God lies at the heart of real evangelism. People who share their faith love God and believe that other people's lives would be better if they were in a relationship with God, too."[86]

Reese understands this vivid relationship with God to entail a "trinity of relationships: with God, within the congregation, and with people outside the church whose lives are not centered in Christ." Evangelism "emerges from the interaction of these three sets of relationships."[87] She grounds this theologically in the doctrine of the Trinity itself: "the idea that God is made up of relationships shows us something important about the nature of people and church."[88] This trinity of relationships structures much of Reese's discussion, so we will follow that pattern here.

We begin with the relationship with God. The sad fact that Reese notes is that "most of us are in mainline churches with a very light emphasis on a relationship with God." Different from the norm are those "that emphasize a growing relationship with God for its members, board, and pastors." "I don't want to sound critical," she says, "but visiting one of these vibrant churches makes attending many of our mainline congregations feel like going to a Lions Club meeting—a good thing, certainly, but not the real thing."[89] The truth is most of us "only dabble our toes at the edges of waters of faith. Few of us have a clue how vivid and powerful life with Christ can be."[90]

---

83. Reese, *Unbinding the Gospel*, 13.
84. Reese, *Unbinding the Gospel*, 4.
85. Reese, *Unbinding the Gospel*, 9.
86. Reese, *Unbinding the Gospel*, 4.
87. Reese, *Unbinding the Gospel*, 5; see also 15, 59.
88. Reese, *Unbinding the Gospel*, 58.
89. Reese, *Unbinding the Gospel*, 61.
90. Reese, *Unbinding the Gospel*, 15.

Sharing the Faith

The second element of this trinity of relationships is life within the church. If persons in the church "are devoted to staying alive in Christ and have a spiritual life that is sustained over time, if the congregation puts a long-term focus on helping people be in primary contact with God, then healthy relationships have a much better chance of developing."[91] Thus vibrant churches "contain people who are attending to spiritual disciplines and are alive in Christ." Such "congregations, where relationships within the church are nurtured and where the congregation tries to work together in the Spirit, change people's lives."[92] Those changes in people's lives do not remain in the church. They "move out into everyone's lives and all their other relationships. The power of the loving church can't stop at the door, or it will turn inward and fade." The church, she says, "is an igniter of faith, an instigator of growth that affects your whole life."[93]

This leads to the third element of the trinity of relationships, that with persons outside the church. Evangelistic churches prepare their members for faith sharing. As do "many good churches," they "concentrate on helping people grow in their faith lives through spiritual practices. But the evangelistic churches also hone in, with laser-like focus, on helping their members articulate and share their growing faith," through sermons, small groups, and financial priorities. "They train people to recognize and articulate their faith."[94]

If one belongs to a congregation like this, a key practice of evangelism is simply inviting persons to church. The Mainline Evangelism Project found that new members "understand two things best: that God loves them and the church loves them." They are most satisfied when "they feel loved, accepted and comfortable in the church, and they are learning about God (Jesus, Spirit) and growing in spirituality."[95]

Evangelism occurs in and through ordinary things. For churches, "sharing the mystery of God is a sacred gift contained in the practical structures of sermons and small groups, newcomer's dinner parties, and signs for the parking lots. The holy is encased in the pragmatic."[96] The same can be said for personal faith sharing. "It's seeing who needs to be prayed for.

---

91. Reese, *Unbinding the Gospel*, 63.
92. Reese, *Unbinding the Gospel*, 65.
93. Reese, *Unbinding the Gospel*, 65.
94. Reese, *Unbinding the Gospel*, 97.
95. Reese, *Unbinding the Gospel*, 74.
96. Reese, *Unbinding the Gospel*, 105.

It's waiting for an opening in a conversation with that friend to mention church or your faith." It can simply be inviting someone to church.[97]

What motivates and guides the entire evangelistic ministry—actually, all ministry—is God. Because of this Reese insists on the centrality of prayer. "Prayer," she says, "is the way individuals, small groups, and congregations grow and become vivid. It is a habit, a discipline," and "is more about receiving from God than it is about asking God for things or working hard at intercession. . . . It results in lightness and energy and excitement."[98]

The truth is that "we need to rely as much on God for pragmatic guidance as we can stand!"[99] Yet "trusting God for guidance is counter-intuitive," especially for "self-reliant Americans." We have a tendency to start out trusting God, only to then "snatch the reins from the Spirit's fingers."[100] This is why, in the second edition of *Unbinding the Gospel*, Reese has added a forty-day prayer journal designed to enable persons to make prayer a habitual and ingrained part of their lives. Unless persons and congregations become people of prayer, they will not rely on God, and any evangelistic efforts will be fatally compromised at the outset.

That would be tragic. People are in need of genuine good news. For as Reese says,

> Life with Christ is reality. It is joy. It is hope. It is salvation. It matters more than anything in the world. It is life that infuses and subsumes the world. In despair, we have hope in God. In fear, the shattering surrender of Christ on the cross shines live glory on us. This is the heart of faith. This is the good news.[101]

The Centrality of Relationships

As distinct as these four approaches to faith sharing are, they have in common a focus on relationship. Foundational to all else is a relationship with God. It is the Holy Spirit that motivates and guides the faith sharer and congregational evangelism, and it is the Spirit that enables hearers to respond. Our need to rely on God is why they so strongly emphasize prayer.

97. Reese, *Unbinding the Gospel*, 112.
98. Reese, *Unbinding the Gospel*, 51.
99. Reese, *Unbinding the Gospel*, 42.
100. Reese, *Unbinding the Gospel*, 52.
101. Reese, *Unbinding the Gospel*, 105.

Second, it is Jesus in his relationship with God and others who is our primary model for faith sharing. Jesus reaches out to all, not from a stance of superiority but humility. He respects the worth and dignity of all people, and genuinely listens to them. At the same time, he embodies the love of God such that he, at times, radically challenges cultural norms.

Third, salvation is not purely individual and future but present and communal. Faith sharing may be person to person, but the invitation is to enter into a community that worships God, cares for one another, and participates in God's mission in the world. It is in community, in relationship with God and each other, that we receive and live out a new life in Christ, formed and shaped by love.

PART THREE
Bringing Good News

CHAPTER 5

Word and Deed

> An individual gospel without a social gospel is a soul without a body and a social gospel without an individual gospel is a body without a soul. One is a ghost, the other, a corpse.
>
> —E. STANLEY JONES[1]

LUKE MAKES THIS OBSERVATION about the ministry of Jesus: "Soon afterwards he went on through cities and villages, proclaiming and bringing good news" (Luke 8:1). We are used to thinking of the good news as something that is proclaimed. What is so striking here is Luke's insistence that it is also brought. Luke understands the good news to be conveyed by word and deed.

We can place this within a larger theological framework. The message of Jesus was the good news of the kingdom, and throughout the New Testament the kingdom—the age to come—is desired as both future and as an anticipation already present. From this perspective, Jesus embodies the kingdom in all he says and does. Led by the Spirit, the church, called by Paul "the body of Christ," is to be a present witness to the reality of the kingdom yet to come in fullness.

The implication for evangelism is clear: the good news is not only shared verbally but also through actions. It is these acts of love that both manifest the life of the kingdom and give integrity to the words that proclaim it.

---

1. Jones, *Unshakable*, 67–68.

The authors we examine in this chapter have made this central to their understanding of evangelism. Although their ways of doing it are diverse, they all insist that word is incomplete without deed. Whether they define evangelism as proclamation and then link it to actions or place both word and deed within their definition of evangelism, the two are and must remain inseparable.

Ronald J. Sider: Incarnational Kingdom Christianity

"Most churches today," Ron Sider observes, "are one-sided disasters." While suburban churches draw people to Jesus, praising God in nice buildings, those new Christians "seldom learn that their new faith has anything to do with wrenching, inner-city poverty just a few miles away." Other churches lobby for social change but "understand little about the daily presence of the Holy Spirit" and would be shocked at the suggestion they should "invite their neighbors to accept Christ." It is this "lopsided Christianity" that Sider seeks to remedy.[2]

To examine the underlying issues, Sider analyzes four divergent models of evangelism and social concern. We cannot do justice to Sider's analysis of these models here, but a brief description will, I suspect, enable recognition of each.

The *Individualist Evangelical* model seeks, largely through proclamation, the conversion of persons who then act as salt and light in the world. *Radical Anabaptists* also focus on persons but share the gospel by both word and deed and see the church as witness to an alternative community. The *Dominant Ecumenical* model is the most complex, having liberal, conservative, and Roman Catholic subtypes, but in general seeks to evangelize both persons and social structures through word and deed. The *Secular Christian* model focuses purely on political action to change social structures.[3]

Sider believes much can be learned from these models but finds them all inadequate. He proposes instead a fifth model, *Incarnational Kingdom Christianity*.[4]

To summarize Jesus' ministry, Sider quotes Matt 9:35: "Jesus went through all the towns and villages, teaching in their synagogues, preaching the good news of the kingdom and healing every disease and sickness." As

---

2. Sider, *Good News*, 26.
3. Sider, *Good News*, 27–45.
4. Sider, *Good News*, 45.

"eternal Word-become-flesh," he "was the perfect combination of word and deed."[5] Jesus communicated the kingdom through "words and wonders, preaching and miracle, both gentle invitation and sharp confrontation."[6]

Jesus not only announced the arrival of the kingdom of peace and justice, "he also fed the hungry and welcomed the socially ostracized into his new community." In fact, this "new redeemed community" was itself a manifestation of the kingdom. It was a holistic ministry: "sick bodies, broken spirits, and disrupted relationships with God all received his gentle healing touch."[7] Jesus commanded his disciples to do the same.[8] Jesus and his disciples were "a disturbing kingdom community."[9] This was a direct challenge to "Satan and his demonic forces," who Jesus saw as the power "behind wicked persons and twisted social patterns."[10] He criticized the rich and identified with the poor, defied cultural norms in welcoming the socially marginalized and women, challenged political and religious leaders,[11] and defied violent revolutionaries with his "peaceful path to messianic shalom."[12]

Jesus' crucifixion seemingly brought an end to his disruption of the status quo, but in raising Jesus from the dead, God showed that "Jesus was truly the Messiah and that his messianic kingdom had begun."[13] With the coming of the Holy Spirit at Pentecost, the redeemed community of Jesus continues and grows, intended by God "to be a little miniature now of the coming kingdom." The church communicates the good news of the kingdom "by word and deed: by presentation, miracles, acts of mercy and justice, and living out the gospel as a winsome example to others."[14]

But more than the church is involved in the dawning of the kingdom. The early church believed the kingdom relates to persons, social structures, and creation itself. The crucified and risen Jesus "was the key to history," and "at his return he would complete his victory over every rule and authority,

---

5. Sider, *Good News*, 71.
6. Sider, *Good News*, 72.
7. Sider, *Good News*, 72.
8. Sider, *Good News*, 52.
9. Sider, *Good News*, 60.
10. Sider, *Good News*, 61.
11. Sider, *Good News*, 61–70.
12. Sider, *Good News*, 68.
13. Sider, *Good News*, 73.
14. Sider, *Good News*, 75.

Part Three: Bringing Good News

even death itself."[15] The dimensions were cosmic, and, with the resurrection and Pentecost, the reign of Jesus has already begun.[16]

This has huge implications for how we understand salvation and conversion. Salvation "is personal and corporate, individual and social,"[17] with the ultimate goal "to bring the entire creation to wholeness."[18] Conversion involves "a radical transformation of our relationships with both God and neighbor";[19] evangelism in the modern period has been "biblically inadequate" in that it has focused only on personal sin and our relationship with God.[20]

Within his incarnational kingdom model, Sider argues that evangelism and social action must not be confused with one another, yet they are at the same time inseparable. They are distinguished from one another by their intention. Sider defines evangelism as "that set of activities whose primary intention is inviting non-Christians to embrace the gospel of the kingdom, to believe in Jesus Christ as personal Savior and Lord, and to join his new redeemed community."[21] This involves both verbal proclamation and visible demonstration. We evangelize by works of love as well as words and witness to the gospel through transformed lives and churches.[22]

"Social action," in contrast, "is that set of activities whose primary goal is improving physical, socioeconomic, and political well-being of people through relief, development, and structural change."[23] Social action does not require verbal proclamation,[24] and its goal is not to invite people into a relationship with God but to improve their lives. "Feeding the starving, ending slavery, and promoting political freedom and economic justice have their own biblical justification whether or not those who benefit ever accept Christ."[25]

---

15. Sider, *Good News*, 74.
16. Sider, *Good News*, 75.
17. Sider, *Good News*, 95.
18. Sider, *Good News*, 94.
19. Sider, *Good News*, 104.
20. Sider, *Good News*, 105.
21. Sider, *Good News*, 163.
22. Sider, *Good News*, 163.
23. Sider, *Good News*, 163.
24. Sider, *Good News*, 162.
25. Sider, *Good News*, 161.

While distinct, evangelism and social action are necessarily interrelated. Evangelism promotes social action in a number of ways. A biblically faithful evangelism upholds Christ as Lord as well as Savior, and "will call on people to repent of involvement in unjust social structures."[26] Furthermore, "again and again, history has shown that new Christians born again by the power of the Spirit are powerfully transformed and consequently change history." This is not automatic, Sider warns; Christians must be "taught about the social implications of the gospel" if they are to make positive change.[27]

Such faithful evangelism leads to faithful churches. When a church "breaks through the sinful barriers of racism, class prejudice, and oppression," the fact of its "existence has a powerful influence on the larger society."[28] Such a church is both a "visible demonstration of the gospel" in its life together and "leavens the whole social order."[29]

Social concern also aids evangelism. While "silence on injustice undermines evangelism," when persons are cared for in the name of Jesus, "our acts of mercy open hearts to the gospel." We stand with the poor and marginalized not as evangelistic strategy, but out of love. Yet "when our genuine compassion also has an evangelistic dimension, we rejoice."[30]

Sider recognizes that churches that focus on either evangelism or social action may do some good. But that falls short of the holistic nature of the kingdom. "Christian mission," Sider concluded, "works best when evangelism and social concern come together in the name and power of Jesus."[31]

Orlando E. Costas: Liberating News

Like Mortimer Arias, Orlando Costas writes from the perspective of the Latin American poor. He proposes a theology of contextual evangelization, and states its central theme this way:

> Evangelization implies bearing witness to the God who saves us from the misery of the human condition. It is an intensely personal and social witness that requires immersion in a particular

26. Sider, *Good News*, 173.
27. Sider, *Good News*, 174.
28. Sider, *Good News*, 175.
29. Sider, *Good News*, 176.
30. Sider, *Good News*, 179.
31. Sider, *Good News*, 183.

sociohistorical context and participation in the struggles of humanity. An evangelistic witness is a person who is not ashamed to let everyone see and hear about his or her experience of God, who identifies with and appropriates the fears and hopes of others, and who from that vantage point shares lovingly, even passionately, the gospel in word and deed.[32]

Costas has several definitions of evangelism throughout his writing, each designed to make a particular point. His most succinct describes evangelization as "the process by which God, through the power of the Holy Spirit, makes possible the hearing and reception of the gospel concerning Jesus Christ."[33] Another highlights testimony in defining it as "the storytelling of God's saving message as it has become an integral part of our lives as people of faith."[34] In yet another, he makes clear that "the transmission of the gospel" is "to those who have yet to hear or receive its message for the first time, as well as those who, although they are part of a sociocultural situation where the gospel has been proclaimed and collectively received, have not had the joy of adequately appropriating it in their personal lives and social relations."[35]

Costas develops his theology of contextual evangelization by way of three propositions centered on context, divine initiative, and praxis. Beginning with the first, he describes evangelization as "a witness that takes place in a given social and historical context."[36] Humanity does not exist in the abstract," he argues, there are only persons in concrete situations. And, he adds, "evangelization always deals with people who have both sinned and been sinned against."[37] Thus, in evangelizing we approach another as someone who shares "the same precarious existence as everyone else, and who is part of the same world of sinners and victims of sin."[38]

Biblical examples of contextual evangelization are found by Costas in Deutero-Isaiah and Esther in the Old Testament and the Gospel of Mark in the New. In Mark's Gospel, Costas notes that Jesus came from the despised and marginalized region of Galilee, and Galilee was the focus of his

---

32. Costas, *Liberating*, 21.
33. Costas, *Liberating*, 28.
34. Costas, *Liberating*, 71.
35. Costas, *Liberating*, 18.
36. Costas, *Liberating*, 21.
37. Costas, *Liberating*, 22.
38. Costas, *Liberating*, 23.

Word and Deed

ministry. There, he announces that the kingdom of God is near, not only as a future hope, but as a new world that "had come within the reach of everyone." The breakthrough of the kingdom was "vividly demonstrated in the miracle narratives," but even more in the death and resurrection of Jesus.[39]

Having established his ministry, Jesus then moves from the Galilean periphery "to confront the powers centered in Jerusalem with the radical message of the kingdom of God."[40]

But it would not stop there. The resurrection of Jesus enables the disciples to both understand the necessity of the cross and "that Jesus was God's kingdom in person." With that "new understanding, they were now ready to evangelize the nations."[41]

While Galilee is itself a particular context, it has universal implications for evangelism in every context. First, "contextual evangelization should have a sociohistorical foundation based on the periphery." It begins in the marginalized places in society and "works from the bottom up," where it can be "credibly announced as a message of liberating love, justice, and peace" and enable the oppressed to have hope and to struggle for justice.[42]

Second, "evangelization is by its very nature public"; "it takes place amid the multitudes."[43] The "Galilean multitudes can be found everywhere," he says, and when they "are evangelized, everybody hears about it," including government, religious leaders, the well-off, and the comfortable. And as we see in Mark, they often "become irritated and threatened," and move to stifle the hope that the gospel has evoked "among the harassed multitudes."[44]

The third implication "is that evangelization has a global scope."[45] It addresses persons "in their sociohistorical reality everywhere on this planet."[46]

Having looked at Costas's first proposition concerning context, we can now move to the second, divine initiative: "Evangelization involves persons addressed by a holy and loving God with the liberating news of Jesus Christ

---

39. Costas, *Liberating*, 55.
40. Costas, *Liberating*, 55.
41. Costas, *Liberating*, 61.
42. Costas, *Liberating*, 62.
43. Costas, *Liberating*, 62.
44. Costas, *Liberating*, 64–65.
45. Costas, *Liberating*, 66.
46. Costas, *Liberating*, 67.

in the power of the Holy Spirit."[47] God "addresses each and every human being in his or her time and space."[48]

Costas understands evangelization to be grounded in the dynamic Trinitarian activity of God. The Holy Spirit is the power of evangelism in two ways: as an "external force" the Spirit anoints the witness; as an "internal force" the Spirit presents Christ, convicts, creates faith, and gives new life which marks the community and sends transformed people into liberating service.[49] The cross of Jesus Christ mediates the reconciliation accomplished through his death and is the criterion through which we evaluate our evangelistic practice.[50] The resurrection of Jesus reveals the liberating rule of the Father, inaugurating "a new order of life." It is the kingdom of God—this devotion to Christ as Lord and bearing witness to his liberating love and rule—that is the goal of evangelization.[51]

Central to the message of evangelism is who this Jesus is. In the incarnation the "Son of God emptied himself of his glory, taking upon himself the human condition, submitting himself to a state of weakness and suffering death." Jesus "lived in poverty, and in his ministry gave preferential option to the poor."[52] Both the humanity and divinity of Jesus must, therefore, be understood "from the perspective of the poor." The poor reveal a critical aspect of the identity of God: "In them, we see God's human face."[53]

The third principle of evangelization has to do with praxis: "Evangelization involves persons and communities working for the transformation of their respective life situations." By praxis Costas means "creative and transforming action" accompanied by critical reflection in order "to make Christian obedience ever more effective."[54] A personal experience of grace is necessary but not sufficient for evangelization to be authentic. The "transforming impact" of the gospel must also be seen in social and historical contexts. Those "reborn into a new life and hope" thus "need to

---

47. Costas, *Liberating*, 23.
48. Costas, *Liberating*, 24.
49. Costas, *Liberating*, 77–79.
50. Costas, *Liberating*, 80–81.
51. Costas, *Liberating*, 82–83.
52. Costas, *Liberating*, 27.
53. Costas, *Liberating*, 27–28.
54. Costas, *Liberating*, 30.

demonstrate the power of the Spirit's presence through a new lifestyle of freedom, service, justice, and peace."[55]

Transforming action requires a base, a place from which it emerges. That base is the congregation.[56] "The gospel," Costas says, "has been committed to a community, is transmitted by that community, and demands a community experience."[57] The congregation is "where the gospel is manifested and lived in its most concrete reality" and "is the starting point for the diffusion of the gospel in the world."[58]

The ultimate spiritual base for contextual evangelization is God. "It is to understand God as an eternal community of love, God as mission and unity who seeks and reconciles, sends and calls." Conversion leads to a reorientation of "one's life in the direction of God's kingdom and its justice." The evangelistic task of the church is to bear witness to that kingdom "under the sign of the cross," and to serve that kingdom in the present as it awaits the fullness of the kingdom "in faith and hope."[59]

David M. Gustafson: Gospel Witness

"Gospel witness," says David Gustafson, "is about more than sharing the gospel with others. It is about whom we worship, who we are, what we receive, what we say, and what we do." Gospel proclamation, which is how Gustafson understands evangelism, cannot be separated from the lives of Christians and congregations without losing its integrity.[60]

The witness of Christians and churches is rooted in the mission of God in which they are participants.[61] This mission, which is the context within which evangelism occurs, is described by Gustafson this way:

> God's purpose in history is not simply to redeem people from sin and offer them a heavenly life but to create a new humanity that exists in the world as a sign, witness, and foretaste of God's kingdom, participating in his mission in the world.[62]

---

55. Costas, *Liberating*, 30.
56. Costas, *Liberating*, 133.
57. Costas, *Liberating*, 134.
58. Costas, *Liberating*, 135.
59. Costas, *Liberating*, 149.
60. Gustafson, *Gospel Witness*, 1.
61. Gustafson, *Gospel Witness*, 7, 17.
62. Gustafson, *Gospel Witness*, 6; see also 261.

This mission is expressed in two divine mandates: The *creation mandate* (or *cultural mandate*) is given to all humanity "to be fruitful and multiply, to rule over the earth, to care for God's creation and creatures, and to maintain order, peace, and justice in the world." The *disciple-making mandate* (or *gospel mandate*) is given to the church to announce the good news and make disciples. The two mandates "come together in word and deed in the mission of the church."[63] Verbal witnessing "to the gospel is embedded in practical demonstrations of love that address human needs."[64]

Jesus carried out both of these mandates in his ministry, announcing the in-breaking of the kingdom in word and demonstrating it in deed.[65] He "announced the inauguration of *his*" messianic kingdom, which "was now present and operative in him."[66] The gospel tells the story of Jesus—his life, death, and resurrection.[67] That story is both within and fulfills the full biblical story, from creation and fall, through Israel and the coming of Jesus, to the mission of the church and the fullness of the kingdom.[68]

Evangelism, then, "is the verbal proclamation of the person and claims of Jesus, communicated by words that are meaningful to listeners."[69] It "is an *introduction* to a relationship with the triune God," "an invitation to the life of a Christian disciple," and "a means of *initiation* into the kingdom of God through faith in Jesus Christ."[70] The essence of evangelism is communicating this gospel; "the goal is to make disciples."[71]

The primary agent in evangelism is the Holy Spirit. The Spirit illumines persons' understanding of the truth of the gospel, convicts them of sin, leads them to repentance, and calls them to "believe in and follow after Jesus Christ."[72] "Alongside the work of the Holy Spirit" is Christian witness. "God uses the faithful presence and words of Christians, individually and

---

63. Gustafson, *Gospel Witness*, 19; see also 103–4, 260.
64. Gustafson, *Gospel Witness*, 20; see also 108.
65. Gustafson, *Gospel Witness*, 30.
66. Gustafson, *Gospel Witness*, 40.
67. Gustafson, *Gospel Witness*, 40–42.
68. Gustafson, *Gospel Witness*, 42–47.
69. Gustafson, *Gospel Witness*, 21.
70. Gustafson, *Gospel Witness*, 21–22.
71. Gustafson, *Gospel Witness*, 22.
72. Gustafson, *Gospel Witness*, 127; see also 201, 124.

collectively, along with the gospel and works of the Spirit to bring seekers to repentance and faith."[73]

Those who proclaim the gospel do so in ways appropriate to the context. We are called "to communicate the gospel accurately and relevantly." Contextualization, if done well, is both "faithful to the historic, apostolic message of the gospel and the missional task of communicating it to particular people at a particular time."[74]

Gustafson rejects the transactional understanding of conversion as a single event,[75] instead seeing it as "a process with a turning point marked by a crisis moment of repentance and belief." Correspondingly, "gospel witness should not be viewed as a once-for-all activity but as a series of activities alongside the process of conversion that leads to making disciples of Jesus Christ."[76] This makes evangelism relational in nature and conversational in practice.[77]

Relationality is central to our humanity as persons created in God's image. "Because the triune God is divine-persons-in-relation," Gustafson says, "love, community, and relationships are intrinsic to his being." God's disposition is toward self-communication. Humans "are rational, moral, emotional, and social beings able to communicate, exercise conscience, and show love."[78] Thus relationality is central to Gustafson's entire discussion of evangelism as well as specific topics, such as his description of three forms of apologetics as rational, experiential, and relational (the last of which is a communal demonstration of the love of God).[79]

Thus, both personal and communal evangelism are relational. Personal evangelism is telling one's faith story in a way that points to the gospel. It is sharing with another person the difference Christ has made in one's life.[80] It is motivated by love for God, a "desire for God's glory and praise,"[81] and love and compassion for one's neighbor.[82] It is energized by living under the

---

73. Gustafson, *Gospel Witness*, 131.
74. Gustafson, *Gospel Witness*, 51.
75. Gustafson, *Gospel Witness*, 125.
76. Gustafson, *Gospel Witness*, 22.
77. Gustafson, *Gospel Witness*.
78. Gustafson, *Gospel Witness*, 22–23.
79. Gustafson, *Gospel Witness*, 163–69.
80. Gustafson, *Gospel Witness*, 75–77.
81. Gustafson, *Gospel Witness*, 60–61.
82. Gustafson, *Gospel Witness*, 62–65.

reign of Christ, abiding in Scripture, prayer, and "being filled with the Holy Spirit."[83] In addition, personal evangelism requires us to be intentional in engaging relationships with others, mirroring the intentionality of God and especially the ministry of Jesus.[84] It is incarnational in that we embody what we speak in particular contexts.[85] Following Jesus, it calls us to be "faithfully present" to others, to identify with others, and to serve others.[86]

Communities witness to others when they embody the gospel, as shown "by their reconciliation, unity, and life together with one another."[87] But they also witness through inviting persons to small gatherings such as Bible studies or book studies. These are *centered-set* gatherings in which all are welcome, with the goal of moving persons toward Christ, the center. The "order of a centered-set gathering is belonging, believing, behaving." This is "in contrast to a *bound-set* gathering where the order is . . . believing, behaving, belonging."[88] The strength of the centered-set gathering is that it provides "a safe and accepting environment" in which to explore the gospel and its implications for life. It is much like the gatherings in households that marked the early church.[89]

The centered-set approach encourages "a long view of evangelism" which enables more time for study, reflection, and conversation as well as observing how Christians live. This corresponds to conversation seen as a process over time. This does not negate the "short view" in which one briefly presents the gospel, an approach that is especially helpful when a seeker "asks 'what must I do to be saved' (Acts 16:30)."[90]

Evangelism for Gustafson is part of the overall gospel witness. The church is called to be a "faithful presence" in the world, to both "make disciples and serve the common good of our neighborhoods and cities."[91] We hope for a heavenly city, but that hope "does not eclipse our desire to see the kingdom of God break into human history." Rather, it expands our vision "and feeds our passion for personal sacrifice and our compassion for service

---

83. Gustafson, *Gospel Witness*, 67–73.
84. Gustafson, *Gospel Witness*, 82–83.
85. Gustafson, *Gospel Witness*, 84–85.
86. Gustafson, *Gospel Witness*, 85–88.
87. Gustafson, *Gospel Witness*, 176.
88. Gustafson, *Gospel Witness*, 186.
89. Gustafson, *Gospel Witness*, 187.
90. Gustafson, *Gospel Witness*, 189–90.
91. Gustafson, *Gospel Witness*, 260.

in daily life." "Living with a vision of heaven does not stifle our passion to serve those with temporal and eternal needs," Gustafson says, "it fuels it."[92]

Mark R. Teasdale: Abundant Life

For Mark Teasdale, the divine promise of salvation is best expressed as "abundant life." In this, he is drawing on John 10:10, where Jesus is the good shepherd who brings abundant life to the sheep. That abundant life includes not only eternal life but a deep caring for persons in this world as well as the next.[93] In addition to providing a more biblically, holistic understanding of salvation, abundant life gives us language to share our faith within today's secular culture.[94]

Here is how Teasdale describes evangelism that is centered on the promise of abundant life:

> Participating in abundant life means that we believe and practice the entire gospel. The gospel proclaims that God provides abundant life to all creation through Jesus Christ in the power of the Holy Spirit. This abundant life overflows into this world and the next. That means we should care for all that happens in this world, including working for the common good. It also means we do not lose sight of sin, repentance, and eternity.[95]

While Teasdale believes the language of abundant life communicates well in today's American culture, he also argues for adopting purely contemporary terminology when needed. Thus, in describing the three aspects of abundant life, he uses "the terms *standard of living*, *quality of life*, and *eternal life*."[96]

The first two of these are concerns Christians share with adherents of other religions or no religion at all. Thus, Christians can and should partner with all who seek to serve the common good. "As we do this," he says, "we will gain credibility to share with them that we believe what we are doing is part of how we experience salvation: participating in the abundant life of God by receiving God's provisions and sharing them with others." Then, we

---

92. Gustafson, *Gospel Witness*, 164.
93. Teasdale, *Abundant*, 10–12.
94. Teasdale, *Abundant*, 12.
95. Teasdale, *Abundant*, 15.
96. Teasdale, *Abundant*, 15.

can share our belief that abundant life also includes salvation from sin and death through Jesus Christ.[97]

Let's look at these three components of abundant life more closely. By *standard of living* Teasdale means "the ability to consume what we need and want," understood as involving both access to these goods and their affordability. The emphasis placed by Jesus on meeting physical needs shows that God wants everyone to have "a good standard of living," and for those who have received this "portion of abundant life" to share with those in need.[98]

Those in poverty do not have an adequate standard of living. As Teasdale notes, the impact of poverty is more than deprivation of physical needs. It can also lead to social isolation and a decrease in emotional health.[99] Through humanitarian aid religious and secular organizations seek to alleviate poverty and suffering, including for victims of major disasters or persecution.[100]

While not his primary goal, Jesus devoted a significant portion of his ministry to improving standards of living through caring for others. He also taught his followers to do the same, as in his parable of the sheep and the goats (Matt 25:31–46). In this passage and Jas 2:14–17 it is clear that those who claim to follow Jesus will be held accountable for their caring for the standard of living of others.[101]

The motive for aiding others, however, is not to escape judgment. It is to love others as Jesus did. We can show this by following "the example of Jesus, who was willing to have his own life disrupted and interrupted so that people who have been ostracized could rejoin society." Early Christians not only cared for those in need but welcomed them "into their houses and monasteries."[102] Hospitality and treating all persons with dignity were marks of Christian community.[103]

The concern for human dignity leads to the second dimension of abundant life, *quality of life*. This "refers to how much we enjoy our lives";[104] "to

---

97. Teasdale, *Abundant*, 14.
98. Teasdale, *Abundant*, 16.
99. Teasdale, *Abundant*, 83.
100. Teasdale, *Abundant*, 86–91.
101. Teasdale, *Abundant*, 92–95.
102. Teasdale, *Abundant*, 96.
103. Teasdale, *Abundant*, 96–97.
104. Teasdale, *Abundant*, 17.

the level of well-being a person feels."[105] Among the causes of a low quality of life in wealthy nations is loneliness, which not only leads to sadness but to a wide array of mental and physical health problems.[106] The goal of ministry is to help persons "develop lasting happiness,"[107] not "hedonistic happiness" which is immediate pleasure that does not last, but "eudaimonic happiness," which is a kind of contentment in which persons understand "their purpose in life and" feel fulfilled as human beings "when pursuing it."[108]

Jesus shows us the central way to increase the quality of life is "through forging relationships and building communities."[109] He did this with his disciples. But he also forged relationships with others, such as the Samaritan woman. Not only did he enhance her quality of life by crossing religious, ethnic, and gender barriers to establish a relationship; through her telling others about him, Jesus was able to establish a community that improved the quality of life for the entire village.[110]

As Teasdale notes, "While being in any community allows us to receive a portion of God's abundant life," we receive "a fuller experience of the abundant life of God" through "being in a community gathered around Jesus that both receives God's goodness and shares in God's mission." We not only participate in abundant life as individuals; we grow into abundant life with others.[111]

Quality of life is improved through our "simply taking time to be involved with other people in a way that meets them as they are, pays attention to them, listens to them, supports them, and shares our best with them."[112] It "increases even more when people integrate with a community that calls them to live for a greater good than just satisfying their personal desires."[113] It is through participating in such Christian communities that many are brought to conversion.[114]

---

105. Teasdale, *Abundant*, 106.
106. Teasdale, *Abundant*, 107.
107. Teasdale, *Abundant*, 111.
108. Teasdale, *Abundant*, 110.
109. Teasdale, *Abundant*, 115.
110. Teasdale, *Abundant*, 117–18.
111. Teasdale, *Abundant*, 120.
112. Teasdale, *Abundant*, 130.
113. Teasdale, *Abundant*, 133.
114. Teasdale, *Abundant*, 131–32.

This leads to the third aspect of abundant life, *eternal life*. This is what makes abundant life distinctively Christian; without it the church becomes simply "one more humanitarian agency."[115] As John 3:16 makes clear, "abundant life extends beyond the physical world," and Jesus Christ is "the unique way God has provided to save people so they will share in God's goodness rather than be condemned by the judgment of God." It also means "that the abundant life of the kingdom will claim final victory by extending from this world into eternity, where chaos will be no more."[116]

Eternal life is a gracious gift of God through Jesus Christ, received by faith. Saved by faith, we are forgiven of our sins and reconciled to God.[117] We are saved not only from God's judgment but from death itself.[118] But salvation is much more than this: it is a new life in which we participate. As Teasdale says,

> The abundant life of God flows through us now as well as into eternity, unbroken by physical death. In addition, we do not just receive abundant life; we participate in it. We are invited to believe in the Son and to join in his mission to bring abundant life to all creation.[119]

For Teasdale, to experience salvation is to participate in abundant life.[120] Salvation, then, is not merely a concept but something we experience: "We receive and share salvation in an ongoing way." To do so, we must "do more than just articulate our message; we must embody our message in how we speak, act, and move through our daily lives."[121] This is how we participate in abundant life and bring its promise to a world in need.

Howard A. Snyder: Kingdom Evangelism

Biblically, salvation means the healing of creation. Howard Snyder thus argues that the scope of salvation is much wider than is commonly believed. "Of course," he says, "the gospel is about justification by faith, atonement,

---

115. Teasdale, *Abundant*, 19; see also 138.
116. Teasdale, *Abundant*, 138.
117. Teasdale, *Abundant*, 140.
118. Teasdale, *Abundant*, 141.
119. Teasdale, *Abundant*, 136; see also 169.
120. Teasdale, *Abundant*, 34.
121. Teasdale, *Abundant*, 169.

Word and Deed

forgiveness, and new birth. But the larger truth that encompasses all of these is healing—complete healing, creation restored, true *shalom*."[122] As we will see, this expansive understanding of salvation has profound implications for evangelism.

Although this view of salvation is abundantly clear in Scripture, it has been largely missed by the church. The story of why that has happened is complex and is told by Snyder in some detail. But at the heart of the story is "the theological divorce of earth from heaven." This led, among other things, to the idea that salvation is for the soul and not the body and that materiality is of little importance.[123] This dualism of heaven and earth became increasingly pervasive and was fully dominant by 1500. "The chasm between earth and heaven could be bridged only through the sacraments and mystical experience. At death, the soul escaped earth and entered the timeless bliss of a spiritual heaven.[124] Salvation was now about going to heaven, and the biblical premise of the healing of creation was almost fully eclipsed.

Snyder insists, with Calvin and Wesley, among many others, that God's goal is not to destroy and replace creation but to refine and renew it.[125] To do this, God seeks to heal four alienations that resulted from the human fall into sin. Snyder calls this fourfold alienation "the ecology of sin: alienation from God, internal alienation within each person (alienation from oneself), alienation between humans, and alienation from and within nature." These "multiple alienations interweave, interconnect, and mutually reinforce each other." They cannot be treated separately. If healing these is God's mission, then Christian mission must focus "on healing the four alienations or divisions that result from the fall."[126]

Central to Snyder's concern is to restore to its proper theological place God's concern for the earth. The evidence for this is throughout Scripture, but aside from the creation story itself, the basis is the covenant God made after the flood in Gen 9. This "is a three-dimensional covenant" between God, Noah and his family, and every living creature. The covenant "makes a new beginning. The plan of salvation," Snyder says, "really begins here, not

---

122. Snyder, *Creation Healed*, xiv.
123. Snyder, *Creation Healed*, 4.
124. Snyder, *Creation Healed*, 26.
125. Snyder, *Creation Healed*, 59–60.
126. Snyder, *Creation Healed*, 68, 117.

Part Three: Bringing Good News

with the calling of Abraham."[127] Moreover, this covenant is not temporary; it is "an everlasting, ongoing covenant."[128]

Examining the Old Testament, Snyder finds a continuing pattern of relationship between God, the people, and the land: God gives the land to nourish the people and calls and blesses the people to care for and enjoy the land.[129] This initially applies to Israel and the land of promise, but God intends for Israel to be "God's priestly people among nations, a contrast society to show who God is and what God intends." God is the God of all nations and the entire earth, and Israel is "to bring *shalom* to the whole creation." The fulfillment of Israel's calling occurs in Jesus Christ, who is reconciling the entire world to himself.[130] The mission of God is being accomplished "through Jesus Christ in the power of the Holy Spirit." It is from God's mission that "the church derives its mission."[131]

In light of this mission, how are we to understand evangelism? "In its broadest and deepest sense," says Snyder, "evangelism means announcing and embodying the reign of God." While centered on personal faith, the "*circumference* of evangelism" is "all that is included in the good news of God's kingdom."[132] Because "kingdom evangelism" is as comprehensive as the reign of God, Snyder envisions it as having four dimensions involving conversion, disciplining, justice, and culture.

"*Conversion evangelism* is proclaiming and showing by our lives that Jesus Christ is Savior and Lord." This "is preeminently the work of the church . . . not just individuals or specialized organizations—though first and last it is in the work of the Spirit."[133] While many see this as the whole of evangelism, Snyder argues that understanding falls short of the fullness of the kingdom.[134]

"*Discipling evangelism* refers to the church making disciples, not just converts or church members." The goal is a community "that shows forth the character of Christ and the power of the Spirit in its social context." It

---

127. Snyder, *Creation Healed*, 119.
128. Snyder, *Creation Healed*, 120.
129. Snyder, *Creation Healed*, 124–25.
130. Snyder, *Creation Healed*, 126–27.
131. Snyder, *Creation Healed*, 128.
132. Snyder, *Creation Healed*, 141.
133. Snyder, *Creation Healed*, 142.
134. Snyder, *Creation Healed*, 143.

embodies reconciliation between persons from different classes, genders, races, and ethnicities.[135]

"*Justice evangelism* means living out the righteousness and justice of God's reign within the church's social context—locally and globally." This includes concern for poverty, the environment, oppression, militarism, and the like. Snyder notes that "Evangelism that does not include this justice dimension is not really evangelism in the full biblical sense." This dimension also includes "eco-evangelism—proclaiming and embodying the good news to and for the land, the physical world."[136]

"*Culture evangelism* means shaping the world's societies and cultures through the truth and virtues of God's reign." It includes "engaging society in all sectors," whether that be economics, politics, education, the arts, science, or the media.[137]

Snyder says these four dimensions of evangelism are all intertwined. Its comprehensiveness means that every disciple can be and is called to be engaged in some aspect of kingdom evangelism.

The good news is that God is at work healing all four alienations through reconciling us with God, us to ourselves, us to others, and us to the earth itself.[138] The healing of creation

> is an eschatological claim in three ways: First, it means that the end or *telos* of history foresees complete healing, restoration, and reconciliation—complete *shalom*. Second, it means the church's present being and mission are defined by this end. Finally, it means that, ultimately, God's economy or *oikonomia* and eschatology are one.[139]

"God's intent," Snyder says, "has never been to take his people out of the world." This means "the church is called to be God's healing community here and now and for eternity."[140] Because the church is Trinitarian, grounded in what God is doing through Christ and in the power of the Holy Spirit, it "is at the same time *incarnational* and *eschatological*." It is incarnational as "the

---

135. Snyder, *Creation Healed*, 143.
136. Snyder, *Creation Healed*, 143.
137. Snyder, *Creation Healed*, 143–44.
138. Snyder, *Creation Healed*, 146–50.
139. Snyder, *Creation Healed*, 156.
140. Snyder, *Creation Healed*, 167.

visible body of Christ. It is eschatological because it now lives out—and so becomes the agent of—the hope of creation finally healed."[141]

Bearing Witness to the Kingdom of God

Whether they consider social concern as a part of or a partner with evangelism, for these authors the two are inseparable. They challenge us to think of salvation as more than personal, extending it to society and creation itself. They also insist salvation is present as well as future, in this age as well as the age to come. Salvation is about this gift of a new life that death cannot take from us.

They insist that through receiving this new life, we, as persons and as churches, bear witness to the reality of the kingdom through our life together, hospitality to others, working to meet human needs, and caring for creation itself. In meeting human needs and creation care, we join with those who are not Christians to work together for the common good.

This raises the issue of Christian identity: if the work we do to alleviate suffering or bring justice is like that of others, what makes this work distinctively Christian? Our authors see it as an anticipation of the coming kingdom and look to the life of Jesus to shape both evangelism and social concern. But more than this, they recognize that Christians know Jesus was crucified and risen, the ground of hope in a world afflicted by hunger, death, suffering, and injustice. It is that hope that sustains participation in God's mission, and it is that message that offers good news to all.

---

141. Snyder, *Creation Healed*, 179.

CHAPTER 6

Evangelism with Power

> A 21st-century reformation will demand reinserting the supernatural into the heart of Christianity. This will result not only in a sounder biblical theology but also a more powerful missional church.
>
> —HWA YUNG[1]

IN 1972, DEAN M. Kelley published a book examining the decline of mainline Protestant denominations in America called *Why Conservative Churches are Growing*. He argued that the central reason for the decline is, unlike evangelical and Pentecostal churches, the mainline churches have failed to provide what only religion can provide, a sense of the meaning and purpose of life. They were not enabling persons to look at the world from the perspective of God's revelation, a way of making sense of things that the world cannot provide on its own. Instead, in a quest for relevance, mainline churches have become involved in an array of social programs that, while good, are no different from what secular agencies provide.

There is much to commend in this insight. But one story meant to illustrate it, drawn from his former pastor, Morgan Phillips, seemed to point to something more. Here is the story in full:

> Peter and John were walking in the temple at the hour of prayer. Beggars were pleading for alms as usual, and one who daily lay at the gate asked their help. What is the *Christian* answer? . . . the

1. Yung, "21st Century Reformation," 33.

conventional morality tale would propose one or another of several exemplary endings:

1. They could give the beggar some money;
2. They could help him find some useful employment suitable for the handicapped;
3. They could encourage him through various supportive techniques to overcome his personal problems and recover his self-respect;
4. They could even explore the possibilities of obtaining . . . therapy which would eliminate his disability.

Possibly any one or all of these responses might have proved helpful, but the two disciples made none of them. Instead, Peter replied, "*I have no silver and gold, but I give you what I have; in the name of Jesus Christ of Nazareth, walk!*"[2]

For Kelley, this story shows "that religious organizations have a contribution to make to the human predicament that is different from the technological interventions of secular groups," that is, "to give *meaning* to the situation: purpose, promise, and possibility."[3] But if we take the story as it is, the distinctive gift of Christianity to the situation is more than meaning: it is a manifestation of the power of the Holy Spirit, a real anticipation in this particular healing of the eschatological healing of creation to come. It is an encounter with the living God in the form of signs and wonders.

Healing, casting out demons, and raising the dead to life all marked the ministry of Jesus and that of the early church. It was essential to the good news and a critical aspect of what it meant for the kingdom of God to draw near. The authors we will consider in this chapter are not only committed to evangelism in word and deed but place an emphasis on those deeds that are signs and wonders. Their reliance on the Holy Spirit in evangelism entails an openness to the miraculous.

David Watson: Proclamation and Demonstration

When David Watson examines the ministry of Jesus and that of the early church, he finds (as we noted in chapter 1) that proclamation of the gospel

---

2. Kelley, *Conservative Churches*, 135 (ellipses and italics original).
3. Kelley, *Conservative Churches*.

is linked to a demonstration of the gospel.[4] As the scriptural accounts make clear, "you cannot separate in the evangelistic ministry of Jesus, proclamation and demonstration, preaching and acting, saying and doing."[5] The same connection is found in Paul's letters and the book of Acts. For example, in Acts 8, when Philip is evangelizing in Samaria, it is said that the people "gave heed to what was said by Philip, when they *heard* him and *saw* the signs which he did." Those signs included casting out demons and healing. "Here was powerful evangelism," Watson says, "not only because of the faithful announcement of the good news of God's Kingdom, but also because of the good deeds that accompanied the good words."[6] Watson concludes (as was cited in chapter 1) that from the New Testament era to the present, "unless there is a demonstration of the power of the Spirit, the proclamation of the gospel will be in vain. It will not be evangelism."[7]

In light of this, Watson invites us to enlarge our understanding of "the word of God." He finds it remarkable that where one would expect to read in Acts that the church grew, we find instead Luke telling us it is the word that grew, multiplied, and spread.[8] The word, says Watson, is more than Scripture. It was the word of God that created the heavens and the earth, and Jesus was the word incarnate. The word comes to us visually as well as audibly, in art as well as traditional preaching. The word of God, in short, is God's communication in all its forms to humanity.[9]

How, then, was the word communicated in the early church? Watson finds a rich array of methods, all with evangelistic import.

First, there is preaching and teaching. In emphasizing the need for a demonstration of the gospel, Watson does not want "in any way to minimize the proclamation of biblical truth." At Pentecost, he notes, those observers of the apostles had no way to understand what was happening until Peter preached.[10] In Acts the "disciples took every conceivable opportunity . . . to proclaim Christ," regardless of personal risk.[11] Watson also notes the absence of "the careful methods and strategies that so characterize

---

4. Watson, *I Believe*, 27.
5. Watson, *I Believe*, 28.
6. Watson, *I Believe*, 29.
7. Watson, *I Believe*, 30.
8. Watson, *I Believe*, 41.
9. Watson, *I Believe*, 43.
10. Watson, *I Believe*, 45.
11. Watson, *I Believe*, 48.

Part Three: Bringing Good News

evangelistic campaigns of today"; instead the disciples eagerly made use of the openings given to them by the Holy Spirit.[12]

The second way the word is communicated is through the church. Jesus was attractive to ordinary people and the oppressed because of his "lifestyle, the simplicity of his teaching, his obvious compassion, his reality, and integrity."[13] Likewise, the church is the body of Christ, and it is through the church "that Christ today expresses himself to the world."[14] People long for acceptance and "need to feel God's presence before they will listen to God's word." The church, therefore, "needs to become a loving, caring, welcoming fellowship which radiates the joy of Jesus Christ."[15] God, says Watson, is "concerned not only with personal salvation . . . but also with the establishment of his kingdom on earth." God "wants us to become a new society, a living community that will demonstrate, by its new lifestyle, new values, and new relationships," God's purpose for the world.[16]

A third means of communication is through signs and wonders. Watson finds Western culture today to be "astonishing similar to that facing the early church." The need for "a demonstration of the power of Christ" is as strong today as it was then.[17] Watson gives two examples of what he means. One was of a nonbeliever who came to Watson's church at the invitation of a friend, and upon hearing "two prophecies: two inspired utterances, given by the Spirit of God through two members of our congregation," found the second spoke directly to her. She experienced God's presence, she related, "something terrifying yet wonderful," and gave her life to Christ.[18] The second was an ex-boxer whose partial paralysis was healed by God.[19]

The fourth means is prayer and praise. In the book of Acts, the disciples "devoted themselves to prayer," waiting for the Holy Spirit to be poured out on them. Then, at Pentecost, filled with the Spirit, they began not with preaching but praise.[20] Watson recounts instances where "God has revealed his glory and spoken with power in direct response to worship and

---

12. Watson, *I Believe*, 49; see also 134.
13. Watson, *I Believe*, 49.
14. Watson, *I Believe*, 50; see also 135.
15. Watson, *I Believe*, 51.
16. Watson, *I Believe*, 135.
17. Watson, *I Believe*, 52–53.
18. Watson, *I Believe*, 53.
19. Watson, *I Believe*, 54.
20. Watson, *I Believe*, 54.

praise," including the Spirit falling afresh upon the congregation, nominal Christians filled with the Spirit, and persons converted "through the power of praise, sometimes without any preaching at all."[21]

Fifth is social action and service. Watson decries the false dichotomy between a personal and social gospel, noting that Jesus cared for bodies and minds as well as a person's spiritual condition and taught us to love our neighbor.[22] He cites Samuel Escobar, who said serving others "is not optional." Evangelism and social action "go together," Escobar said, for while we seek to get "the transforming message of Christ" to others, it is those made new by the gospel "who sometimes need to transform the structures of society so that there may be less injustice, less opportunity . . . for evil, for exploitation."[23]

Sixth is suffering, something the early church knew well. Watson believes that it is often "through suffering that God can speak powerfully." He notes that suffering is not always heroic but can be found "in the loneliness, frustration, perplexity, and afflictions . . . experienced in tough and unglamorous situations where Christians may toil away for years, with very little outwardly to show for their labours." It is also frequently through suffering that God's word is planted by the Spirit in our hearts, enabling us to "speak that word with added authority and power."[24]

The seventh and final means for communicating the word is the most essential: the power of the Holy Spirit. The "great purpose" of the gift of the Spirit is "to make us more effective in our witness and evangelism." When "the Spirit is present in power, the evangelistic work at the Church will flow naturally and spontaneously."[25] When it is not, "there will be little evangelism."[26]

The lack of the Spirit makes all the other means ineffective. Preaching becomes "a lifeless orthodoxy," the church becomes disunited and not loving, signs and wonders are counterfeit, prayer and praise are "either dangerously emotional or depressingly formal," social action is no different

---

21. Watson, *I Believe*, 55.
22. Watson, *I Believe*, 57–58.
23. Escobar, "Evangelism," 16–17; Watson, *I Believe*, 58–59.
24. Watson, *I Believe*, 61.
25. Watson, *I Believe*, 169.
26. Watson, *I Believe*, 61.

than that of secular organizations, and suffering leads "to self-pity or a self-centered persecution complex—it will not speak of Christ."[27]

In the early church, "the power of the Spirit was manifestly present because" the disciples "were totally committed to Christ and also to one another." Our individualism is why that commitment is lacking in the contemporary church, "and consequently, there is so little power or even motivation when it comes to evangelism."[28] Watson insists that "the Church must become a witnessing community, controlled and empowered by the Spirit of God before the reality of Christ can be seen as well as heard."[29]

What is needed is for congregations to be devoted to prayer and, through repentance and obedience to God, to be filled with the Spirit.[30] It may be that in our day God is not raising up individual evangelists but seeking "to renew congregations and bring to life local churches," enabling "the whole body of Christians when empowered by the Spirit of God," to "effectively communicate Christ."[31] The same Spirit that empowered the early church for effective evangelism can empower congregations today.

John Wimber: Power Evangelism

As a pastor, John Wimber had a passion for evangelism but was discontented with how it was being practiced. Certainly, there needed to be a message that presented the gospel. But in addition to the intellectual element there seemed to be an intuitive aspect that was not being addressed. He learned from Peter Wagner that evangelism was not just disseminating information but must also be persuasive, and the goal should not be to elicit decisions but to make disciples. But it was his later encounter with Wagner's positive view of Pentecostalism that proved decisive in helping Wimber fully rethink evangelism. He abandoned his belief that the charismatic gifts had ceased after the apostolic age and embraced the role of the Holy Spirit in evangelism.[32] "Once I accepted the fact that all the spiritual gifts are for

---

27. Watson, *I Believe*, 61.
28. Watson, *I Believe*, 273.
29. Watson, *I Believe*, 174.
30. Watson, *I Believe*, 180–85.
31. Watson, *I Believe*, 183.
32. Wimber, *Power Evangelism*, xvii–xix.

today," he said, "I found a key for effective evangelism: combining the proclamation with the demonstration of the gospel."[33]

Wimber had been an active consultant in the church growth movement. I agree with William Abraham's assessment that Wimber's theological journey led not to a new variation of church growth methodology but to an approach fundamentally at odds with that methodology. Wimber's emphasis on eschatology and his "more demanding conception of discipleship" distinguished his power evangelism from church growth methods.[34] But most importantly, unlike church growth, Wimber "completely subordinates planning and programs to the direct guidance of the Holy Spirit in the church."[35] While not a fully developed theology, Abraham finds Wimber's proposal to be "a significant development in modern evangelism."[36]

Wimber's theology of evangelism has three major components: the kingdom of God, power encounters, and the influence of worldviews. Underlying all three is an understanding of the power of the Holy Spirit.

Drawing on the work of New Testament scholar George Eldon Ladd, Wimber argues that in Jesus Christ, "the future age, the kingdom of God" has "invaded the present age, the kingdom of Satan."[37] Thus, Wimber says,

> This explains the twofold pattern of Christ's ministry, repeated wherever he went: first *proclamation*, then *demonstration*. First, he preached repentance and the good news of the kingdom of God. Then he cast out demons, healed the sick, raised the dead—which proved he was the presence of the kingdom, the Anointed One.[38]

Jesus' miracles not only show who he is, but also shows "us what the kingdom of God is like," revealing "glimpses of God's love, peace, and joy."[39] They are present anticipations of the future: casting out demons points to the final demise of Satan, healing points to the end of suffering, and raising of the dead points to the end of death itself.[40]

---

33. Wimber, *Power Evangelism*, xx.
34. Abraham, *Logic of Evangelism*, 88–89.
35. Abraham, *Logic of Evangelism*, 89.
36. Abraham, *Logic of Evangelism*, 90.
37. Wimber, *Power Evangelism*, 5.
38. Wimber, *Power Evangelism*, 6.
39. Wimber, *Power Evangelism*, 91.
40. Wimber, *Power Evangelism*, 92.

Part Three: Bringing Good News

The church is both a witness to the kingdom and "the instrument of the kingdom," but only God can establish the kingdom.[41] Thus, power and authority comes only from God. Jesus gave his disciples power and authority to cast out demons and heal the sick, and that same power is available to all Christians today through the Holy Spirit.[42]

For the second component of his theology of evangelism, Wimber drew upon missionary anthropologist Alan Tippert's concept of a power encounter. For Tippert, thinking in a missionary context, a power encounter occurs when persons see the superior power of God over tribal gods when meeting human need, as in the case of healing sickness or confronting demonic possession.[43] Wimber includes healing and conflict with demons as examples of power encounters but defines it more broadly: "Any system of force that must be overcome for the gospel to be believed is cause for a power encounter." What is overcome in a power encounter is unbelief, which "is the kingdom of Satan, albeit a far less visible form of him than demons or illness." When we become vehicles of the Spirit and unbelievers are converted, "the kingdom of God defeats the kingdom of Satan."[44]

The "ultimate power encounter" was at the cross. "Great power was released" on Good Friday: "the earth shook, rocks split, the sun stopped shining for three hours, . . . the Temple curtain was torn in two," "tombs were opened." "Life was radiating from the death of Christ," Wimber concludes, "it shook a creation that was under the reign of evil." With "the resurrection and ascension, Christ came out the victor, and Satan the loser." This secures salvation for all who have faith in Christ. But we live between the resurrection and the coming of the kingdom in fullness, and many who are still under the reign of Satan need to experience that victory in their own lives.[45]

Power encounters are hard to accept among Western Christians because they "are difficult to control" and "do not fit rational thought." They are transrational in nature.[46] Yet phenomena like persons falling to the floor under the power of the Spirit have occurred in religious awakenings in the past, including in the ministries of "John and Charles Wesley, George

---

41. Wimber, *Power Evangelism*, 7.
42. Wimber, *Power Evangelism*, 11; see also 31.
43. Wimber, *Power Evangelism*, 18–19.
44. Wimber, *Power Evangelism*, 16.
45. Wimber, *Power Evangelism*, 20.
46. Wimber, *Power Evangelism*, 23.

Evangelism with Power

Whitefield, Charles Finney, and Jonathan Edwards."[47] In Wimber's own church such phenomena occurred when a guest preacher asked the Holy Spirit to come. Wimber and his staff were "extremely upset," and church members left. But Wimber was reassured of their authenticity by a reliable fellow pastor as well as those prior examples in history.[48] Most important, as the supernatural phenomena continued over the next several months, was the fruit it produced.

> New life came into our church. All who were touched by and who yielded to the Holy Spirit—whether they fell over, started shaking, became very quiet and still, or spoke in tongues—accepted the experience and thought it was wonderful, drawing them closer to God. More importantly, prayer, Scripture reading, caring for others, and the love of God all increased.[49]

Whether among the unchurched or churched, if a power encounter is truly of God, it will bear fruit consistent with the kingdom of God.

Power encounters are an intrinsic part of power evangelism. Wimber defines power evangelism as "a presentation of the gospel that is rational, but that also transcends the rational. The explanation of the gospel comes with a demonstration of God's power through signs and wonders." The form the power encounters can take includes "words of knowledge, . . . healing, prophecy, and deliverance from evil spirits." It is the demonstration of power that overcomes resistance and encourages receptivity to the gospel.[50]

Wimber contrasts power evangelism with programmatic evangelism. In programmatic evangelism, the message is presented through rational argument, usually to passive listeners. It is usually a prepared message delivered to anyone and everyone and is primarily seeking a decision.[51] Power evangelism contains within it the "heart of programmatic evangelism, a simple presentation of the gospel." Yet it is quite different. Instead of a preprogrammed message, "those practicing power evangelism depend on the immediate illumination of the Holy Spirit to give pertinent information for each encounter." Thus, each instance of evangelism "is initiated by the Holy Spirit for a *specific* place, time, person, or group."[52] Programmatic

---

47. Wimber, *Power Evangelism*, 25.
48. Wimber, *Power Evangelism*, 24–25.
49. Wimber, *Power Evangelism*, 26.
50. Wimber, *Power Evangelism*, 35.
51. Wimber, *Power Evangelism*, 45.
52. Wimber, *Power Evangelism*, 46.

evangelism, while it may have some beneficial results, is fundamentally incomplete as it lacks the corresponding "demonstration of the kingdom of God in signs and wonders."[53]

The dependence on the Holy Spirit includes the element of a divine appointment. This "is an appointed time in which God reveals himself to an individual or group through spiritual gifts or other supernatural phenomena."[54] An example is when the Holy Spirit leads someone, often through persistent thoughts, to go to a particular place or speak to a particular person. It often includes a word of knowledge when the Spirit prompts you to say something related to a person's life that you could not have otherwise known. This is an "integral part of power evangelism."[55]

The third component of Wimber's theology of evangelism is the influence of worldviews, a concept he appropriates from Charles Kraft. All cultures necessarily have worldviews, although most within each are not conscious of it.[56] Worldviews provide *explanations* "of how and why things are and how and why they continue to change." They "serve as a basis for *evaluation*, for judging and validating experience." They also provide "*psychological reinforcement* for a society's way of life."[57] While worldviews vary in their openness to new ideas, they are always changing. Worldviews have "an *integrating function*" enabling cultures to incorporate new ideas and experiences even as others are rejected.[58]

The Western worldview "assumes that nothing exists except matter" and "seeks a rational explanation for all experience." Those in the West "often live as though the material world is more real than the spiritual" and "exclude from reality all phenomena that cannot be measured scientifically."[59] Hence, it is highly resistant to supernatural phenomena, in contrast to many other cultures in Asia, Africa, and Latin America. A consequence of this is that while persons may have faith in Jesus Christ, they lack the "faith that produces miracles," something Wimber himself initially lacked.[60] This way of phrasing things may convey a wrong idea—Wimber is not saying

53. Wimber, *Power Evangelism*, 47.
54. Wimber, *Power Evangelism*, 51.
55. Wimber, *Power Evangelism*, 52.
56. Wimber, *Power Evangelism*, 67.
57. Wimber, *Power Evangelism*, 68.
58. Wimber, *Power Evangelism*, 69.
59. Wimber, *Power Evangelism*, 70–71.
60. Wimber, *Power Evangelism*, 111; see also 43.

faith produces miracles in a cause-and-effect way but is really speaking of having an expectant faith in what God can do.

There are two other aspects of Wimber's theology that need further clarification. With regard to divine healing, Wimber (along with all others discussed in this book who are open to it) rejects the "if you have faith you will be healed" theology that is common to Word of Faith advocates. He recognizes that not everyone is healed, and although, because God is love, God is always inclined toward healing, it is never automatic.[61]

With regard to the demonic more needs to be said than what is found in *Power Evangelism*. It is clear Wimber regards demons as spiritual beings opposed to the kingdom of God. What is not clear is how demonic activity is to be distinguished from other phenomena such as mental illness or ordinary sin. Much damage has been done by practitioners of deliverance ministry who failed to make such distinctions. In a subsequent book, *Power Healing*, Wimber recognizes the problem and argues that such things as bad habits, sin, and physical and emotional illness are not "always or even frequently caused by demons, only that their cause *may* be from the influence of demons." Moreover, causes can be complex, "a combination involving psychological, physical, and demonic factors."[62] Wimber's discussion in this book is at least an initial attempt to address an issue fraught with difficulties.

Wimber argues that intrinsic to "the modern Western worldview is a desire to control everything—people, things, events, even future events."[63] Yet Christians are called to go against the grain and instead "submit our lives to the control of the Holy Spirit, to ask it to actualize all that it has for us, to release the gifts."[64] And finally, against our tendency to take charge, "we must learn to wait on God, allowing him to speak, act, lead."[65] In power evangelism we "yield control of our lives to the Holy Spirit, learning to hear and do its will, risking all we have to defeat Satan and to advance the kingdom of God."[66]

---

61. See Wimber, *Power Healing*.
62. Wimber, *Power Healing*, 102.
63. Wimber, *Power Evangelism*, 70.
64. Wimber, *Power Evangelism*, 151.
65. Wimber, *Power Evangelism*, 155.
66. Wimber, *Power Evangelism*, 156.

Part Three: Bringing Good News

Gary Tyra: Prophetic Speech and Action

"Have you ever," Gary Tyra asks, "felt 'led,' 'prompted,' or 'impressed' to speak or act toward another person or group of persons on God's behalf, whether to evangelize or edify or equip?"[67] Tyra argues that this sense of the Holy Spirit prompting is not exceptional but the intended norm for all Christians and is the primary way the Spirit works to accomplish God's mission.[68] He finds a multitude of examples in both the Old and New Testaments and attributes attentiveness to the Spirit's leading to the phenomenal growth of Pentecostalism in the twentieth century. He seeks to encourage Western evangelicals, whether Pentecostal/Charismatic or not, to adopt what is in effect a different way of being Christian through showing the intrinsic connection between this work of the Holy Spirit and mission.[69]

For Tyra, mission involves "*both* gospel proclamation toward the end of disciple-making *and* a loving engagement in social action toward the goal of a more peaceful, just, humane society, and a clean, healthy environment."[70] While the mission of God extends beyond individual humans, "holding disciple-making, social action and creation care in healthy tension," it is disciple-making that is "at least the heart of missional activity."[71]

Tyra understands mission as the work of the Trinity. All three persons work together to restore people to "the life-giving community . . . that is at the heart of the Trinity," not only regenerating and sanctifying persons but enabling "their participation in the ministry of reconciliation as well."[72] Given that the Father and Son have sent the Spirit into the world for this purpose, Tyra concludes "*that being missional is the heartbeat of the Holy Spirit.*"[73]

In his survey of the whole of Scripture Tyra finds prophetic speech and action as a major form of empowerment by the Holy Spirit. Prophetic speech is not "foretelling, but forth telling"; "to say something to God or on behalf of God to others, as a result of the prompting of the Spirit."[74]

---

67. Tyra, *Holy Spirit*, 13.
68. Tyra, *Holy Spirit*, 12.
69. Tyra, *Holy Spirit*, 130.
70. Tyra, *Holy Spirit*, 24.
71. Tyra, *Holy Spirit*, 27.
72. Tyra, *Holy Spirit*, 30–31.
73. Tyra, *Holy Spirit*, 30.
74. Tyra, *Holy Spirit*, 41.

Likewise, prophetic action is "doing something toward others on behalf of God at the Spirit's prompting."[75] But more than this, Tyra finds a "biblically discernible connection between prophetic activity and a missional faithfulness and hopefulness."[76] This is most evident in the account of the early church in Acts. He believes that we need today to imitate the missional practices shown in Luke-Acts,[77] and that "at least some" of our own missional activity "be conducted in a prophetic manner, unmistakably empowered by the Holy Spirit."[78]

Tyra notes that some Pentecostal and Charismatic scholars divide ministry practices in the book of Acts "into two broad categories: Spirit-enabled miraculous signs (works) and Spirit-inspired sermons (words)." While he does not say this is wrong, he instead wants to distinguish "between a ministry *means* and a ministry *end*." From that perspective, a prophetic ministry in the early church can be understood as pursuing three ends: "*evangelism* (bringing people to faith in Christ), and *edification* (building people up in their walk with Christ), and *equipping* (providing the various kinds of support necessary for people to accomplish the unique mission they have received from Christ)." All of these ends are pursued with prophetic speech and action.[79]

With this overarching approach to mission, Tyra can now offer a definition of prophetic evangelism. It refers

> to sermons (verbal presentation of the gospel) and acts of compassion that tend to be delivered in an extemporaneous and spontaneous manner as a result of an explicit sense that the disciple is being prompted by the Holy Spirit to do so in a particular way at a particular time.[80]

He further specifies that "the *prophetic acts of compassion* can be *spectacularly miraculous* (such as exorcisms and physical healings) or *subtly miraculous* (such as sacrificial sharing of one's resources with those in need or a willingness to be reconciled with previously estranged enemies)."[81] Tyra follows the same pattern in defining prophetic edification and prophetic

75. Tyra, *Holy Spirit*, 46.
76. Tyra, *Holy Spirit*, 75.
77. Tyra, *Holy Spirit*, 77.
78. Tyra, *Holy Spirit*, 34.
79. Tyra, *Holy Spirit*, 79.
80. Tyra, *Holy Spirit*, 80.
81. Tyra, *Holy Spirit*, 80.

equipping.[82] He offers Ananias of Damascus (Acts 9:10–20) as an especially helpful model for all these aspects of prophetic mission.[83]

As he explores the work of those who argue that the nature of the church is missional, Tyra argues that "the goal of missional communities" is twofold: "to engage in a faithful *representation* of the reign of God incarnated into a particular ministry location," and using "methodological innovations" that "are the result of an imaginative engagement in the process of ministry *contextualization*."[84] He believes prophetic speech and action aid in accomplishing both of these goals.

With regard to contextualization, Tyra notes that missional church literature envisions "an imaginative dialogue between the scriptural text and the cultural contexts."[85] Drawing on the importance of prophetic activity in both the early church and among Christians in the Majority World, Tyra argues that this is actually "a conversation with three entities, not two: the biblical text, the cultural context, and the Spirit of mission!" The role of the Spirit "needs to be made more explicit."[86]

The Holy Spirit also enables the missional church to represent a foretaste of the kingdom community.[87] Given that love is "integral to who the Spirit is and what" the Spirit "is about, it should not surprise us to discover him encouraging church members to speak and act toward others in the loving, edifying ways."[88] The missional church serves people through prophetic action, which can "be either small and personal, or bold and big" (such as working for creation care or changing socioeconomic structures). Prophetic action, as has been said, can be spectacularly miraculous or subtly miraculous.[89] Spirit-prompted prophetic speech can also represent the kingdom through prophetic sermons or ministry conversations.[90]

For Tyra, the Holy Spirit is a missionary Spirit, an evangelistic Spirit. To be a faithful and hopeful missionary people he urges us to listen to the

---

82. Tyra, *Holy Spirit*, 89, 95–96.
83. Tyra, *Holy Spirit*, 98.
84. Tyra, *Holy Spirit*, 132.
85. Tyra, *Holy Spirit*, 138.
86. Tyra, *Holy Spirit*, 139; see also 135, 141.
87. Tyra, *Holy Spirit*, 149.
88. Tyra, *Holy Spirit*, 150.
89. Tyra, *Holy Spirit*, 152.
90. Tyra, *Holy Spirit*, 156–57.

promptings of the Holy Spirit with the same attention and obedience as was found in the early church.

Experiencing Life in the Kingdom

These authors share a deep conviction that the life of the coming kingdom can break into the present through the power of the Holy Spirit. Like all the authors in this book, they find love for God and others to be the most important manifestation of that life. But they go further in emphasizing signs and wonders as anticipation of a kingdom in which there is no sickness or death, no sin or evil. These are powerful demonstrations of the good news that evangelism proclaims.

They also place great importance on the promptings of the Holy Spirit in initiating an evangelistic encounter. Western Christians have been enculturated to deny or ignore such promptings and need to cultivate an openness and attentiveness to the Holy Spirit.

They are also convinced that our individualistic Western culture hinders us from seeing the communal nature of salvation. The Holy Spirit not only seeks persons but creates community. This Spirit-formed and Spirit-led community is in itself a witness to the powerful presence of the life of the age to come.

PART FOUR

Kingdom and Community

CHAPTER 7

Evangelistic Community

The only hermeneutic of the gospel is a congregation of men and women who believe it and live by it.

—LESSLIE NEWBIGIN[1]

EVANGELISM, AS PRACTICED IN the nineteenth and early twentieth centuries, had become highly individualistic. Whether it was a preacher concluding an evangelistic sermon with an altar call or a Christian sharing the gospel one-on-one with another person, the message was to individuals and the hoped-for response was individual decisions.

By the latter part of the twentieth century, there was growing dissatisfaction with this way of evangelizing. The problem was not with the concept of personal salvation through justification and sanctification—that remained a central promise of the gospel. The problem was the awareness that people were not simply autonomous individuals as the Western Enlightenment had assumed but were shaped by the contexts in which they were embedded. There was the larger cultural context which so powerfully affects our assumptions, way of life, and how we see the world. And there were much more local communities, including the church, that through their own stories and practices shape the lives and outlooks of their participants.

Rather than simply proclamation, evangelism began to be seen as occurring in the interplay of the gospel, the cultural context, and the local

---

1. Newbigin, *Gospel in a Pluralistic Society*, 227.

church. This led to a variety of new approaches to evangelism that took seriously all three of these factors. Where they disagreed was on their exact understanding of the three and the manner in which they are related. In this chapter, we'll look at four distinct ways of thinking about evangelism and the church in light of culture.

The Church Growth Movement

It would be hard to overestimate the impact of the church growth movement on both global mission and the church in America. While exceedingly controversial in its early decades, its insights and methods have permeated the way a multitude of church pastors and denominational leaders think of evangelism. Yet, for all of that, the movement still has its critics, including many of the persons discussed in this book.

The founder of the church growth movement is Donald A. McGavran, who developed its central principles while serving as a missionary in India for the Disciples of Christ. McGavran himself does not claim to be the sole originator of church growth—he was influenced by others, and none more than Methodist Bishop J. Waskom Pickett and his 1933 book *Christian Mass Movements in India*. "I lit my candle at his fire," McGavran wrote,[2] spurring him to over two decades of research on why churches were or were not growing.

It was very clear to McGavran that, in India, some churches were, in fact, growing while most were not. McGavran said that he

> knew perfectly well that church growth is dependent on the action of the Holy Spirit, but since God works in orderly ways and, according to Scripture, does not want any to perish, I believed the Holy Spirit wanted more growth than we were getting. I came to believe that nongrowth is a disease but a curable disease.[3]

Leaving his position as a missionary administrator, McGavran "spent seventeen years in planting churches." What he learned he published in 1955 as *The Bridges of God*, arguably the first church growth book.[4] He then extended his research to other countries in Asia and Africa, leading to his 1959 book *How Churches Grow*. His culminating work *Understanding*

---

2. McGavran and Hunter, *Church Growth*, 14.
3. McGavran and Hunter, *Church Growth*, 16.
4. Wagner, "Donald A. McGavran," 16.

Evangelistic Community

Church Growth was published in 1970, has gone through three editions, and remains the standard textbook on church growth. Colleagues of McGavran, like C. Peter Wagner and Win Arn, produced books and other resources directly applying McGavran's approach to the American church.

McGavran is very clear about the theological foundation for the church growth movement: It is "based on the biblical judgment that men and women without Jesus Christ are truly lost and God wants them found."[5] McGavran develops this most fully in chapter 2 of *Understanding Church Growth*, where he contrasts a search theology with a harvest theology. Search theology, which was dominant at the time McGavran was writing, says "that in evangelism the essential thing is not the finding, but going everywhere and preaching the gospel."[6] Any emphasis on results was "fiercely attacked"; "missionary writers" vied "with one another in deprecating mere numbers."[7] McGavran believes a search theology "is not biblically justified. . . . *God wants his lost children found.*"[8] In contrast, Jesus emphasizes sending "laborers into *his* harvest," which McGavran understands as going to populations receptive to the gospel.[9] This practice of going to "where people responded" was also standard for the church in the New Testament.[10] "Indeed," concludes McGavran, "God commands an ardent searching for the lost *in order to find them.*"[11]

The principle of receptivity—that you put most of your resources toward reaching populations that are receptive to the gospel at the time they are receptive—is one of the central insights of the church growth movement. A second is related to it and is, according to George G. Hunter III, the key strategy of the church growth movement: "The faith spreads most naturally and contagiously along the lines of the social networks of living Christians, especially new Christians." People are most responsive "when the invitation is extended to them from credible Christian friends, relatives, neighbors, and fellow workers from within their social web."[12]

---

5. McGavran and Hunter, *Church Growth*, 19; see also Wagner, "Donald A. McGavran," 16–17.
6. McGavran and Wagner, *Understanding Church Growth*, 24.
7. McGavran and Wagner, *Understanding Church Growth*, 26.
8. McGavran and Wagner, *Understanding Church Growth*, 27.
9. McGavran and Wagner, *Understanding Church Growth*, 27.
10. McGavran and Wagner, *Understanding Church Growth*, 29.
11. McGavran and Wagner, *Understanding Church Growth*, 30.
12. McGavran and Hunter, *Church Growth*, 30.

Part Four: Kingdom and Community

Extensive research continues to show that this is by far the most common way persons become involved in a Christian community. Social networks, in McGavran's words, are the "bridges of God."

Another major insight is the "people movement theory." How people make decisions varies from culture to culture. While Western culture is highly individualistic, for most people in the world important decisions are made by the community. Therefore, evangelism in those cultures "had to be through the encouragement of a multi-individual, interdependent conversion process whereby members of families, extended families, clans, villages, and tribes would become Christian at the same time."[13]

Perhaps the most controversial element of church growth theory is the homogenous unit principle (HUP). Put succinctly by McGavran, it is that "People like to become Christians without crossing racial, linguistic, or class barriers." "The world's population is a mosaic," McGavran says, "and each piece has a separate life of its own that seems strange and often unlovely to men and women of other pieces."[14] The most obvious barriers are linguistic and cultural—McGavran is a sharp critic of missions that either overtly or subtly expect converts to adopt the culture of the missionary. He seeks to honor the particularities of each culture and advocates a contextualized gospel. He also recognizes that the church is called to a unity that transcends racial, ethnic, and class divisions, but notes that it applies to those who, having been "baptized into Christ, have put on Christ." But to require that of non-Christians as "a prerequisite for salvation" is erecting a barrier to their becoming a Christian.[15] People should not have to join another culture to be Christians.

That, in general, people are more comfortable in not crossing racial or class barriers may be a valid observation, but when turned into a strategy for church growth it elicits strong criticism. René Padilla argued that in the apostolic church, "The breaking down of the barriers that separate people in the world was regarded as *an essential aspect of the gospel*, not merely as a result of it."[16] While McGavran sees evidence of the HUP in Scripture, Padilla's own examination points to multicultural churches in the New Testament. Thus, he concludes, "the use of the homogenous unit principle for church growth has no biblical foundation. Its advocates have taken as

13. Wagner, "Donald A. McGavran," 17.
14. McGavran and Wagner, *Understanding Church Growth*, 163.
15. McGavran and Wagner, *Understanding Church Growth*, 169.
16. Padilla, "Unity of the Church," 29.

their starting point a sociological observation and developed a missionary strategy; only then, a posteriori, have they made the attempt to find biblical support."[17] A much more extensive critique, which also summarizes the debate, is found in the book by Bruce W. Fong.[18] From a different angle, Skip Bell points out that while the HUP may have made sense in the time it was proposed, in the twenty-first century, we are seeing increasing numbers of multicultural churches in America and persons who are drawn to their diversity."[19]

Another controversial proposal by McGavran is his distinction between discipling and perfecting. Discipling, he says, is "helping a people . . . turn from non-Christian faith to Christ. Discipling was to be followed by perfecting, that is, by the whole complex process of growth in grace, ethical improvement, and the conversion of individuals in that first and succeeding generations."[20] According to Wagner, McGavran was concerned "that too many mission activities had been diverted to perfecting when the original mission charter demanded discipling."[21]

Win Arn sees disciple-making as a relational alternative to evangelism understood as a verbal presentation of the gospel to elicit a response. Disciple-making seeks a behavioral change.[22] Thus, "Effective disciple-making strategies should provide a variety of opportunities for non-Christians to be with other Christians to observe a variety of believers in a variety of situations."[23] Arn points out that in giving the Great Commission, Jesus said to make disciples, not just verbally present the gospel.

Critics note that in the Great Commission, Jesus also says to teach them to obey what he has commanded (Matt 28:20). For the proponents of church growth, the teaching aspect of the command has to do with perfecting, not discipling. The critics argue that teaching is part of what it means to make disciples, and to omit it at the beginning is to invite a misunderstanding of what it means to follow Jesus. It is to envision discipleship without, say, the emphasis on the kingdom of heaven that is pervasive throughout the Gospel of Matthew.

17. Padilla, "Unity of the Church," 29.
18. Fong, *Racial Equality*, 18.
19. Bell, "What Is Wrong," 19.
20. McGavran and Wagner, *Understanding Church Growth*, 123.
21. Wagner, "Donald A. McGavran," 18.
22. Arn, "Evangelism or Disciple Making?," 59.
23. Arn, "Evangelism or Disciple Making?," 60.

Part Four: Kingdom and Community

Church growth theory, by its very nature, is not static. It is research driven, and further research leads to new insights. In addition, some church growth proponents have seriously wrestled with the issues raised by critics. One such proponent is George G. Hunter III, whose recent work has expanded the traditional church growth concern for cultural relevance to include emotional relevance, highlighted the role of "radical outreach" to the marginalized, and emphasized acting out of a social conscience as aspects of growing churches.[24] Hunter notes, writing in 2009, "most of us in the Church Growth Movement have mellowed; we now present our insights in more nuanced ways than before." The still "indispensable contribution" of the movement is "informing evangelization within and across cultures." Most importantly, "We know the goal of evangelism is more than just getting people into churches and enrolled for heaven. Churches are called to produce the kind of disciples who know that they are the 'salt of the earth' and 'the light of the world.'"[25]

Darrell L. Guder: Continuing Conversion of the Church

As we saw in chapter 2, Darrell Guder is among those who argue that "the center or core of the *missio Dei* is evangelization: the communication of the gospel."[26] Mission, for Guder, is witness, which "serves as an overreaching term drawing together proclamation (*kerygma*), community (*koinonia*), and service (*diakonia*)" as its "essential dimensions."[27] He suggests evangelism itself be redescribed as "evangelization," "which is closer to New Testament usage," resists reduction to a "method or program," and emphasizes "the ongoing, dynamic, process character of the church's witness."[28]

Guder then seeks to develop his theology of evangelization as a form of witness. But central to this theology is a further aspect of evangelization:

> If the Christian community is to carry out its mission of gospel witness, then its evangelization will be directed both to itself as well as to the world into which it is sent. . . . For the sake of its evangelistic vocation, the continuing conversion of the church is essential.[29]

24. Hunter, *Apostolic Congregation*, 31, 34–35. See also Hunter, *Radical Outreach*.
25. Hunter, *Apostolic Congregation*, xxi–xxii.
26. Guder, *Continuing Conversion*, 49.
27. Guder, *Continuing Conversion*, 53.
28. Guder, *Continuing Conversion*, 25.
29. Guder, *Continuing Conversion*, 26.

Evangelistic Community

We will discuss why Guder argues for the ongoing evangelization of the church in the pages ahead, but first let's examine more fully his understanding of witness.

Guder sees God's mission in creating a world and then redeeming it when it went astray as good news, and the primary vocation of the church is to witness to that good news. Scripture "is not a collection of universal ideas" but an account of "a particular, specific history as the event of God's self-disclosure." It is through God's encounter with Israel that "the good news that God is loving and purposeful enters into human history and becomes knowable."[30] The motivation for God's mission is God's compassion,[31] and "results in the sending of Jesus," whose "mission was God's mission," carried out in the same compassion that God had shown to Israel.[32]

At "the very heart of the good news" Jesus "brought and embodied" is the kingdom of God, which is at the same time both present and yet to come.[33] This kingdom "is defined by the very character and action of God," and to enter into it is to be liberated "from all that separates from God."[34] The presence of the kingdom in Jesus through forgiving sins, healing, forming a new community, and the like confronted a world in which the reign of God was resisted, leading to his death on the cross.[35] But that death was itself central to the mission of Jesus. However problematic the cross of Jesus was to people then and is to people today, it became the heart of the good news in the New Testament. His death for our sins was the culmination of his mission and demonstrated "the depth and comprehensive character of God's love for the world."[36]

With the resurrection of Jesus, "the message and the messenger merged, the king and the kingdom came together."[37] Mission now not only proclaims the kingdom of God but is itself a manifestation of the kingdom of God. The risen Jesus "sends his disciples into the world" as a furtherance of his mission, a mission "defined by the entire event of the life, teaching,

---

30. Guder, *Continuing Conversion*, 29.
31. Guder, *Continuing Conversion*, 32.
32. Guder, *Continuing Conversion*, 33–34.
33. Guder, *Continuing Conversion*, 36.
34. Guder, *Continuing Conversion*, 37.
35. Guder, *Continuing Conversion*, 39.
36. Guder, *Continuing Conversion*, 41.
37. Guder, *Continuing Conversion*, 44.

Part Four: Kingdom and Community

proclamation, and passion of Jesus."[38] It was the empowering presence of the Holy Spirit at Pentecost that "equips the apostolic community to become God's missionary people." The church, then, exists for mission.[39]

God's mission takes place in history, in the form of "events in which God encounters us and enable us to recognize it is God who is speaking and acting." This incarnation in history reaches its "climax and ultimate purpose" in Jesus Christ. As an event in history it "could be witnessed, it could be reported and put into words."[40] As the good news is shared to all the world, "this witness may be translated into every human setting, since Jesus may be met and known in every human setting."[41]

Translatability, then, is a necessary aspect of mission. This is not simply the translation "from one language to another," but from one culture to another, wherein the gospel finds "tangible expression" within the receiving culture.[42] But this "process of gospel translation is profoundly interactive. As the gospel is heard within a culture, and as a missionary people is formed within it, that culture will also be challenged." Cultures reflect human sinfulness; thus, "the impact of the gospel will be both affirming and critical of all cultures."[43] This "includes the continuing conversion of the translator—evangelists themselves,"[44] because each "particular culture's translation of the gospel contributes a witness that corrects, expands, and challenges all other forms of witness in a worldwide church."[45]

Yet God's loving mission in history carries with it a necessary risk: because of sin, humans can "encounter God's Word and work in history" only "to ignore it, to reject it, to distort it, or to manipulate it"[46]—in other words, to control it. Sin, Guder argues, can be understood "as the constant attempt to bring under human control what we are not qualified to control."[47] The risk this poses to translatability "is that sinful humans are its agents." We

---

38. Guder, *Continuing Conversion*, 46.
39. Guder, *Continuing Conversion*, 51.
40. Guder, *Continuing Conversion*, 80.
41. Guder, *Continuing Conversion*, 81.
42. Guder, *Continuing Conversion*, 83.
43. Guder, *Continuing Conversion*, 85.
44. Guder, *Continuing Conversion*, 89.
45. Guder, *Continuing Conversion*, 90.
46. Guder, *Continuing Conversion*, 74.
47. Guder, *Continuing Conversion*, 76.

Evangelistic Community

"never divorce" ourselves "from the desire to bring this powerful and radical gospel under control."[48]

Even apart from sin, translation of the gospel leads to its reduction. This reduction occurs both in "translation in the narrower sense, from one language to another, and in the broader sense, from one culture to another." While translation can also "uncover dimensions of a message which have not been" previously recognized, at the same time, reduction almost always occurs.[49] This reduction can only be overcome by the Holy Spirit, "which empowers the translating, the proclaiming, and the hearing of the biblical witness as God's Word."[50]

Reduction becomes a more serious problem when, through sin, we seek to control the gospel. We then treat "our unavoidable reductions" as absolutes and "assert that our way of understanding the Christian faith is a final version of Christian truth." We "enshrine one cultural articulation of the gospel as the normative statement for all cultures."[51] This Guder calls reduction*ism*, a way of distorting the gospel that has afflicted the church throughout history. The most common way this occurs, he says, "has been to diminish the historical particularity of Jesus by reducing him and his message to a set of ideas . . . often connected with a codified ethic and managed thematically within the church's rites and celebrations."[52]

The "most profound reductionism of the gospel" today is the making of a "fundamental dichotomy between the benefits of the gospel and the mission of the gospel." The focus is on individual salvation separated from the purpose of grace, which is to empower the people of God "to become Christ's witnesses."[53] The effects of this reductionism range "throughout every dimension and expression of Christian thought and action," trivializing "God as it makes God into a manageable deity" as well as reducing how church and mission are understood.[54]

The missional community was never intended to only proclaim a verbal message, but to be a witness "in every dimension of its existence" to the new reality inaugurated in Jesus Christ. The "essential differentness" of this

---

48. Guder, *Continuing Conversion*, 93.
49. Guder, *Continuing Conversion*, 98.
50. Guder, *Continuing Conversion*, 99.
51. Guder, *Continuing Conversion*, 100.
52. Guder, *Continuing Conversion*, 101.
53. Guder, *Continuing Conversion*, 120.
54. Guder, *Continuing Conversion*, 131–32.

community, as it is shaped by the Holy Spirit, is manifested "in the relationships of Christians with one another" as well as taking on the character of a "servant who radically refuses every form of force and coercion." It is this "essential differentness" from the culture that "provokes sinful Christians to try to bring" the gospel "under control," leading to reductionism.[55] Maintaining the integrity of its mission is why the continuing conversion of the church is so essential.

The implications of this theology of evangelization for the church are manifold. While the particular shape of a local congregation "will differ from place to place, from culture to culture," Guder argues that it is essential to the mission of God that "The people of God . . . have a visible, tangible, experiencable shape." It is the work of the Holy Spirit to "form mission communities so that the gospel may be incarnated in particular places, to be the witness to Jesus Christ."[56] But in any culture, there are aspects "which are hostile to the gospel, or conversely, which are threatened by the gospel. Much of the reductionistic process is related to such cultural hostility."[57]

Thus, to be renewed, a local church must confront its reductionism. This is a work of the Spirit. But a local church can invite renewal by beginning with the biblical witness and asking "Scripture the questions that will open us up to a reviving encounter with the gospel."[58] "The Holy Spirit shapes God's people for mission . . . as the community 'indwells' Scripture." Through this, the people "are learning to think Christianly; they are learning how to see the world through the eyes of Jesus" and become "effective translators of the gospel into their world."[59]

Central to encountering and celebrating Christ is the integrity of public worship.[60] This, Guder says, "is the most sensitive indicator of the spiritual health or lack of it in the body of Christ."[61] The central issue, Guder believes, is not the style of worship—"of organs versus guitars, baroque versus rock"—but "a general lack of understanding of what worship is really

---

55. Guder, *Continuing Conversion*, 137–38.
56. Guder, *Continuing Conversion*, 146.
57. Guder, *Continuing Conversion*, 147.
58. Guder, *Continuing Conversion*, 151.
59. Guder, *Continuing Conversion*, 160.
60. Guder, *Continuing Conversion*, 153.
61. Guder, *Continuing Conversion*, 154.

all about."⁶² Worship is God-centered and, as such, "is the first and central form of witness to the world." What the world needs to see is "a community of people who love the God they are addressing, who love each other, and who desire to carry their God's love into the world."⁶³

The continuing conversion of the church is necessary to fulfilling its vocation as a witness to Jesus Christ. The ongoing renewal of the church has been an essential aspect of God's work from the beginning. "The Holy Spirit began the conversion of the church at Pentecost," Guder notes, "and has continued that conversion throughout the pilgrimage of God's people from the first century up to now. The conversion of the church will be the continuing work of God's Spirit until God completes the good work begun in Jesus Christ."⁶⁴

Brad J. Kallenberg: Evangelism as Communal Practice

Western culture, which has been shaped for centuries by Enlightenment-based modernity, is now moving into postmodernity. While some bemoan this, Brad Kallenberg does not. "After all," he says, "modernity has been no friend of the church." So instead of gnashing his "teeth at the onrush of postmodernity," Kallenberg wonders "whether postmodern philosophy might provide a long-awaited remedy to a Christianity grown somewhat ill through an overdose of modernity."⁶⁵

Kallenberg explores this through first identifying three significant differences between modern and postmodern understandings of persons, language, and epistemology. Then, he invites us to rethink our understanding of conversion and evangelism in light of these postmodern insights. It should be noted that the forms of postmodernism Kallenberg is drawing upon are not that of the French deconstructionists but of philosophers like Alasdair MacIntyre, Ludwig Wittgenstein, J. L. Austin, and W. V. O. Quine, who he identifies as part of the "post-critical" strand of postmodernism.⁶⁶

---

62. Guder, *Continuing Conversion*, 156.
63. Guder, *Continuing Conversion*, 157–58.
64. Guder, *Continuing Conversion*, 206.
65. Kallenberg, *Live to Tell*, 13.
66. Kallenberg, *Live to Tell*, 132n2. I identify the two postmodern strands as "ultra-critics" and "post-critics" in *A Future for Truth*; Nancey Murphy distinguishes them as the "Continental" and "Anglo-American" strands in *Beyond Liberalism and Fundamentalism*.

Part Four: Kingdom and Community

The first claim of modernity that postmodernism challenges is sometimes called "generic individualism." It is the belief that "the individual is always prior to and more significant than the larger group of which he or she is a part"; indeed, a community is simply "the sum of the individual members."[67] In contrast, postmodernism argues for "metaphysical holism," in which "a group may be more than the sum of its individual parts."[68] Groups are seen to "behave like real entities that both constitute each member's identity and have top-down causal influence on them."[69]

Second, modernity holds to "representationalism," the belief "that language is *nothing but* a picture of the world." It is "a neutral depiction of the way the world is."[70] Postmodernity argues instead "that language constitutes the world";[71] it "is the means by which we think and act in the world."[72] If "language is the means by which we think," then the world cannot be treated as "in isolation from language."[73] This postmodern view is called "linguistic holism."[74]

Third, modernity claims "that beliefs are *nothing but* assertions about the way things really are." This understanding, known as "propositionalism," means that the truth or falsity of any statement can be shown through "rigorous testing" by "publicly accessible criteria."[75] In contrast to this is the "epistemological holism" of postmodernity, which holds that our beliefs "about our world form an interlocking set that we share with the rest of our community." The web of beliefs, known as a "paradigm, is very resilient and typically resists change."[76] But when new experience cannot be reconciled to one's reigning paradigm, a crisis can occur that can lead to the old paradigm being replaced by a new one.[77] When this "change comes, it comes all at once."[78]

67. Kallenberg, *Live to Tell*, 16.
68. Kallenberg, *Live to Tell*, 21.
69. Kallenberg, *Live to Tell*, 29.
70. Kallenberg, *Live to Tell*, 16.
71. Kallenberg, *Live to Tell*, 21.
72. Kallenberg, *Live to Tell*, 29.
73. Kallenberg, *Live to Tell*, 22.
74. Kallenberg, *Live to Tell*, 29.
75. Kallenberg, *Live to Tell*, 16.
76. Kallenberg, *Live to Tell*, 29.
77. Kallenberg, *Live to Tell*, 27.
78. Kallenberg, *Live to Tell*, 29.

What might these three shifts to a postmodern perspective mean for our understanding of conversion? First, metaphysical holism means that conversion is best understood as a "change of one's social identity."[79] Kallenberg begins his explanation by distinguishing between two ways of identifying things: analysis and holism. "While analysis identifies an object by disassembling it and labeling its constitutive parts, holism identifies an object by understanding its function in a larger scheme."[80] We are used to thinking in terms of analysis, yet when we try to say something about our own identity, we commonly tell stories. With Alasdair MacIntyre, Kallenberg believes "that our penchant for telling stories is a clue to the irreducibly narrative fabric of our existence."[81] Human actions only make sense "when seen in the context of a string of actions," multiple sets of actions form episodes, and these together "tell the story of a single human life." But that life can only be fully intelligible when understood as part of larger stories: "communal history, human history, the history of the cosmos and perhaps even the story of God."[82]

Such was the case for the conversion of Augustine, who, in coming to believe the gospel, "was not only allowing the story of God to make sense of the past" but "was also allowing it to shape his future by joining its storyline."[83] Through his conversion, Augustine "was graced with a new story and thus a new self that came to him by means of the gospel which simultaneously revealed to him who he was and whose he was."[84] He had acquired a new identity.

Second, linguistic holism points to conversion as acquiring "a new conceptual language."[85] As has shown to be the case for human culture in general, Kallenberg agrees with theologian George Lindbeck "that one's religious world is likewise limited or expanded by the conceptual language one has at one's disposal"—we cannot express an experience unless we have the language to do so.[86] Secular language lacks such notions as "sin" and "grace." Thus, if they are to be part of our understanding and experience, we

---

79. Kallenberg, *Live to Tell*, 32.
80. Kallenberg, *Live to Tell*, 32–33.
81. Kallenberg, *Live to Tell*, 34.
82. Kallenberg, *Live to Tell*, 35.
83. Kallenberg, *Live to Tell*, 37.
84. Kallenberg, *Live to Tell*, 38.
85. Kallenberg, *Live to Tell*, 39.
86. Kallenberg, *Live to Tell*, 40.

Part Four: Kingdom and Community

need to acquire the necessary language through conversion. We do this in two ways. Fluency in a language "is gained by participation in the linguistic community's *forms of life*—that weave of activity, relationships, and speech that gives the community its unique personality." In addition, "we learn a conceptual language" through "our community's stockpile of interpretive stories."[87] Conversion, then, requires participation in the life of a Christian community that is shaped by the story of God.

Third, epistemological holism leads us to understand conversion as a paradigm shift that "involves for the individual an exchange of allegiance from an old community to a new one."[88] Kallenberg's focus here is on how we read Scripture. If we try to understand the Bible by way of some other story, we will misunderstand it. We "cannot properly read the Bible," he argues, "until the text ceases to become the object that one views and becomes, instead, the lens itself through which one sees."[89] With theologian Hans Frei, Kallenberg suggests we read Scripture as a realistic narrative, much as people did prior to modernity. Because those "precritical readers" understood the world of the New Testament to be continuous with that of the Old, they found it "possible to tell the story of the whole of history in a unified and cumulative way." This, in turn, "implied the continuity of the biblical world with the reader's own world," and because of that, they saw the need to "understand and evaluate" their lives and communities "in terms of fit or lack of fit with the biblical story."[90]

Thus, "the meaning of the story cannot be separated from the story itself because there is no non-narrated place to stand to judge the correspondence between the story and its meaning." The meaning of the story is the story itself, told through characters, plot, and setting.[91] Modern readers try to understand the text by placing it within a larger story of human history and culture. But like precritical thinkers, postcritical persons place human history and culture within the larger biblical story and "submit themselves to the text as Scripture in a way that allows the text to interrogate them."[92]

This postmodern understanding of conversion, in turn, enriches

---

87. Kallenberg, *Live to Tell*, 41.
88. Kallenberg, *Live to Tell*, 42.
89. Kallenberg, *Live to Tell*, 43.
90. Kallenberg, *Live to Tell*, 45.
91. Kallenberg, *Live to Tell*, 45.
92. Kallenberg, *Live to Tell*, 46.

the practice of evangelism in at least three ways. First, our notion of evangelism must be broadened so that we insist on embodying the story in the web of relationships that constitutes our identity. Second, evangelism must engage others in conversations spoken in our conceptual language. And third, evangelism must enlist the outsider in the telling of the gospel story.[93]

With regard to embodying the gospel, Kallenberg challenges the common assumption that evangelists should "*translate* confusing concepts into the language of the believer."[94] To do so inevitably compromises the concepts because it places them in a context outside Christianity. "Sometimes," Kallenberg says, "what cannot be plainly spoken may nevertheless be shown."[95] "It is the pattern of the believing community's relationships that embodies the story of Jesus in concrete terms that outsiders can comprehend."[96]

Second, Kallenberg argues since "conversion involves the acquisition of a new conceptual language, then evangelism must be akin to teaching a foreign language to people who do not yet speak it."[97] Here again, our attempt to translate Christian concepts into the language of non-Christians undermines conversion. To become fluent in another language includes more than grammar—one must "participate in the form of life of the language's speakers." Therefore, to be fluent in Christian conceptual language "is to participate in activities such as forgiving one's neighbor, giving thanks to God, and worshipping with other believers."[98]

Kallenberg's third point about evangelism relates to how paradigms shift. "Beliefs," he notes, "come in interlocking sets." Persons do not change "beliefs one at a time until conversion is complete." Rather, conversion is the fruit of an ongoing conversation, likely marked by tension as the new gospel paradigm clashes with the old. When conversion comes, it will not happen "incrementally, but all at once."[99] Evangelism, then, must assist in a paradigm shift "by being dialogical in style and by, wherever possible, enlisting potential converts in the telling of the story."[100]

---

93. Kallenberg, *Live to Tell*, 48.
94. Kallenberg, *Live to Tell*, 51.
95. Kallenberg, *Live to Tell*, 52.
96. Kallenberg, *Live to Tell*, 50.
97. Kallenberg, *Live to Tell*, 54–55.
98. Kallenberg, *Live to Tell*, 57.
99. Kallenberg, *Live to Tell*, 61.
100. Kallenberg, *Live to Tell*, 64.

Kallenberg's approach involves patience, listening, and invitation into a community that seeks to live out the story of God. It creates the conditions that assist the work of the Holy Spirit in enabling persons to change their allegiance to a new story and community and thereby enter into new life in Christ.

Bryan Stone: The Church as Witness

For Bryan Stone, the central challenge "of practicing evangelism in a post-Christendom culture" is to do so "without at the same time playing by the rules of that culture."[101] The problem is not "*whether* we can reach unchurched people but rather *how* we reach them."[102] It is here that the increasing marginalization of the church may be an advantage, for "it is precisely from a position of marginality that the church is best able . . . to bear witness to God's peaceable reign in such a way as to invite others to take seriously the subversive implications of that reign."[103]

What is needed is not demonstrations of the gospel's intellectual credibility or practical usefulness[104] "but rather saints who have taken up the way of the cross and in whose lives the gospel is visible, palpable, and true."[105] Evangelism is "a fundamentally subversive activity, born out of a posture of eccentricity" (living at the margins) "and out of the cultivation of such deviant practices as sharing bread with the poor, loving enemies, refusing violence, forgiving sins, and telling the truth."[106] Stone's thesis, then, "is that the most evangelistic thing the church can do today is to be the church—to be formed imaginatively by the Holy Spirit through core practices such as worship, forgiveness, hospitality, and economic sharing into a distinctive people in the world, a new social option, the body of Christ." To put it succinctly, the church does not "need an evangelistic strategy. The church is the evangelistic strategy."[107]

In developing his argument, Stone, like Brad Kallenberg, draws upon the thought of moral philosopher Alasdair MacIntyre and postliberal

---

101. Stone, *Evangelism After Christendom*, 13.
102. Stone, *Evangelism After Christendom*, 14.
103. Stone, *Evangelism After Christendom*, 11.
104. Stone, *Evangelism After Christendom*, 11.
105. Stone, *Evangelism After Christendom*, 12.
106. Stone, *Evangelism After Christendom*, 13.
107. Stone, *Evangelism After Christendom*, 15.

theologian George Lindbeck. But his primary inspiration is the Anabaptist theology of John Howard Yoder, which understands the church as an embodied witness to the world of a new reality.[108] Evangelism, at its heart, is the church being that witness.

More precisely, Stone identifies evangelism as a practice of the church. A practice is more than a skill. Just as the practices of baseball or medicine involve a range of skills and activities, so does evangelism.[109] Drawing on MacIntyre, Stone argues that "the goods that are realized in carrying out a practice are 'internal' to that practice."[110] This is critical, for to associate a practice with external goods—in the case of evangelism, growth in church membership—causes the practice to lose its integrity and to become a mere instrument for attaining that external goal.[111] This in turn has an impact on "the standards of excellence by which we judge a practice." If evangelism is evaluated in terms of external goods such as church growth or number of conversions, "the church ceases to have any good reason to practice evangelism *well* or virtuously."[112]

A practice is a cooperative activity in which "the goods internal to a practice are impossible apart from a community of other practitioners . . . with whom we share and at times criticize standards of excellence and purposes internal to the practice," enabling the practice to grow and change over time.[113] Thus, "a practice is never static or finished, and its standard and purposes may be enlarged and extended" as it develops.[114]

How, then, do we determine the goods internal to the practice of evangelism? Again, drawing on MacIntyre, Stone identifies three elements that are necessary to know the *telos* (goal) of evangelism as well as its inner logic. Practices, he says,

> are finally unintelligible considered in the abstract apart from (a) a *narrative* or story that provides unity, meaning, and direction both for our lives and for our practices, (b) the *tradition* in which the question about the internal goods of a practice . . . is embodied

---

108. Stone, *Evangelism After Christendom*, 21–22.
109. Stone, *Evangelism After Christendom*, 31.
110. Stone, *Evangelism After Christendom*, 30.
111. Stone, *Evangelism After Christendom*, 31–32.
112. Stone, *Evangelism After Christendom*, 34.
113. Stone, *Evangelism After Christendom*, 35.
114. Stone, *Evangelism After Christendom*, 36.

socially within a community and thereby extended over time, and (c) the dispositions or *virtues* that sustain our practices.[115]

Stone spends the remainder of his book examining each of these elements in great detail.

The narrative that shapes Christian practices is "a particular story—the story of the people of God."[116] In contrast to other ancient religions, this is "the story of a people and their having been chosen, called, liberated, and led by God from among the nations as a new and holy nation."[117] Israel was called to be "a living testimony to the rule of God," a rule that the prophets described as "*shalom*, a term that weaves together peace and justice in the context of a Spirit-created community where human flourishing, blessedness, and wholeness" is extended to the entire creation.[118]

The story continues with the coming of Jesus, who both proclaims and embodies the reign of God "in ways that were both continuous and discontinuous with what came before him."[119] For Jesus, God's reign is fundamentally social, involving the gathering of a new community marked "by tangible practices of eating, sharing, meeting, and service."[120] The life of this community was counter to the prevailing social order and served as a living critique of that order, which would eventually lead to Jesus' execution.[121] The message of Jesus, most especially, was one of peace, "a pattern in which domination is exchanged for servanthood, punishment for forgiveness, and ethnocentrism for enemy-love."[122] While all of these would be characteristic of *shalom*, what is new in Jesus' message is that this reign of God has concretely broken into this present age and is offered to all "as both a *gift* and a *demand*," an invitation to receive and a summons to change.[123] Evangelism in light of this "is ultimately eschatological from beginning to end"; not preparing persons for "the end" but inviting them "to be transformed by the end that has already made itself present."[124]

---

115. Stone, *Evangelism After Christendom*, 37–38.
116. Stone, *Evangelism After Christendom*, 55.
117. Stone, *Evangelism After Christendom*, 63.
118. Stone, *Evangelism After Christendom*, 70.
119. Stone, *Evangelism After Christendom*, 77.
120. Stone, *Evangelism After Christendom*, 79.
121. Stone, *Evangelism After Christendom*, 80.
122. Stone, *Evangelism After Christendom*, 81.
123. Stone, *Evangelism After Christendom*, 82–83.
124. Stone, *Evangelism After Christendom*, 85.

Evangelistic Community

The resurrection of Jesus not only confirmed for the early church his message of the in-breaking reign of God but was seen as "initiating the events of the end of time." Jesus "must now be proclaimed as the One through whom this new age had actually begun to dawn."[125] The second confirmation was the coming of the Holy Spirit at Pentecost creating the church, "a new social option."[126] Its mission was to spread the good news of this new possibility while living together as a community marked by joy and unity,[127] "a living demonstration that the end of time has come."[128]

Stone notes several aspects of this story that enable it to shape a people. "Learning to be Christian," he says, "is not just learning *about* a story; it is learning to live *into* a story."[129] The story helps us remember, not in the sense of recalling to mind but as "the saturation of our lives," such that the beginning of the story "is our beginning, its journey our journey, its end, our end."[130] It engenders hope, "called forward by the promise of the end of our journey together," thus providing the practice of evangelism its *telos*.[131] It provides two critical resources for evangelism: memory and suspicion. We are in continual need of "persons who can help us remember the story and tell it faithfully," and of "persons who raise suspicions about our storytelling, ask new questions, and are even able to tell the story *against* tradition."[132]

Stone identifies two rival narratives that have subverted and continue to subvert evangelism. The first is the Constantinian "story of the church's forgetting its journey and making itself at home in the world."[133] The second is the story of modernity, a rejection of the Constantinian story and the Christendom it produced. It "is the story of a world that believes itself to have 'come of age,'" of the creation of an autonomous secular realm where individual selves are free to pursue their own ends and free of the direct influence of the church.[134] Within the story of modernity, salvation becomes a private matter, and evangelism is reduced to "either a matter of rational

---

125. Stone, *Evangelism After Christendom*, 101.
126. Stone, *Evangelism After Christendom*, 102.
127. Stone, *Evangelism After Christendom*, 103.
128. Stone, *Evangelism After Christendom*, 104.
129. Stone, *Evangelism After Christendom*, 109.
130. Stone, *Evangelism After Christendom*, 55–56.
131. Stone, *Evangelism After Christendom*, 56.
132. Stone, *Evangelism After Christendom*, 60.
133. Stone, *Evangelism After Christendom*, 116.
134. Stone, *Evangelism After Christendom*, 131–32.

technique, planning, and strategy aimed at promoting and defending the rationality, effectiveness, or usefulness of the gospel," or an exercise in "rhetorical persuasion."[135] This is precisely the error Stone sees church growth theorists like George Hunter, despite their good intentions, to have fallen into.[136]

Stone's second element necessary for identifying the *telos* of evangelism is tradition embodied in a community. The narrative of the gospel is not only "told by a people but also embedded in and constitutive of that people, even while being retold, embellished, and reconstructed by them."[137] It is this ongoing conversation that, over time, constitutes a tradition. Thus, a living tradition "is never a static, finished ... achievement but is a dynamic process that is responsive to ever-changing historical circumstances."[138] Thus, the church not only interprets the narrative "but also finds itself interpreted by the narrative and formed into it."[139]

A church formed by this narrative has a life in contrast to that of the world. In political terms, instead of "a politics of domination, exclusion, national idolatry, and individualistic rights," the church is called to be "a new and extraordinary social existence where enemies are loved, sins are forgiven, the poor are valued, and violence is rejected."[140] In economic terms, instead of "an economics of scarcity, consumption, greed, utility, and competition," the church is marked by "eucharistic fellowship and sharing."[141] Stone argues this radical "difference from the world" does not diminish the credibility of the church's witness but instead "is a necessary condition of that witness and is intrinsic to the church's invitation to the world to accept that witness as truth."[142] Evangelism conceived in this manner "is an eschatological activity" because it invites persons to see the world and live their lives in accordance with the reign of God,[143] "an eschatology that is both peaceful and cruciform."[144]

---

135. Stone, *Evangelism After Christendom*, 135.
136. Stone, *Evangelism After Christendom*, 144–51.
137. Stone, *Evangelism After Christendom*, 172.
138. Stone, *Evangelism After Christendom*, 41.
139. Stone, *Evangelism After Christendom*, 172.
140. Stone, *Evangelism After Christendom*, 178, 179.
141. Stone, *Evangelism After Christendom*, 178, 199.
142. Stone, *Evangelism After Christendom*, 176.
143. Stone, *Evangelism After Christendom*, 214.
144. Stone, *Evangelism After Christendom*, 224.

Evangelistic Community

This eschatological church is not something we make "but is a creation and gift of the Holy Spirit."[145] The politics of evangelism is "pacifist," understood as "a fundamental orientation that arises . . . from trust that the Spirit goes before us so that we need not be anxious, manipulative, or controlling" and "the conviction that Jesus alone is normative for the Christian's action in the world."[146] Evangelism (and apologetics) is "primarily an aesthetics," not so much an argument to be made but a way of life embodied in community. "Evangelism is a way of living openly, engagingly, virtuously—and therefore *beautifully* before a watching world."[147]

Evangelism "is shaped by the kind of conversion for which it calls and for which it hopes."[148] Conversion "is not simply a decision or an experience but the acquisition of a way of life that is embodied and passed along in community."[149] Understood this way, conversion takes time and is necessarily preceded by "an incorporation into the church," which provides the "language and practice" to enable us to desire and move toward the transformation offered by Christ.[150]

The third element for identifying the *telos* of evangelism is "dispositions, or virtues," that are "learned and cultivated over time."[151] These "excellences of character" are defined and formed through the practices of communal tradition and "are not merely instrumental to the good life; they are constitutive of it."[152] While virtues may be described as teleological in that they "order us toward good ends," Christian virtues are more accurately described as eschatological in that they are "not a matter of our own efforts" but are rather due to "our participation in and witness to an end that has already been gifted to us in Christ."[153] Because they are acquired in community, the church can be described as a school of virtue.[154]

If we look for a model of evangelistic virtue, Stone argues it should not be "the revivalist or megachurch pastor" but the martyr whose "pattern of

---

145. Stone, *Evangelism After Christendom*, 228.
146. Stone, *Evangelism After Christendom*, 229.
147. Stone, *Evangelism After Christendom*, 236.
148. Stone, *Evangelism After Christendom*, 258.
149. Stone, *Evangelism After Christendom*, 259.
150. Stone, *Evangelism After Christendom*, 263.
151. Stone, *Evangelism After Christendom*, 43.
152. Stone, *Evangelism After Christendom*, 44.
153. Stone, *Evangelism After Christendom*, 280.
154. Stone, *Evangelism After Christendom*, 281.

life and death . . . exhibits a radical and paradigmatic loyalty to Jesus."[155] He identifies four virtues that are especially important for evangelistic practice: presence "with and for others,"[156] patience, courage, and humility.[157]

If, Stone concludes, "the ordinary and peaceable nonconformity of the church *is* its evangelistic witness," then "cruciformity rather than triumph, growth, and expansion will be among the primary marks of evangelism practiced well." Virtuous evangelism will not be known for its expertise but in the faithfulness of its discipleship.[158]

Church and Culture in Tension

Moving from evangelism understood as calling for a decision by autonomous individuals leads inevitably to considering culture and community, those larger contexts in which persons are formed and shaped—people whose stories provide meaning for their lives and enable their understanding of the world. The central question then becomes how culture and Christian community relate. What we see in this chapter are various responses to that question, motivated by different concerns.

The church growth movement resists the conflation of Christianity and Western culture, which was characteristic of much missionary activity prior to the mid-twentieth century. It also seeks to raise awareness of the cultural barriers in local churches that make them inhospitable to, say, younger generations. It calls for contextualizing the gospel in order to reach people in culturally relevant ways, honoring rather than denigrating their cultural practices.

While finding this translation of the gospel into cultural forms necessary, Darrell Guder sees it at the same time as a risk. All cultures participate in the fallenness of creation, and translation always entails the reduction of the gospel, compromising its message. Unlike church growth theory, Guder does not see culture as neutral. To avoid our sinful tendency to absolutize a reduced gospel, the church itself needs continual conversion.

Brad Kallenberg and Bryan Stone place even greater emphasis on the tension between church and culture. Christianity is a way of life shaped by the story and reign of God. To attempt to translate it into a form that is

---

155. Stone, *Evangelism After Christendom*, 282.
156. Stone, *Evangelism After Christendom*, 285.
157. Stone, *Evangelism After Christendom*, 284–306.
158. Stone, *Evangelism After Christendom*, 315.

understandable in terms of human culture is to change its meaning entirely. The Christian community has its own story, language, and practices, and it is only in that context that the gospel can be understood. The best way to communicate the gospel to the world is to embody it as a community and offer the story of God as an alternative paradigm to the dominant stories of the culture.

Of course, all of these authors recognize the necessity of contextualization in the sense of worship and preaching being in the language of the people and praise being done through indigenous styles and instrumentation. The issues that divide them are much larger and have to do with failure to honor and engage the culture of others on one hand and compromising the integrity of the gospel on the other. This may not be in the end a problem to be solved, but a tension that we live in.

CHAPTER 8

Evangelism as Initiation

> I was more convinced than ever, that the preaching like an Apostle, without joining together those that are awakened, and training them up in the ways of God, is only begetting children for the murderer.
>
> —JOHN WESLEY[1]

THIS QUOTE FROM WESLEY raises a critical question: "When we are finished with evangelism, do we end up with Christians?" Wesley was aware that the churches in his day were filled with nominal Christians who, though baptized, knew nothing of the new life promised by the gospel. He also knew that awakening persons to their situation, whether they be regular church attenders or not, was necessary yet insufficient to lead them to that new life promised by the gospel.

Robert Webber, using different language, puts the question this way: "How can our evangelism produce not only converts but disciples who grow in faith and become active members of the church?"[2] Many who have that concern join Webber in calling for an expansion of the definition of evangelism from proclamation to a process of initiation. They also reject the common idea that evangelism is completed when it elicits a decision for Christ. Instead, evangelism is constituted by a range of practices that enable

---

1. Wesley, *Works*, ed. Jackson, 3:144.
2. Webber, *Ancient-Future Evangelism*, 13.

persons to begin a lifelong journey of Christian discipleship and growth. We will look at three examples of this understanding of evangelism.

Robert E. Webber: Recovering the Catechumenate

Robert Webber argues that an evangelism that results in making disciples "is a process," "takes place over a period of time," and "brings new believers to spiritual maturity."[3] We do not need to look far to find a model for this sort of evangelism, for it was practiced by the ancient church, which "brought evangelism, discipleship, and spirituality together in a unified process of faith formation."[4] Webber finds this holistic approach throughout the New Testament and the pre-Constantinian church in which believing, behaving, and belonging were united. Thus,

> the process of formation was not left to the mere hope that the new converts would mature. Instead, the church's approach to new converts was to take them by the hand and walk them through an intentional, life-giving process of formation that assured they believed the faith handed down by the apostolic community, that they learned how to behave like a Christian, and that they became active participants in the new community to which they now belonged.[5]

Over time, this unitive process fell apart, although something much like it was recovered by John Wesley.[6] Webber is convinced that we need to restore third-century practices of evangelism to the church today, and has advocated this in a series of books, culminating in *Ancient-Future Evangelism*.[7] He is not alone—others, such as Daniel Benedict and Patrick Keifert, have offered similar proposals.[8]

This is not to say Webber seeks to simply replicate the earlier model. Instead, he looks at the principles that underlay that model in order to develop a process of Christian formation for a postmodern culture.[9]

---

3. Webber, *Ancient-Future Evangelism*, 13.
4. Webber, *Ancient-Future Evangelism*, 18.
5. Webber, *Ancient-Future Evangelism*, 24.
6. Webber, *Ancient-Future Evangelism*, 33.
7. *Celebrating our Faith* (1986); *Liturgical Evangelism* (1992); *Journey to Jesus* (2001); *Ancient-Future Evangelism* (2003).
8. Benedict, *Come to the Waters*; Keifert, *Welcoming the Stranger*.
9. Webber, *Ancient-Future Evangelism*, 36.

Part Four: Kingdom and Community

Let's first look at the ancient model, as described by Hippolytus in *The Apostolic Tradition*. It consisted of four steps of Christian formation linked by rites of passage:

> Inquiry
> *Rite of Welcome*
> Catechumenate
> *A Rite of Enrollment*
> Purification and Enlightenment
> *Rite of Baptism*
> Mystagogue[10]

Inquiry was for the seeker, who is called to turn to and follow Jesus and is made aware of the cost of discipleship.[11] Welcomed into the community, the new disciple was now a catechumen, that is, one who is instructed "in the faith and in Christian life." After two or three years of instruction, the catechumen was enrolled in the list of those seeking baptism. During Lent, they underwent an intense period of formation called *purification and enlightenment*, with an emphasis on spiritual warfare.[12] The disciple was baptized on Easter morning and then entered a time of instruction lasting until Pentecost, called *mystagogue*, in which they reflected "on the mystery of faith, especially the meaning of baptism and the Eucharist, and they were taught to care for the poor and needy."[13]

Webber summarizes the emphasis in each stage of the process in this way:

1. Evangelize into the gospel of Jesus Christ.
2. Disciple into the church, its worship, its Scripture, its disciplines.
3. Spiritually form into the ethic and lifestyle of faith.
4. Assimilate into the church through a discovery of gifts, the Christian vocation of work, and caring for the poor and needy.[14]

This is, in short, how disciples are made. It recognizes "that discipleship is a matter of the heart, the will, and the intellect." Thus, formation is not

---

10. Webber, *Ancient-Future Evangelism*, 44.
11. Webber, *Ancient-Future Evangelism*, 44.
12. Webber, *Ancient-Future Evangelism*, 45.
13. Webber, *Ancient-Future Evangelism*, 45–46.
14. Webber, *Ancient-Future Evangelism*, 48.

simply going through the motions, but "in every stage is a matter of the heart's intention."[15]

In adopting this process for today, Webber advises churches to not be legalistic but attend to "the spirit of the ancient model." He suggests a general pattern for today would look like this:

> Evangelize the seeker
> *first passage rite*
> Disciple the hearer
> *second passage rite*
> Spiritually form the kneeler
> *third passage rite*
> Assimilate the faithful into the church
> Christian vocation[16]

Webber believes the passage rites, which mark the transition from one stage in the process to the next, to be essential. Ritual does not replace the verbal but complements it. "The word communicates to the verbal and cognitive side of the person," he argues, "whereas the symbol communicates to the emotive side of the person."[17]

While traditionally the third passage rite was baptism, Webber recognizes churches that practice infant baptism would need to alter the process.[18] Daniel Benedict discusses this same issue and advocates "profession of faith and reaffirmation of the baptismal covenant" for those already baptized.[19]

There are three theological insights that leads Webber to see the necessity of a process that links evangelism with formation for a postmodern culture. First, "conversion happens within community." It is not only intellectual assent but involves "taking one's place within the body of people who confess Christ and seek to live out the kingdom of Jesus."[20]

Second, "knowing God in community requires a participation in the language of the community." Webber rejects an evangelism that is grounded on meeting the felt needs of people. "Unconverted people don't know their need in any comprehensive way" because they lack "the language to identify

15. Webber, *Ancient-Future Evangelism*, 47.
16. Webber, *Ancient-Future Evangelism*, 53.
17. Webber, *Ancient-Future Evangelism*, 49.
18. Webber, *Ancient-Future Evangelism*, 51.
19. Benedict, *Come to the Waters*, 22.
20. Weber, *Ancient-Future Evangelism*, 39.

Part Four: Kingdom and Community

their sinful condition nor to describe the redemption that is brought by Jesus. They need to learn the language of faith." If the church simplifies its language to the point of losing it, "the church has destroyed the linguistic tools it needs to provide the converting person with a language that provides meaning and depth to the personal spiritual formation."[21]

Third, "the process of discovering a new language within the church creates a paradigm shift. The converting person's way of perceiving reality takes a huge leap into a new way of believing, belonging, and behaving." This is through coming to know the story of God, a story that can only be learned in the Christian community.[22]

Webber examines each of the four stages of initiation in detail. Here, we will focus on the first stage, evangelism itself. Drawing on the early church, Webber identifies "three principles for evangelism in a secular/spiritual culture: we must be open to all; we are to preach, teach, enact, and live an exclusive Christian message; and we need to create a community that not only looks after its own but cares for the needs of the world."[23]

With regard to the first of these principles, the church must be a place of hospitality. Weber cites with approval two themes on hospitality found in the early church: "The first is that Christians must recognize themselves as strangers in the world. The second is that Christians must recognize strangers as Christ."[24] Studies by others have shown how the early church grew primarily through social networks, most especially friends. Webber believes that today such social networking "will primarily happen where people eat together in homes of Christians and in neighborhood communities where faith is shared."[25]

The second principle is to proclaim the Christian message through word and action. The entire "creation is under sin and death," but "God's mission is to free creation (nature and people) from death and deliver creatures and creation into life—life in this world and life eternal." At the heart of this message is that "God in Christ is the one who recapitulates, that is, restores and renews the entire universe."[26]

---

21. Webber, *Ancient-Future Evangelism*, 39.
22. Webber, *Ancient-Future Evangelism*, 40.
23. Webber, *Ancient-Future Evangelism*, 57.
24. Oden, "God's Household," 39, cited in Webber, *Ancient-Future Evangelism*, 57.
25. Webber, *Ancient-Future Evangelism*, 58.
26. Webber, *Ancient-Future Evangelism*, 137–38.

Third is building community. "The missional church . . . evangelizes primarily by immersing the unchurched in the experience of community."[27] Postmodern culture emphasizes knowing through participation; thus, evangelism invites persons to participate in "a community that embodies the truth." "Postmodern evangelism," Webber argues, "is not so much an argument but a display."[28] An evangelizing community also "proclaims, sings, teaches, and enacts truth" through worship. Evangelism immerses the unchurched in worship, and faith is born through that participation.[29]

Christianity, Webber concludes, "must stop reinventing itself in cultural accommodation and instead return to the countercultural vision of the faith embodied in a community of committed people." The "future evangelism and Christian formation," he says, "will take place in community."[30]

William J. Abraham: Initiation into the Kingdom of God

To "develop a coherent content of evangelism," William Abraham argues, we "must begin with eschatology." "Whatever evangelism may be," he says, "it is at least intimately related to the gospel of the reign of God that was inaugurated in the life, death, and resurrection of Jesus of Nazareth."[31] For Abraham, the kingdom of God is a past, present, and future reality. "We live," he says,

> suspended between the times. God's kingdom has come, and all creation is invited to share in the blessings of salvation; God's kingdom is yet to come, and all creation is invited to strain toward the final consummation of God's justice and love with eager anticipation.[32]

When Abraham examines how the gospel spread initially in the New Testament, he finds it was not due to a prepared program of evangelism, a dutiful obedience to the Great Commission, or through the efforts of professional evangelists utilizing public relations techniques. Rather, "the Holy Spirit was present in the community, bringing in the reign of God and

27. Webber, *Ancient-Future Evangelism*, 62.
28. Webber, *Ancient-Future Evangelism*, 62–63.
29. Webber, *Ancient-Future Evangelism*, 63.
30. Webber, *Ancient-Future Evangelism*, 165.
31. Abraham, *Logic of Evangelism*, 17.
32. Abraham, *Logic of Evangelism*, 32.

inspiring the disciples to speak boldly of the mighty acts of salvation that God had wrought through the life, death, and resurrection of Jesus Christ."[33]

From this eschatological perspective and careful attention to what the early church actually did, Abraham argues that defining evangelism as proclamation is too narrow. It neither represents the breadth of the New Testament practice nor, in its focus on individual conversion, takes account of the communal nature of the gospel.[34] Defining evangelism as church growth is likewise deficient. Although he commends the church growth movement for its ecclesial focus and sociological insights, he finds that it tends to ignore or dilute crucial theological claims, and subtly ignores the radical social and corporate demands of the gospel for repentance and justice.[35] Moreover, while emphasizing church membership, "church growth theorists give little or no attention to what it is to be incorporated and grounded in the kingdom of God."[36]

Evangelism, then, involves enabling persons to come under the reign of God through beginning to participate in a community. Abraham thus proposes that evangelism be defined as "a set of intentional activities which is governed by the goal of initiating people into the kingdom of God for the first time."[37] The focus, he insists, should not be on ourselves or on a particular institution but on what God has done and is doing through Christ and the Spirit. From the standpoint of the kingdom of God, we can, in turn, see what it means for the church to be a kingdom community.[38]

Abraham identifies six intentional activities that together constitute initiation into the kingdom of God. The first is *conversion*, the experiential dimension of initiation, which designates "what happens to people when they are confronted with the gospel of Jesus Christ in a personal manner."[39] Abraham places conversion firmly in relation to the kingdom of God. "Entry into the kingdom of God is not a casual affair," Abraham notes; one cannot be "confronted with the rule of God" and have "life go on as usual."[40]

---

33. Abraham, *Logic of Evangelism*, 37–38.
34. Abraham, *Logic of Evangelism*, 49–61.
35. Abraham, *Logic of Evangelism*, 82, 85.
36. Abraham, *Logic of Evangelism*, 83.
37. Abraham, *Logic of Evangelism*, 95.
38. Abraham, *Logic of Evangelism*, 98.
39. Abraham, *Logic of Evangelism*, 120.
40. Abraham, *Logic of Evangelism*, 121.

Evangelism as Initiation

The second activity is *baptism*, the communal dimension of initiation. Baptism is a means of grace through which persons are initiated into the eschatological community.[41] "Christian experience," he argues, "is inescapably social in character. We depend crucially on the traditions, the rites, the ethos, the visions, and the conceptuality of a community to shape and sustain our moral and spiritual commitments."[42] Conversion and baptism, the personal and the communal, are complementary.

The third activity is initiation into the *rule of life*, or the Christian moral tradition. The new Christian is invited to appropriate that tradition as his or her own, the heart of which is the "command to love God with all one's heart and to love one's neighbor as oneself."[43]

The fourth activity, learning the *rule of faith*, is the intellectual dimension of initiation. The reign of God necessarily entails seeking to understand "the significance of what God has done in Jesus of Nazareth" and a vast array of related issues.[44] Abraham suggests the Nicene Creed as the place to begin—it is brief, ecumenical, and contains the essentials for a beginning Christian.[45]

The fifth activity is life in the Spirit, the operational dimension of initiation. The Holy Spirit comes not only to draw people to Christ but "to sustain and equip the body of Christ to continue the works of the kingdom today."[46] The Spirit empowers each member of the community for service through the distribution of spiritual gifts.[47] Abraham encourages a recovery of the full work of the Spirit, "including that mysterious, dynamic activity represented by direct manifestation both to individuals and to the gathered community."[48]

The sixth activity is learning *spiritual disciplines*, the disciplinary dimension of initiation. These include, most especially, the Eucharist ("the most profound means of grace the church knows"),[49] prayer, fasting, reading

---

41. Abraham, *Logic of Evangelism*, 130.
42. Abraham, *Logic of Evangelism*, 133.
43. Abraham, *Logic of Evangelism*, 134.
44. Abraham, *Logic of Evangelism*, 144.
45. Abraham, *Logic of Evangelism*, 147, 151.
46. Abraham, *Logic of Evangelism*, 152.
47. Abraham, *Logic of Evangelism*, 153.
48. Abraham, *Logic of Evangelism*, 157.
49. Abraham, *Logic of Evangelism*, 160.

the Scriptures, fellowship, and hymns. The key is not to master them all but to receive them as gifts that enable our growth as Christians.[50]

Evangelism, then, is a "polymorphous activity" "more like farming or educating than raising one's arm or blowing a kiss." Many of the actions involved in accomplishing these six activities—things like proclamation, teaching, conversation, prayer—are practices found throughout the church and its ministry. "What makes the actions evangelism is that they are part of a process that is governed by the goal of initiating people into the kingdom of God."[51]

It also follows that if evangelism is understood in this way, no single agent is involved. Abraham identifies four agents, beginning with the most important.

> The primary agent is the triune God who has created us in his own image, who has acted decisively in Jesus of Nazareth for the liberation of the cosmos, and who has come in the person of the Holy Spirit to make known the work of Christ and to empower God's people to live as his disciples and to participate in his activity in the world.[52]

Andrew Kinsey rightly notes that for Abraham, the "power of God's rule in Jesus of Nazareth through the activity of the Holy Spirit provides the theological horsepower to the various dimensions or activities of initiation." The "primary horizon is theological, not anthropocentric. . . . Without such divine agency, the scaffolding of the house of evangelism crumbles."[53]

The second agent for Abraham "is the church, which is called to embody the rule of God," nourish those called to evangelize, and share in their evangelistic activity. "The third agent is the evangelist, whose task is to proclaim the good news of the kingdom and ensure that those who respond are appropriately grounded in the rule of God in history." The "fourth agent is the person or persons evangelized," who hear the gospel, "respond in faith and repentance, open themselves generously to the work of the Holy Spirit, and gladly own the responsibilities and privileges of the kingdom of God."[54] As Kinsey observes, "There is simply no way of separating the

---

50. Abraham, *Logic of Evangelism*, 162.
51. Abraham, *Logic of Evangelism*, 104.
52. Abraham, *Logic of Evangelism*, 103.
53. Kinsey, "Evangelism as Initiation," 45.
54. Abraham, *Logic of Evangelism*, 103–4.

human element from the divine initiatives" in the various activities that comprise initiation into the kingdom.⁵⁵

Abraham draws three implications for ministry from this understanding of evangelism. First is the critical importance of authentic worship. "If God is not celebrated and adored as Lord in worship," he says, "it is highly unlikely that God's rule will be celebrated and welcomed anywhere else." To speak of initiation "into the rule of God will be vacuous and empty."⁵⁶

The second is for proclamation. When what God has done in Jesus Christ "is not announced, it will not be known."⁵⁷ Telling the story is central to proclamation. "What matters," says Abraham, "is that the good news of the kingdom can be transmitted with flair and in culturally fitting forms."⁵⁸ By proclamation, Abraham does not mean only preaching. The gospel is also proclaimed through "basic instruction" and "dialogue and conversation." Because "the word proclaimed and the invitation to respond are staggering in their proportions and utterly incredible to most people who stop to think about them," the "whole process" of proclamation "should be soaked in prayer and sensitivity to the Holy Spirit."⁵⁹ It is the Spirit who convicts and converts.

Third is a need to recover the catechumenate. "We need," he says, "a specific, official, public institution that will ensure that the various dimensions of initiation . . . are encountered by those who enter into the rule of God."⁶⁰ By this, he does not mean organizing the six dimensions of initiation into an orderly sequence. Since they are all interrelated, that would not be possible. Instead, the goal should be for "completeness and balance."⁶¹

"Evangelism," Abraham argues, "cannot be the primary activity and preoccupation of the church." "The first task of the church," he says, "is to worship: to bow down before the Lord of glory, to celebrate God's love and majesty, and to invite God to rule over the length and breadth of all creation."⁶² Yet evangelism is essential and "enjoys a unique relation to the other ministries of the church." Without evangelism there would be no

---

55. Kinsey, "Evangelism as Initiation," 46.
56. Abraham, *Logic of Evangelism*, 168.
57. Abraham, *Logic of Evangelism*, 170.
58. Abraham, *Logic of Evangelism*, 171.
59. Abraham, *Logic of Evangelism*, 171.
60. Abraham, *Logic of Evangelism*, 174–75.
61. Abraham, *Logic of Evangelism*, 175.
62. Abraham, *Logic of Evangelism*, 182.

church and no ministries of the church. Evangelism is necessary as one of its goals "is to establish agents of the kingdom who are irrevocably committed to doing the works of the kingdom."[63] Thus, says Abraham, "There is . . . no necessary conflict between evangelism and other ministries of the church, especially if we relate evangelism to initiation into God's reign of justice and mercy."[64]

Scott Jones: Initiation Into Discipleship

As important as Jesus' "commands to 'make disciples,' 'proclaim the good news,' and 'be [Christ's] witnesses'" are, Scott Jones argues they "must be subordinate" to the two greatest commandments to love God and love one's neighbor. This is the heart of Jones's vision of evangelism. "If the whole of Christian life is to be understood as loving God and neighbor, then part of that love is the ministry of evangelism." The one evangelizing "must be motivated and guided by love."[65]

Thus, while Jones agrees that the focus on the reign of God by William Abraham and Mortimer Arias leads to a more holistic understanding of evangelism, in the end, he finds it insufficient.[66] Instead, he agrees with Walter Klaiber that "love of God is the fundamental category and the reign of God is the expression of that love."[67] For Jones, love is God's essence: "God creates, redeems, and saves the world because God is love." "God's evangelistic love of the world," he says, is "the central message of Scripture."[68]

There is a second concern that governs Jones's theology of evangelism. Jones believes evangelism has gone astray when it has failed to hold in tension such things as divine and human action, its invitational nature with proclamation and church growth, its personal and communal nature, its being distinct yet "related to other aspects of Christian discipleship," and its relation to social justice.[69] The best "way of balancing all of these polarities," he believes, is to understand evangelism "as an interrelated set of practices

---

63. Abraham, *Logic of Evangelism*, 183.
64. Abraham, *Logic of Evangelism*, 184.
65. Jones, *Evangelistic Love*, 16.
66. Jones, *Evangelistic Love*, 27–32.
67. Jones, *Evangelistic Love*, 32.
68. Jones, *Evangelistic Love*, 33.
69. Jones, *Evangelistic Love*, 16.

Evangelism as Initiation

in a congregational context."[70] The congregation is the primary locus of evangelism.

Jones proposes "a threefold formula of the church's task—worship, formation, and witness—corresponding to the three objects Christians are called to love in the Great Commandments. By worship we love God. By formation, we love ourselves. By witness, we love others." These are the ways the church responds to the reign of God, and each of these three has a transforming impact on the others.[71] Bearing witness for Jones consists of both words and actions.[72] As a people who bear witness, the church has a missionary nature, at one and the same time a holy people distinct from the world and a community of love and hospitality to the stranger.[73] "Mission, therefore, is a combination of bringing people together and nurturing their identity as a separated people on the one hand, and sending them out to serve God in all they do on the other hand."[74]

With these foundations in place, Jones develops his theology of evangelism. He begins by critically reflecting on the definition of evangelism proposed by William Abraham. Jones considers "Abraham's most significant contribution to the theology of evangelism is his focus on the concept of initiation in its broad sense." It is, says Jones, "a brilliant insight" in that it "at once connects and shows the relationships among all the competing definitions of evangelism."[75]

Jones finds much to appreciate in Abraham's theology. Abraham's "use of 'intention' allows for a wider range of actions to be construed as evangelistic," providing needed flexibility for a theology of evangelism. Because what one is being initiated into determines the character of the initiation process, Abraham rightly argues that being initiated into the kingdom "will have its own unique logic and grammar."[76]

Yet there are some aspects of Abraham's theology of evangelism that Jones finds troubling. The most important is this: "By focusing on the initiation into the reign of God and by requiring the church and the evangelist to be agents who are active, however subordinately in the process, Abraham

---

70. Jones, *Evangelistic Love*, 17.
71. Jones, *Evangelistic Love*, 55.
72. Jones, *Evangelistic Love*, 58.
73. Jones, *Evangelistic Love*, 61.
74. Jones, *Evangelistic Love*, 62.
75. Jones, *Evangelistic Love*, 66.
76. Jones, *Evangelistic Love*, 67.

Part Four: Kingdom and Community

has, in fact, limited the extent of God's reign to the reach of the church."[77] Because all the elements of initiation into the reign of God are tied to the church, Jones argues that for Abraham, "where there is no church, there can be no reign of God."[78]

Jones has identified an area of unclarity here, which Abraham seeks to address in a subsequent article. Jones finds this to be an improvement but still inadequate.[79] The heart of Jones's concern is that Abraham's proposal compromises God's sovereignty. We should not, he says, "limit the reign of God to the ministry of the church. It is God who is at work saving the world, and clearly, God will use those persons and save those persons whom God chooses to use and save."[80] While this quote misleadingly sounds a bit like a claim for predestination of the elect, which Jones would emphatically reject, his main point is this: "it is highly presumptuous to suppose that God is not at work outside the church."[81]

From one angle, Jones's concern about God's sovereignty is well-taken. As he says, "God is graciously reigning on earth in partial ways now" and will bring "about the fullness of God's reign in the future."[82] This is true whether or not there is a church or whether or not the church is faithful. We could extend his argument to say Jesus is the risen Lord, whether we acknowledge it or not. But I think Abraham's focus is on something else that is also crucial. He speaks of the kingdom of God as something we enter—we become, in effect, citizens of—and that entry is transformative. The rule of God is over all creation, but the conscious and active human participation in that kingdom is in Israel and the church, actual historical communities.

The difference may be indicated in their choice of synonyms: for Jones, "reign of God" emphasizes sovereign rule; for Abraham, "kingdom of God" has the connotation of an entity of which one is a part.

Jones seeks to address Abraham's concerns while not compromising the sovereignty of God through his own definition of evangelism "as the set of loving, intentional activities governed by the goal of initiating persons

---

77. Jones, *Evangelistic Love*, 69.
78. Jones, *Evangelistic Love*, 70.
79. Jones, *Evangelistic Love*, 70–72.
80. Jones, *Evangelistic Love*, 73.
81. Jones, *Evangelistic Love*, 73.
82. Jones, *Evangelistic Love*, 72.

Evangelism as Initiation

into Christian discipleship in response to the reign of God."[83] This maintains the centrality of love which is so foundational for Jones's theology. Too often so-called evangelism has failed "to love adequately the persons being evangelized." It is love that "is the chief criterion for the adequacy of evangelism."[84]

The activities Jones has in mind are Abraham's six plus one more: faith sharing. "Any account of Christian discipleship," Jones argues, "must include the missionary character of each Christian."[85] What makes these seven activities evangelism is "the intention behind them" which is "to initiate persons into discipleship."[86] These activities are also the key to understanding how evangelism "is connected with other ministries" of the congregation. "Because discipleship has seven aspects (baptism, cognitive commitment, spiritual gifts, spiritual disciplines, conversion, morality, and faith-sharing), the life of discipleship is simply a continuation of each of these seven."[87]

The focus on the reign of God in the definition emphasizes "that evangelism is not a purely human activity." God's purposes are central. "We serve a God who is a God of justice, reconciliation, and peace, and who is going to save the world. Our ministries are in response to the saving activities of God."[88]

While each Christian tradition has its own distinctive understanding of discipleship, Jones illustrates how the seven aspects of discipleship can be correlated with the three steps of John Wesley's way of salvation: "repentance, justification, and sanctification."[89] Repentance he defines as "the turning away from sin, evil, and other gods and toward the one true God."[90] Here, a person is seeking, investigating, or becoming initially involved in some way. This "often involves trying out one or more of the seven aspects of Christian discipleship."[91]

---

83. Jones, *Evangelistic Love*, 114.
84. Jones, *Evangelistic Love*, 115.
85. Jones, *Evangelistic Love*, 74.
86. Jones, *Evangelistic Love*, 116.
87. Jones, *Evangelistic Love*, 117.
88. Jones, *Evangelistic Love*, 118.
89. Jones, *Evangelistic Love*, 76.
90. Jones, *Evangelistic Love*, 79.
91. Jones, *Evangelistic Love*, 80.

Part Four: Kingdom and Community

In justification, persons come to know their sins are forgiven and that they are accepted by God, changing their relationship to that of a child of God. The aspect of baptism especially relates to this step in the way of salvation.[92] Also related is the aspect of cognitive commitment, "the intellectual acceptance of the gospel."[93]

Sanctification denotes a life increasingly governed by love, having the mind that was in Christ, "living by the Spirit."[94] Because sanctification has to do with growing in one's capacity to live according to the two greatest commandments, that is, to love God, self, and others, Jones organizes his discussion around the three corresponding tasks of the church he described earlier: worship, formation, and witness.[95]

With regard to *worship*, the relevant aspects are some of the spiritual disciplines: worship itself, Eucharist, prayer, and fasting. These are all focused "on our love for God."[96] While these are all formative, other aspects are more directly related to personal *formation*: conversion and the spiritual disciplines of study and fellowship.[97] Connected to *witness* and our love for others are the aspects of morality, spiritual gifts, faith sharing, and the spiritual discipline of hospitality.[98]

Turning to the practice of evangelism, Jones notes that the gospel has always been enculturated.[99] He offers three theological bases for enculturation. First is the incarnation: "Since Christ is God put into human flesh, the gospel can be put into their languages and cultural forms."[100] Second is the universality of the message of good news. "Universality and incarnational theology combine," Jones argues, "to provide the theological rationale for translating the gospel into cultural forms that will carry Christianity's essential message to reach new persons."[101] A third basis is theological anthropology. Because humans themselves are historical in nature and live in

---

92. Jones, *Evangelistic Love*, 81–82.
93. Jones, *Evangelistic Love*, 82.
94. Jones, *Evangelistic Love*, 84.
95. Jones, *Evangelistic Love*, 85.
96. Jones, *Evangelistic Love*, 86–88.
97. Jones, *Evangelistic Love*, 88–93.
98. Jones, *Evangelistic Love*, 93–98.
99. Jones, *Evangelistic Love*, 121.
100. Jones, *Evangelistic Love*, 124.
101. Jones, *Evangelistic Love*, 125.

distinct cultures, our love for others requires us "to love the person's culture as well as the person."[102]

Jones strongly advocates getting to know the community and culture that surrounds and "shapes the lives of the person one is trying to reach." "Evangelism must," he says, "begin where the person is."[103] While Jones takes seriously the danger of the church turning the gospel into a consumer product, he, nonetheless, is sympathetic to the church growth movement's focus on the felt needs of persons.[104] "From a Christian perspective," he says, "this felt need may be the first stirring of an awareness of a need for God."[105]

We see the same nuance in his evaluation of the homogeneous unit principle. He is, on one hand, sympathetic to arguments from critics of church growth theory that the church should be a foretaste of the kingdom, a new humanity in which the barriers of race, class, and ethnicity are removed. They believe the church fails to attract people because it is not distinct enough from the dominant culture. On the other hand, he affirms church growth advocates like George Hunter, who says that the reason people avoid Christianity is they do not want to be like people they see in church, "that the real barrier is that the church is strange in ways that are unimportant."[106]

Jones concludes that homogenous units that "are culturally formed by ethnicity, language, and other factors . . . can be a valid starting place for a Christian journey." But new believers must "be shaped in ways that will help them appreciate the diversity of God's people."[107] The "homogeneous unit principle is helpful when taken as an indication of where people are and how to connect the gospel to their lives" but "heretical if taken as a description of the goal of the reign of God."[108]

The Necessity of Beginning the Journey of Discipleship

Most, if not all of the authors we have examined in this book would agree that the point of salvation is not a onetime decision but to begin a process

---

102. Jones, *Evangelistic Love*, 125.
103. Jones, *Evangelistic Love*, 127.
104. Jones, *Evangelistic Love*, 127–31.
105. Jones, *Evangelistic Love*, 127.
106. Jones, *Evangelistic Love*, 130.
107. Jones, *Evangelistic Love*, 131.
108. Jones, *Evangelistic Love*, 132.

Part Four: Kingdom and Community

of growth in discipleship and sanctification. It is to receive, live out, and grow in a new life in Christ. They would also insist that personal salvation cannot be understood apart from Christian community and/or the reign of God. As we saw in the last chapter, some explicitly link evangelism with the life and some of the practices of the Christian community.

What makes those considered in this chapter distinct is that they understand getting persons started on the journey of discipleship to be intrinsic to the practice of evangelism. They question the adequacy of any practice of evangelism that fails to fully initiate persons into the Christian life. This means that for them, there can be no evangelism adequate to the gospel that is not organically linked to a local church that has the practices that enable persons to enter that life of discipleship.

PART FIVE

Learning from Tradition

CHAPTER 9

A Cloud of Witnesses

> The history of evangelism is a diverse litany. Male and female, rich and poor, itinerant and local, Catholic and Protestant, extreme and natural, public and private. Evangelists come in all shapes and sizes.
>
> —PRISCILLA POPE-LEVISON[1]

AS WE HAVE SEEN, many who write on evangelism look to Scripture, and most especially the ministry of Jesus and of the early church, as sources for its theology and models for its practice. This is entirely appropriate and has born much fruit. But these are not the only sources of evangelistic insight. Whether called by that name or not, evangelism has been thought about and practiced throughout church history, and there is much to learn from its practitioners.

In this chapter we will look at approaches that draw upon the Christian tradition for fresh insights on evangelism, including unlikely or often ignored sources.

---

1. Pope-Levison, *Models*, 5.

Part Five: Learning from Tradition

Elaine A. Heath: The Mystic Way of Evangelism

The post-Christendom church is in crisis.[2] "Programmatic approaches to evangelism" are inadequate for the situation we face.[3] What is needed to teach the church today about "the theory and practice of evangelism," says Elaine Health, are "the great exemplars of holiness—the Christian mystics."[4] Heath is calling upon the church to learn from these spiritual giants in order to itself be centered on God and renewed in holiness and love.

Evangelism for Heath, "is never coercive, violent, or exploitative." Drawing on William Abraham, she defines evangelism as "the holistic initiation of people into the reign of God as revealed in Jesus Christ." It is a process that "is complete only when" persons are fully "participating in the life of the church in worship, service, prayer, and evangelistic presence in the world." Evangelism "is at the heart of everything we believe and practice as Christians."[5]

By Christian mysticism Heath does not mean private experience in isolation from the world. It "is about the holy transformation of the mystic by God, so that the mystic becomes instrumental in the holy transformation of God's people."[6] It moves persons beyond themselves "into greater depths of divine love."[7] Although many do not seem to attain it, this mystical transformation is intended by God for all Christians. Its fruit is love for God and neighbor; it "is a love enfleshed in action."[8]

Heath organizes her theology of evangelism around "the classical threefold contemplative path" of "purgation, illumination, and union," applying these to the church rather than to individuals.[9] She realizes this is controversial, but points to the biblically grounded "communal nature of the faith," long marginalized in the individualistic culture of Western Christianity, as justification for her approach.[10]

---

2. Heath, *Mystic*, 12.
3. Heath, *Mystic*, 13.
4. Heath, *Mystic*, 14.
5. Heath, *Mystic*, 13.
6. Heath, *Mystic*, 15.
7. Heath, *Mystic*, 16.
8. Heath, *Mystic*, 19.
9. Heath, *Mystic*, 20.
10. Heath, *Mystic*, 124.

Beginning with *purgation*, Heath argues that "the decline of the church in the United States . . . is best understood as a corporate dark night of the soul."[11] She defines a dark night of the soul as

> a divinely initiated process of loss—so that the accretions of the world, the flesh, and the devil may be recognized and released. It is a process of detachment from disordered affections, a process of purgation and de-selfing.[12]

This is an act of divine love, gradually enabling "detachment from enmeshed relationships, compulsions, addictions, and idolatries," giving us "growth, healing, and freedom."[13]

She identifies three signs that the American church is entering a dark night of the soul. There is "dryness and fruitlessness in prayer, religious activity, and life." Second, there is "a loss of desire for the old ways of being religious." Third, there is "a growing desire simply to be with God."[14] But this sense of emptiness is the precondition for renewal. These "exile experiences of loss and marginalization," Heath says, "are what are needed to restore the church to its evangelistic place." It is a marginalized church "that can once again become a prophetic, evangelistic, alternative community," offering a way of life that is "life-giving, loving, healing, liberating."[15]

In her section on *illumination*, Heath draws upon some of those exemplars of holiness to present "the key elements of a contemplative vision for evangelism that should characterize the church emerging from the night."[16] Foundational to this revisioning are insights of Julian of Norwich into original wounds and Hans Urs von Balthasar's doctrine of a nonpunitive atonement. Both direct our attention to how God sees our sinful world.[17]

Julian lived in the fourteenth century in a world consumed by the Hundred Years' War and repeated outbreaks of bubonic plague. Through sixteen visions Julian came to understand, contrary to the church teaching,

---

11. Heath, *Mystic*, 20.
12. Heath, *Mystic*, 27.
13. Heath, *Mystic*, 30.
14. Heath, *Mystic*, 31.
15. Heath, *Mystic*, 26.
16. Heath, *Mystic*, 20.
17. Heath, *Mystic*, 39.

Part Five: Learning from Tradition

"that God's judgment is without wrath, that it will heal the entire cosmos."[18] The reason is that humanity's fall into sin through Adam was not "willful or proud rebellion" but "a consequence of childlike exuberance leading to a mistake." What the "fall is about is wounds: alienation, blindness, fear, suffering, humanity's inability to extricate itself from its fallen place—in short, wounds to body, mind, and spirit."[19]

The story of Adam and Eve is our story—"our loss of innocence and our wounding and our eventual bondage to sin." "Sin," Heath says, "originates in wounds that come from living in this broken world."[20] For this reason God views us with pity, not wrath. This does not make sin any less terrible—as Julian notes, the greatest consequence of sin is the suffering and death of Jesus.[21] But because "love is God's meaning,"[22] God loves all humanity, and considers humanity "worth any suffering that is required to bring about redemption."[23] The Son of God has in his crucifixion and death "taken into himself for all time the wounds and brokenness of the world," bringing healing to our woundedness.[24] It is this "therapeutic view of redemption" which brings "hope to people with all forms of brokenness" that Heath believes "must be a central concern for evangelism."[25]

Hans Urs von Balthasar is a twentieth-century Roman Catholic theologian. His "trinitarian understanding of God's kenotic love" led him to define God's omnipotence (or "almightiness") "as the way in which God loves." Thus, every divine attribute is kenotic, the "divine self-giving love of the Father, Son, and Holy Spirit."[26] Consistent with this is his nonpunitive doctrine of atonement, "in which Jesus, out of loving solidarity with humanity, willingly bears humanity's sin and despair, our god forsakenness." Through the death and resurrection of Jesus salvation is offered to all persons.[27] For von Balthasar, God's grace is evangelistic, influencing the hearts of sinners without overpowering them, evoking their freely given

18. Heath, *Mystic*, 40.
19. Heath, *Mystic*, 44; see also 55.
20. Heath, *Mystic*, 57.
21. Heath, *Mystic*, 44.
22. Heath, *Mystic*, 44, 47.
23. Heath, *Mystic*, 46.
24. Heath, *Mystic*, 44.
25. Heath, *Mystic*, 46, 47.
26. Heath, *Mystic*, 48.
27. Heath, *Mystic*, 49.

assent.[28] Those who respond to God's call embrace "God's mission in this world," and enter "into the trinitarian life of self-giving love."[29]

With this foundation laid, Heath then discusses four more aspects of illumination. We can only provide the briefest sketch of her rich discussion in these chapters, but hopefully it will offer in broad strokes a description of what her vision of illumination encompasses.

First, it involves "embracing holiness for the sake of the world." Holiness is "a complete belonging to God," but it is not a removal from the world. Indeed, suffering "seems to mark the paths of many great saints and mystics," and it is "in the midst of such adversity that these holy ones become testaments of divine love."[30]

Such was the case for Phoebe Palmer, a Methodist and "mother of the nineteenth-century holiness movement," and Father Arseny, "who spent some twenty years in Soviet death camps."[31] The tragic death of her infant daughter coupled with a lack of experiential assurance in her relationship with God brought Palmer to a spiritual crisis. Letting go of a desire for an experience, she trusted the promise of Scripture and fully consecrated her life to God.[32] Himself suffering greatly, Father Arseny "gave himself day after day in prayer, friendship, and love" to his fellow prisoners, a "beacon of hope" in the midst of death and despair.[33] Both were focused on God; both embodied kenosis in giving themselves to others. "This," says Heath, "is the message of holiness the church in America needs." Instead of "numbers, buildings and budgets, the church is starving for holy leadership." It is this holiness that draws persons into relationship with God.[34]

This leads to a second element in illumination which Heath calls "coming home to God." Her exemplars are the nineteenth-century Quaker Thomas R. Kelly and the twentieth-century Roman Catholic Henri Nouwen. Both struggled to find acceptance and identity; both eventually experienced deep depression. But God's love reached out to them "in the center of their depression, penetrating the defenses and limitations of their carefully constructed selves, melting ambition, and calling forth the true beauty that

---

28. Heath, *Mystic*, 49.
29. Heath, *Mystic*, 51.
30. Heath, *Mystic*, 59.
31. Heath, *Mystic*, 60.
32. Heath, *Mystic*, 60–63.
33. Heath, *Mystic*, 64.
34. Heath, *Mystic*, 70.

Part Five: Learning from Tradition

was hidden beneath much fear." Through knowing God's love for them they were each "released to fully give themselves to the world."[35]

A third aspect of illumination is for the church to confess the "three-fold sin" of "sexism, racism, and classism" which have been embedded in American Christianity from its beginnings.[36] Heath's exemplars here are the nineteenth-century African American holiness evangelist Julia Foote and the thirteenth-century founder of the Beguines, Mechthild of Magdeburg. Both faced opposition and persecution as they gave witness through their ministries of the equality of all persons in Christ. They were critics "of self-serving unjust clergy" and lifted up "the love of God for the 'least of these.'"[37] This three-fold sin wounded the church in their days as in ours. The church needs "to retrieve the egalitarian ethos of the gospel" if it is to "regain the moral authority it needs to speak to a world hurtling towards chaos."[38]

The fourth aspect of illumination is redeeming the earth. Heath notes the destructiveness wrought by "the commodification of science and technology" on creation, from rocks to forests to animals to the thirty thousand children who die each day without food or water. "What the church thinks about creation has never been more important," she says; "What the church does about God's creation is a matter of life and death."

Her exemplars are the thirteenth-century monk Bonaventure and the eighteenth-century Quaker John Woolman. For Bonaventure "all creation comes forth from God and returns to God."[39] The incarnation of Christ "is the final perfection of creation," and since "creation mirrors Christ, creation is therefore made in the image of God."[40] Humanity, as both body and soul, is uniquely "mediator for the return of all things to the Creator" and has "responsibility to facilitate the healing of creation."[41] Woolman became a wealthy Philadelphia businessman yet came to reject affluence. He became a missionary in the American colonies advocating "the abolition of slavery, the cultivation of a life of simplicity, respect and care for creation, and the end to unjust systems of labor that created poverty and oppression."[42] They

---

35. Heath, *Mystic*, 80.
36. Heath, *Mystic*, 99.
37. Heath, *Mystic*, 96.
38. Heath, *Mystic*, 100.
39. Heath, *Mystic*, 103.
40. Heath, *Mystic*, 104.
41. Heath, *Mystic*, 106.
42. Heath, *Mystic*, 107.

were both precursors to what Heath calls "eco-evangelism," our "being good news to creation in the name of Jesus."[43]

Having discussed purgation and illumination, Heath now turns to *union*. Here she presents "a vision for ways in which the church can take a contemplative stance, evangelistically living in union with God in day-to-day life."[44] It begins, in the spirit of Julian and von Balthasar, with a hermeneutic of love. We believe "Jesus really does live in the people around us," he is bound to each one in love.[45] As a result,

> when I see people that way, everything changes. How I evangelize changes. Now I see people already being called by the Holy Spirit, already being loved and known by Jesus before I ever meet them. Now I understand that prayer and friendship are the foundation for my relationships with others, in the name of Jesus.[46]

On this foundation, we, like Phoebe Palmer and Father Arseny, give ourselves away to God and to others. "The church," says Heath, "has been at its missional best when giving itself away. . . . It is the way the church is supposed to be."[47] We also, like Thomas Kelly and Henri Nouwen, learn to pray contemplatively, what Heath calls "homing prayer" because it leads us to God and to our true selves.[48] As we receive God's mercy and healing, we extend that same graciousness to others through hospitality.[49]

The church is also in need of a new Pentecost "so radical that the walls of gender, race, and class dissolve in its healing reach."[50] Resisting hierarchies of power, as did Julia Foote and Mechthilde of Magdeburg, the church would have egalitarian leadership and affirm the spiritual gifts of all.[51] The church would also, like Bonaventure and John Woolman, embrace creation care through practices of stewardship (a lifestyle of "simplicity, adequacy,

---

43. Heath, *Mystic*, 111.
44. Heath, *Mystic*, 20.
45. Heath, *Mystic*, 125.
46. Heath, *Mystic*, 125.
47. Heath, *Mystic*, 134.
48. Heath, *Mystic*, 149.
49. Heath, *Mystic*, 157.
50. Heath, *Mystic*, 159.
51. Heath, *Mystic*, 161.

and sustainability"),[52] a simpler use of material resources, and resistance to "unchecked consumerism."[53]

Heath offers a holistic and prophetic form of evangelism grounded in divine love and centered in the church as witness. Through both its hospitality and outreach, its community and engagement in the world, the church embodies the good news it proclaims, and stands as a beacon of hope to a world in distress.

George G. Hunter III: The Celtic Way of Evangelism

The contemporary church in the West is increasingly secular, populated by people "with no Christian memory." It is also urban, out of touch with nature. And it is postmodern, less governed by Enlightenment rationalism and more "peer driven" and "feeling driven."[54] How do we evangelize in the midst of these massive cultural changes? George Hunter believes that Celtic Christianity from the fifth century may show us the way. Hunter is a leader in the church growth movement, "a communication theorist and missiologist, with no credentials . . . for interpreting ancient and medieval history."[55] But he brings his missiological lens to the work of historians like Thomas Cahill and John Finney, plus primary sources, to provide an insightful account of the Celtic way of evangelism and its implications for today.

The story of Celtic Christianity begins with Patrick. Captured at age sixteen by Celtic pirates and sold into slavery to a Druid chieftain in Ireland, Patrick spent the next six years herding cattle. He was a nominal Christian, but as he was in the fields he sensed the presence of the triune God and began to pray throughout the day and into the night. At the same time, he came to understand the Celtic people and their culture, even to love the Celtic people "and to hope for their reconciliation to God."[56] A voice in a dream instructed Patrick to go to a ship that would take him home. He did so and trained to be a priest, serving a parish in England. Then "at the age of forty-eight" he had another dream instructing him to take Christianity to the Celts. The church approved, and Patrick was appointed "as history's first

---

52. Heath, *Mystic*, 172.
53. Heath, *Mystic*, 173.
54. Hunter, *Celtic*, 9.
55. Hunter, *Celtic*, 11.
56. Hunter, *Celtic*, 13–14.

missionary bishop." In 432 "he arrived in Ireland, with a modest entourage of priests, seminarians, and others."[57]

The Celts were among the many "barbarian" peoples who lived just outside the Roman Empire. Since the second century, the church "assumed that reaching barbarians was impossible," because "a population . . . had to be literate and rational enough to understand Christianity, and cultured and civil enough to become real Christians if they *did* understand it."[58]

That was not how Patrick saw it. As Hunter says,

> The fact that Patrick understood the people and their language, their issues, and their ways, serves as the most strategically significant single insight that was to drive the wider expansion of Celtic Christianity, and stands as perhaps our greatest single learning from this movement.[59]

When people know they are understood by Christians, they infer that maybe their God does as well.[60]

The most significant missional innovation was the establishment of what Hunter calls "monastic communities." Although Patrick planted parish churches, these presupposed "a network of towns" alien to Ireland, which had only "temporary settlements of tribal groups" and no good roads. Instead, it was the monastic communities that Patrick founded that fit the culture, and this approach was adopted and extended by Patrick's successors.[61]

Although inspired by the monasteries of Eastern Christianity, these Celtic monastic communities were significantly different. Hunter summarizes it this way:

> Eastern monasteries organized to protest and escape the materialism of the Roman world and the corruption of the Church; the Celtic monasteries organized to penetrate the Pagan world and to extend the Church. The eastern monks often withdrew from the world into monasteries to save and cultivate their own souls; Celtic leaders often organized monastic communities to save other people's souls.[62]

57. Hunter, *Celtic*, 15.
58. Hunter, *Celtic*, 17.
59. Hunter, *Celtic*, 19–20.
60. Hunter, *Celtic*, 20.
61. Hunter, *Celtic*, 27.
62. Hunter, *Celtic*, 28.

Thus, while containing monks and nuns, Celtic monasteries were more diverse, "populated by the priests, teachers, scholars, craftsmen, artists, farmers, families, and children." They were primarily laity and could number over a thousand residents.[63] They were filled with activity, worshipped together daily, learned Scripture, and practiced contemplative prayer.[64]

There were two ways the Celtic communities were unusual compared to Roman Christianity. First, they were more community-oriented than individualistic, supporting one another in their Christian growth.[65] Second, they enabled people to "cope as Christians day by day in the face of poverty, enemies, evil forces, nature's uncertainties, and frequent threats from many quarters."[66] Their contemplative prayers, often Trinitarian in shape and content, were prayed as they engaged in everyday activities, continually directing their hearts to God.[67]

Following Patrick, Columba led a mission to reach the Picts of Scotland, and Aiden did the same to evangelize the Germanic Anglo-Saxons who had invaded England. They too established monastic communities, but also adjusted their work to the language and culture of the populations in which they were in mission.[68]

Hunter identifies five themes that shape the Celtic missionary ecclesiology. First, instead of the single entrepreneur patterns of evangelism familiar to the church today, the Celts evangelized as teams. They would "pray and think together," "inspire and encourage each other," identify and befriend the population, and raise "up a church in measurable time."[69]

Second, the monastic communities "prepared people to live with depth, compassion, and power in mission." There were voluntary times of solitude in nature, conversations with a "soul friend," time within a small group, participation in a common life of meals, work, and worship, and gaining experience in ministry and witness. All this was to root persons "in the gospel and Scriptures," enable them to "experience the presence of the Triune God," and help persons have empowered lives and fulfill their vocations.[70]

63. Hunter, *Celtic*, 28.
64. Hunter, *Celtic*, 28–29.
65. Hunter, *Celtic*, 30.
66. Hunter, *Celtic*, 32.
67. Hunter, *Celtic*, 33.
68. Hunter, *Celtic*, 36–37.
69. Hunter, *Celtic*, 47.
70. Hunter, *Celtic*, 48.

Third, in all these different settings within the life of the community, the people practiced imaginative prayer. This engaged the heart as well as the mind, and through imagery enabled the people to "visualize as well as hear the gospel."[71]

Fourth, is hospitality to strangers. Visitors, who could be seekers or refugees, were welcomed by a porter who would introduce them to the community. The abbot would inquire about their reason for coming and pray for them. They would stay at a guest house and have meals at the abbot's table.[72]

Fifth, the Celtic way of reaching people was in sharp contrast to the Roman way. The Roman approach was to present the gospel message, invite a response, and if it is positive, welcome them into the church. The Celtic way is to welcome persons into the community, where they participate "in conversation, ministry, prayer, and worship," and when they find they believe, "invite them to commit."[73] Evangelism for Celtic Christianity enables "people to belong so that they can believe."[74]

With regards to how the gospel was actually communicated, Hunter offers four inferences. First, Patrick and those that followed him connected to the deepest concerns of the people. "Second, in contrast to the indifference of their capricious gods, the people discovered that their feelings mattered to the Triune God of Christianity." Third, experiencing the providence of God overcame their fears. Fourth, Christianity enabled them to express their emotions "through indigenous oratory, storytelling, poetry, music," etc., in service to God.[75]

Celtic Christianity, as has been said, was highly contextualized. They would build chapels on or near the sacred sites of a people's primal religion, Christianize some of their holy days or rituals, and priests and monks would often adopt the attire of their former priests. The Celtic missionaries "preferred continuity rather than discontinuity, inclusion rather than exclusion."[76]

With regard to theology, contextual awareness led to certain distinctive emphases. The Irish loved paradox and riddles, and their primal

---

71. Hunter, *Celtic*, 48–49.
72. Hunter, *Celtic*, 52.
73. Hunter, *Celtic*, 53.
74. Hunter, *Celtic*, 55.
75. Hunter, *Celtic*, 69–70.
76. Hunter, *Celtic*, 73.

religion posited an "Ultimate Reality" that "was mysterious and complex." Their typical way of thinking about complexity was by way of triads that often linked things thought of as incompatible. Thus, they were very open to a triune God.[77] As a result, the "doctrine of the Trinity became the foundational paradigm for Celtic Christianity."[78] The difference from the Roman understanding was that Celtic theology emphasized the threeness and immanent presence of the Trinity more than Roman theology.[79]

A second example is the death of Christ. The Irish practiced human sacrifice to appease their gods. Patrick preached about a God who is not capricious but loving, and who sacrificed his Son for us, bringing an end to human sacrifice. The Christian "God calls us not to die for him, but to live for him and each other."[80]

Another distinctive aspect of Celtic theology is its love for nature. Although thoroughly biblical and orthodox, their love for creation is in contrast to the more "detached and impersonal" approach of Roman Christianity.[81] Here the biblical emphasis on the goodness of creation connects to the reverence for nature held by the pagan Celts, as well as their actually living in natural settings.[82]

The emphasis on the goodness of creation led to an emphasis on the goodness of humanity. In contrast to the Augustinian understanding of original sin, Celtic theology did not see humans as corrupt but "imprinted with the image of God, full of potential and opportunity, longing for completion and perfection."[83] This in turn produces contrasting understandings of salvation: "For Augustine, Jesus Christ saves us by rescuing us from sin and the consequences of the Fall. For the Celtic apostles, Jesus Christ also comes to complete his good creation."[84]

Hunter admits to being uncomfortable with this element of Celtic theology. The horrors of the twentieth century such as the Holocaust count against their optimistic view of humanity. Yet there is both sin and goodness in most people, and testimonies from converts speak to both being

---

77. Hunter, *Celtic*, 81.
78. Hunter, *Celtic*, 82.
79. Hunter, *Celtic*, 82.
80. Hunter, *Celtic*, 83.
81. Hunter, *Celtic*, 86.
82. Hunter, *Celtic*, 87.
83. Hunter, *Celtic*, 89.
84. Hunter, *Celtic*, 90.

rescued and being completed. The Celtic perspective suggests it is more helpful "to begin with people at the point of their goodness" and to see in persons the possibilities of what they can become through Christ.[85]

Hunter sees in today's secular and postmodern culture in the West echoes of the pagan Celtic culture in which Patrick evangelized.[86] There is much evidence that the Celtic approach of bringing persons into community and conversation connects with persons today as it did in Patrick's day.[87] Local churches can practice hospitality, bishops and church leaders can see themselves as evangelists, a team approach can be recovered, and churches can reach out to their neighbors.[88] Most of all, we can meet people where they are. As Hunter says,

> The gulf between church people and unchurched people is vast, but if we pay the price to understand them, we will usually know what to say and what to do; if they know and feel we understand them, by the tens of millions they will risk opening their hearts to the God who understands them.[89]

Laceye C. Warner: Saving Women

Laceye Warner takes issue with the tendency in contemporary Protestantism to understand evangelism as verbal proclamation, and therefore, "as a practice distinct from social reform and works of charity or mercy."[90] She notes that while evangelists like John Wesley and Charles Finney emphasized preaching, "they both practiced and understood other ministries as evangelistic ranging from small discipleship groups to various forms of compassionate ministries and social reform efforts."[91] Moreover, the sole focus on verbal proclamation overlooks the biblical usage of the good news to "explain the mission *and* message of Jesus."[92]

---

85. Hunter, *Celtic*, 90.
86. Hunter, *Celtic*, 96.
87. Hunter, *Celtic*, 99–100.
88. Hunter, *Celtic*, 117–21.
89. Hunter, *Celtic*, 121.
90. Warner, *Saving Women*, 7.
91. Warner, *Saving Women*, 8.
92. Warner, *Saving Women*, 9.

Part Five: Learning from Tradition

In order to broaden and deepen our understanding of the theology and practice of evangelism, Warner examines the ministries of seven remarkable women. Spanning the period from the eighteenth to the middle of the twentieth centuries, they in their own distinctive ways had a more holistic approach to evangelism. We cannot here provide more than a brief outline of their complex and often courageous stories as told so well by Warner. But we can at least highlight the insights for evangelism she has gleaned from their example.

We begin with *Dorothy Ripley*, born in 1775 in Whitby, England. Her father, one of John Wesley's preachers, was for Dorothy an exemplar she strove to imitate. Although he died when she was eighteen, his encouraging her to preach had lasting impact. His death was the first of a series of tragedies that led her to a deeper faith.[93] It was during this time she began to have mystical visions, including a calling she received during a severe illness to an evangelistic ministry to the African slaves in America.[94]

After receiving a second divine commission, in 1802 Ripley began the first of eight trips to America.[95] From Rhode Island, following divine guidance, she journeyed to Washington to meet with President Thomas Jefferson to seek his "approbation" for her ministry. She also challenged him directly for his having slaves. Jefferson arranged for her to preach to the US Congress (the first woman to do so), which she did again in 1806.[96]

Warner says that Ripley's evangelism was "framed by a Wesleyan emphasis on universal atonement," "offering a salvation that was available to all."[97] She brought her message to slaves and slave owners, as well as "Native Americans, the imprisoned, infirm, and dying," through "visitation and preaching."[98] In confronting slavery she addressed "not only spiritual implications of the sinful system, but also the more provocative social and economic implications."[99]

For Warner, Ripley's grounding her evangelism in a universal atonement is her key contribution. She offered the gospel to all, "regardless of social or political status," including especially "marginalized constituencies."

---

93. Warner, *Saving Women*, 18–21.
94. Warner, *Saving Women*, 23–24.
95. Warner, *Saving Women*, 26.
96. Warner, *Saving Women*, 46–48.
97. Warner, *Saving Women*, 16.
98. Warner, *Saving Women*, 17–18.
99. Warner, *Saving Women*, 15.

While sharing the gospel verbally, she also embodied it "in ministries of compassionate presence and evangelistically motivated social action."[100]

Sarah and Angelina Grimké were born into a family of slave-owning Episcopalians in Charleston, South Carolina. Although Sarah was thirteen years older than Angelina, they "both experienced evangelical conversions in adolescence facilitated by Presbyterian clergy."[101] As they matured in their faith, they became disillusioned with the passivity of local churches regarding slavery, and each joined the Society of Friends.[102]

Sarah moved to Philadelphia, where she was later joined by Angelina. Sarah was greatly influenced by the antislavery writings of John Woolman, a Quaker.[103] Angelina's estrangement from the Presbyterians was strengthened by her abandonment of Calvinism for Arminian and Wesleyan teachings of universal grace and Christian perfection.[104] A turning point in their lives came in 1836 when they attended the American Anti-Slavery Society meeting in New York. They became agents of the Society and conducted a five-month speaking tour on its behalf.[105] They were also drawn into the revivalism and antislavery activism of Charles Finney and Theodore Dwight Weld, the latter of whom would later marry Angelina.[106] In addition to abolitionism, Finneyite revivalism was also committed to the equality of men and women. Building on this foundation, the Grimké sisters carried "the implications for the redemption of sins related to racism and sexism even further."[107]

But the sisters had already developed much of their perspective on these issues prior to their connection with Weld and Finney. It was Angelina's *Appeal to Christian Women of the South*, published in 1836, that elicited their invitation to the American Anti-Slavery Society meeting. This was followed in 1838 by Sarah's *Letters on the Equality of the Sexes*, where she urged women to recognize their equality with men, claim their evangelistic

---

100. Warner, *Saving Women*, 268–69.
101. Warner, *Saving Women*, 58.
102. Warner, *Saving Women*, 58, 65.
103. Warner, *Saving Women*, 67.
104. Warner, *Saving Women*, 71.
105. Warner, *Saving Women*, 73–74.
106. Warner, *Saving Women*, 72, 74.
107. Warner, *Saving Women*, 80.

ministry, cultivate their intellect, interpret Scripture for themselves, and make good use of their talents, especially on behalf of slaves.[108]

Warner believes the most significant contribution of the Grimké sisters is how they "defined sin in its many dimensions—personal, social, institutional." Most of all, they proclaimed the promise of "redemption of those not only captive to pride, but to the lack of self," the latter of which was especially prominent among women.[109]

Julia A. J. Foote was born in 1823 and grew up in a devout Methodist home.[110] Although several traumatic experiences challenged her faith, it was strengthened when her family moved to Albany, New York, and "began attending an African Methodist Church."[111] It was at age fifteen that she was converted at a Methodist quarterly meeting. Seeing her lost condition, she collapsed, fell unconscious, and was carried home and prayed for. Twenty hours later she awoke and rejoiced in her redemption.[112]

Although discouraged from doing so by her parents and church leaders, Foote began to seek freedom from sin through entire sanctification. Encouraged by some older saints, she experienced entire sanctification, feeling in her words "a weight of glory," and finding herself "rooted and grounded in love" and "filled with all fullness of God."[113] It was the "receipt of entire sanctification" that led Foote "to embark upon an evangelistic ministry" that was centered on the promise of a real change in one's heart and life. While her ministry largely consisted of preaching, publication, prayer, and visitation, it "also reached beyond these to address social implications."[114] Among these were advocacy for the right for women to preach and be ordained, the temperance movement, and an end to capital punishment.[115] Warner considers Foote's message of a real change "in and between persons" through entire sanctification, including its social implications, to be her major contribution to the theology of evangelism.[116]

---

108. Warner, *Saving Women*, 59, 92.
109. Warner, *Saving Women*, 269.
110. Warner, *Saving Women*, 106–9.
111. Warner, *Saving Women*, 111.
112. Warner, *Saving Women*, 113.
113. Warner, *Saving Women*, 115.
114. Warner, *Saving Women*, 125.
115. Warner, *Saving Women*, 129–41.
116. Warner, *Saving Women*, 271.

Born in 1839 into a Christian home, *Frances Willard*'s early life was a search for faith. A serious illness led to her making a commitment to God, but she still lacked assurance of salvation.[117] It was at the revival services held at her Methodist Episcopal Church in 1859 that she "offered a public confession of faith in Jesus Christ and repentance of her sins" and acknowledged God's forgiveness. She sought the help of the Holy Spirit to live a life of holiness. She would later experience assurance in the form of a "quiet certitude."[118]

It was 1866, at a meeting led by Phoebe Palmer, that Willard made a fresh consecration of her life to God and experienced entire sanctification, manifested as being filled with joy and love.[119] Because holiness teaching was controversial, Willard was advised to keep her experience to herself, leading her to lose it.[120] Still, "the Wesleyan theme of holiness" would ground "her roles as educator and reformer."[121]

After serving as an educator and the first woman college president in America, Willard became involved in the National Women's Christian Temperance Union (NWCTU). During prayer she received a call from God to speak in support of the right to vote for women as a way to protect home and family from the evils of alcohol.[122] After a brief time serving with Dwight L. Moody's evangelistic team, Willard returned to the NWCTU to become its president in 1879.[123]

Willard's call to ordained ministry and even her election as a lay delegate to General Conference was denied by the Methodist Episcopal Church. In *Woman in the Pulpit* Willard made biblical arguments for the right of women to be ordained and to preach.[124] Through the evangelistic department of the NWCTU Willard deployed numerous women who led Sunday services and practiced fruitful ministry.[125] It was in her combination of evangelistic preaching with temperance and women's suffrage that Warner locates Willard's contribution. Her biblically based evangelistic

---

117. Warner, *Saving Women*, 146–49.
118. Warner, *Saving Women*, 151–57.
119. Warner, *Saving Women*, 154–55.
120. Warner, *Saving Women*, 156.
121. Warner, *Saving Women*, 143.
122. Warner, *Saving Women*, 161.
123. Warner, *Saving Women*, 165–66.
124. Warner, *Saving Women*, 167.
125. Warner, *Saving Women*, 172.

theology refused "to separate social responsibility from evangelism" in contrast "to the emerging and eventually reigning dichotomy of proclamation and social action."[126]

Helen Barrett Montgomery was born in 1861. Her father became pastor of Lake Avenue Baptist Church in 1876, where he encouraged her interest in biblical and classical texts.[127] After attending Wellesley College with a focus on biblical studies[128] she discerned a call to evangelistic ministry in which she would "weave together her gifts for teaching and heart for compassionate ministries."[129] She received a license to preach from Lake Avenue Baptist Church in 1892[130] and would eventually serve as the first woman president of the Northern Baptist Convention.[131] As a leader in the women's ecumenical missionary movement Montgomery combined personal evangelism with social gospel, arguing "that one's personal faith in Jesus Christ could not rightfully be separated from a personal commitment to social activism."[132] But in doing this she faced opposition from a fundamentalist faction that not only rejected the linkage of personal evangelism with social action but also sought to restrict the leadership of women in the church.[133]

Montgomery's major contribution to the theology of evangelism was her remarkable book *The Bible and Missions*. Here she "broke new theological ground by reclaiming the Trinity's missional character as a paradigm for evangelistic ministry."[134] Her emphasis on God as the origin of mission and the One who sends the church to participate in mission anticipated a decade earlier the theology of the *missio Dei* that would become standard in mission circles.[135] Instead of the common practice of works on evangelism focusing only on the New Testament, Montgomery showed how both testaments together present an entire narrative of salvation.[136] Against both an otherworldly fundamentalism and a modernism devoted to a social ethic shorn of the need for conversion, she presented a vision of a church

---

126. Warner, *Saving Women*, 272–73.
127. Warner, *Saving Women*, 186–88.
128. Warner, *Saving Women*, 191.
129. Warner, *Saving Women*, 194.
130. Warner, *Saving Women*, 195.
131. Warner, *Saving Women*, 184.
132. Warner, *Saving Women*, 205.
133. Warner, *Saving Women*, 206.
134. Warner, *Saving Women*, 186.
135. Warner, *Saving Women*, 214.
136. Warner, *Saving Women*, 212–13.

empowered by the Holy Spirit to share in God's work of bringing the kingdom of God to reality in the present.[137]

Warner's final exemplar is *Mary McLeod Bethune*. Born in 1875 in South Carolina,[138] she would become the first African American woman to found a four-year college and to hold a high-level position in the federal government.[139] She was raised in a home steeped in prayer and Scripture,[140] and experienced a conversion containing elements of both justification and assurance.[141] Although educational opportunities for African Americans were limited, she was able to attend schools sponsored by the Presbyterians that formed her commitment to a ministry of evangelism.[142]

Following her graduation she became "the first African American to enroll" in what would become the Moody Bible Institute. It was there, through the prayer of Dwight Moody, that she experienced a baptism of the Holy Spirit, which she later would credit with making "all her thoughts, words, and actions effective."[143] Denied an opportunity to serve as a missionary to Africa, Bethune was appointed by the Presbyterians to teach.[144] Eventually she went to Daytona Beach, Florida, to open the school that would become Bethune-Cookman College, supported by the Methodist Episcopal Church. She then became an active Methodist, serving as a delegate to General, Jurisdictional, and Annual Conferences.[145]

Bethune's evangelistic theology had two central foundations. First was an emphasis on the Golden Rule and love,[146] as exemplified by Jesus Christ. Her desire to imitate Christ "formed not only her own relationship with God in Jesus Christ" but "led her to pray and act evangelistically for others to receive that redemption." It also shaped her call "to care for whole persons in the midst of social and economic oppression."[147] Second, was her "ecclesiology that took seriously a robust eschatology in its dual emphasis upon present Christian discipleship and the fulfillment of God's reign yet

---

137. Warner, *Saving Women*, 218.
138. Warner, *Saving Women*, 225.
139. Warner, *Saving Women*, 223.
140. Warner, *Saving Women*, 226–27.
141. Warner, *Saving Women*, 228–29.
142. Warner, *Saving Women*, 229–35.
143. Warner, *Saving Women*, 236.
144. Warner, *Saving Women*, 238.
145. Warner, *Saving Women*, 239, 251, 259.
146. Warner, *Saving Women*, 241.
147. Warner, *Saving Women*, 244.

to come."[148] It is this eschatological evangelism that "does not merely correspond to a future hope but also a changed present reality" that Warner identifies as Bethune's most significant contribution to evangelism.[149]

At the end of her survey, Warner concludes that

> an eschatological evangelism informed by these women (1) offers the gospel of Jesus Christ to all, (2) in the midst of sins of both pride and lack of self, (3) facilitates a real change in and among persons, (4) enables churches and the multiplicity of its members to understand and fulfill their evangelistic purpose to love and serve the world, (5) while receiving formation from and living into the salvation narrative of the biblical text.[150]

Following their examples, "the contemporary church might embrace a dynamic process in which theology and practices shape and inform each other, leading to an evangelism embodied in vital communities of faith."[151]

A Communion of Evangelistic Saints

What we have seen in this chapter is only a small portion of the rich diversity found in the Christian tradition. But it is enough to suggest the wealth of insight for evangelism that still waits to be discovered or rediscovered.

There is a prejudice in post-Enlightenment Western culture that because past eras and cultures are so different from our own that they have little to teach us. I hope this chapter has set that prejudice to rest. The power in the teaching and example of these past figures lies precisely in its concreteness. How they navigated the very particular challenges of their day is what speaks so powerfully and persuasively to us today.

As evangelism is rethought in light of our postmodern world, we need to draw deeply upon the past for assistance in how to move forward. We also need to broaden our scope as well, learning from our Christian brothers and sisters from across the globe. It is from the communion of saints that we are continually opened to see the varied ways God has and continues to renew persons and communities in love.

---

148. Warner, *Saving Women*, 240; see also 253.
149. Warner, *Saving Women*, 276.
150. Warner, *Saving Women*, 280.
151. Warner, *Saving Women*, 280.

CHAPTER 10

Heirs of the Protestant Reformation

> The saving of anyone is something which is not in the power of man, but only of God. No one can be saved—in virtue of what he can do. Everyone can be saved—in virtue of what God can do.
>
> —KARL BARTH[1]

THE PROTESTANT REFORMERS, LED by Martin Luther, Ulrich Zwingli, and John Calvin, were passionate about the gospel. They believed they had recovered the true gospel of salvation by grace alone and justification by faith alone from centuries of medieval Catholic misunderstanding. They were deeply committed to sharing their message of grace and faith to those still caught in the web of Catholic theology and practice.

But commitment to the gospel did not always mean a commitment to evangelism. As Kelly Fryer has noted, while Luther himself had a "passion for sharing the gospel with those who did not know it," this was not true of the next generation of Lutheran theologians. They "taught that the apostles had already fulfilled the Great Commission" and that any further responsibility for mission "belonged to God alone."[2]

Albert Curry Winn argues that with the rise of Constantinian Christendom, the gospel within the Roman Empire was still good but "it was

---

1. Barth, *Dogmatics*, II/2, 625.
2. Bliese and Van Gelder, *Evangelizing*, 22–23.

hardly considered *news* anymore."[3] This remained the dominant assumption of the medieval church and the Reformation. John Calvin wrote that for the early church the gospel was indeed news, centered on the cross and resurrection and offering salvation to Jew and gentile. Yet for all of Calvin's zeal to convert Catholics to Reformed Christianity, "Calvin seems to assume that the gospel, which had been corrupted and now needs to be purified, is something that everyone has heard about and known about for a long time."[4]

Although the Reformation left an ambiguous legacy about sharing the good news, the Lutheran and Reformed traditions contain rich resources for a theology of evangelism. The first to mine those resources were the Pietists of the seventeenth century. But with the final collapse of Christendom in the West, Lutheran and Reformed theologians have approached their traditions afresh, and have drawn upon them for insight into the shape of evangelism in the twenty-first century. Here we will look at the results of two collaborative teams of theologians, one from the Evangelical Lutheran Church in America (ELCA) and the other from the Presbyterian tradition. They show how Lutheran and Reformed traditions can enrich our understanding of evangelism.

Evangelism in the Lutheran Tradition

Lutherans have a confessional tradition. The irony is, as Richard Bliese and Craig Van Gelder note, that while "united by a common gospel confession that is centered on justification," Lutherans are highly uncomfortable with evangelism.[5] This may be because evangelism is seen as a program, as one of many in the church, highly individualistic and presenting a reduced gospel.[6] To address this disconnect between confessional tradition and evangelistic concern, Bliese and Van Gelder led a group of six theologians whose goal was to reread the "Lutheran confessional heritage" from the perspective of mission.[7] Together they call for the death of evangelism with its programs and reductionist gospel, and the resurrection of an evangelizing

---

3. Coalter and Cruz, *Witness*, 12.
4. Coalter and Cruz, *Witness*, 13–14.
5. Bliese and Van Gelder, *Evangelizing*, 9.
6. Bliese and Van Gelder, *Evangelizing*, 9, 114.
7. Bliese and Van Gelder, *Evangelizing*, 9.

church in which "a culture of evangelizing . . . permeates the life of our church on every level."[8]

The Lutheran tradition has much to offer the entire church with regard to evangelizing. Central to the tradition are Martin Luther's theology of human nature and divine grace. The American optimism concerning human ability has led to a loss of "an understanding of the depths of human sin and evil in the world and, just as important, the majestic power of God's grace in Christ." With that loss comes a focus on human activity that diminishes and obscures the priority of God's activity in salvation: "God *calls* people to faith, . . . *saves* in the waters of baptism, . . . *gives* God's self in bread and wine, . . . *announces* God's word through the voice of regular Christians," and "*is the best interpreter* of God's written word."[9]

With this broad framing of the argument we can now look at the specific contributions of some of the primary authors of each chapter. They are the primary authors in that they drafted those chapters, but all chapters were read and critiqued twice by the entire team, so they present a shared perspective.[10]

Kelly Fryer notes that Lutherans know by heart that "we are saved by grace through faith in Jesus Christ." We have received "the most wonderful gift" but have taken it for granted. Yet there is "a world that lies just outside our door," a world that God loves, which is "groaning in pain" and "hungry for anything that will fill it up and make it whole."[11] This wonderful gift "is not a blanket of forgiveness that we can wrap around us" but a gift of new life, a calling to follow Christ. The gift is at the same time a call to "a life of witness and service and self-giving love, a life that gives itself away for the sake of the world."[12]

We are called to participate in the mission of the triune God. The Father sent the Son, the Father and Son sent the Spirit, and now, through the power of the Spirit, the triune God sends the people of God to be God's witnesses. The goal of God's mission is "a world reconciled and whole," but those who "are God's people *through Christ* know that, in a very real way,

---

8. Bliese and Van Gelder, *Evangelizing*, 115.
9. Bliese and Van Gelder, *Evangelizing*, 5.
10. Bliese and Van Gelder, *Evangelizing*, 8.
11. Bliese and Van Gelder, *Evangelizing*, 12.
12. Bliese and Van Gelder, *Evangelizing*, 13; see also 28–29.

Part Five: Learning from Tradition

the promise of this new day has already arrived."[13] The kingdom is already breaking into the present. Thus, says Fryer,

> We do not participate in mission simply because Jesus tells us to but, rather, because we can't help but get caught up in what God has already done and is doing. The kingdom of God, which is here among us and is yet to come, is the basis of all our hope and the vision that drives us forward in mission.[14]

Fryer argues that the Lutheran doctrine of "justification by grace through faith" has led Lutherans to tenaciously and rightly insist that salvation is a gift of God. But the focus on what God does has made it more difficult to speak about what we are to do. To address this Fryer cites Luther, the Pietists, Søren Kierkegaard, and Dietrich Bonhoeffer, who all insist salvation and discipleship, gift and call, are necessarily connected.[15]

Richard Bliese picks up on this theme of divine initiative and human participation in his chapter. A "renewed vision about evangelizing," he says, is not about the actions of clergy and laity. "It is a vision about God's activity in the world through Jesus Christ and our own identification with that activity." To identify with God's mission is to become an evangelizing church. Evangelizing must be "at the core of the church's self-understanding."[16]

Bliese argues that behind all that has been written about "congregational and spiritual renewal lies one simple quest: to encounter Jesus Christ."[17] The heart of evangelical proclamation is that Jesus is alive and present among us.[18] Salvation itself depends on this. Lutherans have long held that Jesus is present in both word and sacrament as means of grace; to these Bliese adds "the life and witness of the Christian community." This is an incarnational understanding: "God's saving love comes down to us through living words, a bath, a meal, and in the mutual care and consolation among Christians." This is good news indeed, but also can be a hindrance, as it may be hard to hear or see the good news through these concrete actions of sinful people. It takes faith to encounter Jesus in the midst of an all-too-human congregation.[19] The affirmation that Jesus is present "in Word, Sacrament, and Chris-

---

13. Bliese and Van Gelder, *Evangelizing*, 16.
14. Bliese and Van Gelder, *Evangelizing*, 17.
15. Bliese and Van Gelder, *Evangelizing*, 22–26.
16. Bliese and Van Gelder, *Evangelizing*, 35.
17. Bliese and Van Gelder, *Evangelizing*, 35.
18. Bliese and Van Gelder, *Evangelizing*, 38.
19. Bliese and Van Gelder, *Evangelizing*, 39.

tian community" may be the most significant "Lutheran contribution to an ecumenical mission theology of evangelizing."[20]

This is the basis for how Bliese defines evangelizing: "Evangelizing is Jesus coming to people," more precisely, through their "hearing the gospel." A more expanded definition is that "Evangelizing is an acoustical affair in which Christ comes to people within their particular context through the concrete means of grace."[21]

Evangelizing, then, occurs "within an ecclesiological framework." Lutherans have long spoke of receiving the word; this now needs to be balanced by the recognition that the word also sends clergy and laity into mission.[22] Among the changes Bliese advocates to enable an evangelizing church is to call and equip "all the baptized" to go "into the world with full authority to use the means of grace to bring Christ to people,"[23] to open the Eucharist "to all sinners—baptized and non-baptized—announcing that Jesus Christ really comes to them with all his gifts in bread and wine," and making adult catechesis and baptism the norm.[24]

Craig Van Gelder next considers the relation of the evangelizing church to the world. He grounds his theology of the church in this way:

> Our view of God is not complete without having the world in view, with God in relationship to it as both Creator and Redeemer. The gospel is not fully the gospel if it does not have the whole of Creation as its horizon. The church is not fully the church if it does not seek to bring redemption to bear on every dimension of life.[25]

In his survey of the Old Testament Van Gelder finds that participation in God's mission "was more about suffering service than privileged status."[26] This is amply confirmed by the ministry of Jesus and of the early church in the New Testament. While the church has struggled to model this, often amassing power to serve its own interests, it is nonetheless freed by the gospel "to live in vulnerability in relation to the world, where this vulnerability will often lead us to the margins."[27]

20. Bliese and Van Gelder, *Evangelizing*, 41.
21. Bliese and Van Gelder, *Evangelizing*, 45.
22. Bliese and Van Gelder, *Evangelizing*, 46.
23. Bliese and Van Gelder, *Evangelizing*, 46.
24. Bliese and Van Gelder, *Evangelizing*, 47.
25. Bliese and Van Gelder, *Evangelizing*, 51.
26. Bliese and Van Gelder, *Evangelizing*, 53.
27. Bliese and Van Gelder, *Evangelizing*, 54.

Part Five: Learning from Tradition

Jesus Christ both announced and embodied the kingdom of God. The church, empowered by the Holy Spirit, "would carry the message of the good news about the kingdom to the world." Thus the "nature, purpose and ministry" of the church is "formed by the reality, power, and intent of the kingdom of God." This means evangelizing and mission are not just some among many activities the church does but "are embedded as inherent practices in the very nature of the church."[28]

Among the implications of this are these. First, the church is led by the Spirit. The church plans for evangelizing "even as it seeks to discern the leading of the Spirit." Such leading "often comes through conflict, disruption, and surprise," as it did for Peter in Acts 10.[29]

This leads to a second point. Through the Spirit the "gospel brings about a reciprocity," in which "the cultural group that brought the gospel to another context"—as Peter did when he went to bring the gospel to Cornelius—"is itself changed over time by those who receive the gospel."[30]

Third, the church is a social community, a place of "mutual conversation and consolation," and of mutual forgiveness. Its corporate nature is changed by the fruit of the Spirit and its members are empowered for ministry through gifts of the Spirit. Every member contributes to both the life of the community and lives out "their vocation in the world." The fruit and gifts of the Spirit are cultivated through sanctification, "where God's people seek to become conformed into the very image of Christ." As this occurs, "they become a *sign, foretaste* and *instrument* for announcing the presence of the redemptive reign of God in Christ to the world."[31]

The remaining chapters in the book build on the theological foundations in these earlier chapters through discussing concrete practices in the church and addressing difficult issues. Since our primary goal is to present theological reflection on evangelism, we will not examine these chapters here. However, chapter 12 will return to this book for an insightful Lutheran perspective on evangelism in a religiously pluralistic society.

What has been presented is a theologically grounded Lutheran vision of an evangelizing church, and a call for Lutherans to embrace that vision. "It is for the sake of this world that God loves," the authors conclude, "that

---

28. Bliese and Van Gelder, *Evangelizing*, 55.
29. Bliese and Van Gelder, *Evangelizing*, 66, 59.
30. Bliese and Van Gelder, *Evangelizing*, 68.
31. Bliese and Van Gelder, *Evangelizing*, 64.

we must learn to speak the faith with unprecedented boldness, conviction, and integrity."[32]

Evangelism in the Reformed Tradition

Unlike the Lutheran tradition, the Reformed tradition in America, especially in its Presbyterian and Congregationalist forms, has had a robust history of practicing evangelism. As J. Milton Coalter says, the primary issue has been the social and religious changes that have continually called for rethinking that practice. In meeting these challenges, the Reformed tradition has seen Christ as revealed in Scripture "as *the* 'faithful witness'" who "provides his disciples with a clear definition of what faithful outreach is and should be." Thus, the struggle of Reformed communions has been not only to decide "which evangelistic methods fit the times but also which forms of witness continue true to the scriptural vision of Christian discipleship."[33]

But over time this questioning has bred uncertainty. Today "there is a wariness toward techniques that simplistically" equate "membership growth with successful outreach" among some, and a questioning of the entire practice of evangelism among others.[34] To address this "ambivalence about the church's evangelistic mission" a three-year study by a number of scholars was undertaken, culminating in the Faithful Witness Conference in 1993.[35] Eight of the presentations were published in a book edited by Coalter, centered on the Presbyterian strand of the Reformed tradition. While half discussed the history of evangelism, our focus here will be on those essays presenting the theological foundations for witness.

We begin with Albert Curry Winn's discussion of "What is the gospel?" He notes at the outset that neither Scripture nor the Reformed tradition have been "concerned with a program" or "a set of methods"—what he calls "the *ism* of evange*lism*." Instead, their concern is "with the evangel, the gospel."[36]

It was Jesus who first proclaimed the good news. Winn identifies three aspects of that proclamation. First, it "concerned the reign of God,"[37] which

32. Bliese and Van Gelder, *Evangelizing*, 37.
33. Coalter and Cruz, *Witness*, xiii.
34. Coalter and Cruz, *Witness*, xiii.
35. Coalter and Cruz, *Witness*, xiv.
36. Coalter and Cruz, *Witness*, 3.
37. Coalter and Cruz, *Witness*, 4.

Part Five: Learning from Tradition

involves "a great reversal of the values of the present world." "It will belong to the poor instead of to the rich"; "to little children instead of adults." "Tax collectors and prostitutes will go into" it ahead of the religious. "The great ones . . . will be humble." "The last will be first and the first last." This kingdom, although yet to come in fullness, "is already at work in the world."[38] "Jesus' *evangelion*," says Winn, "was indeed *news*, something new, startling, undreamed of. It marked an epoch."[39] Second, "Jesus not only announces the *evangelion* in his teaching and preaching, he demonstrated it; he embodied it." This is shown in his victories over sickness, death, and unclean spirits.[40] Third, Jesus' *evangelion* "was addressed in a special way to the poor."[41]

The crucifixion and resurrection of Jesus led "to dramatic changes in the presentation of the gospel" in apostolic preaching. Most notably, Jesus himself replaces the kingdom at the center of the *evangelion*. This is a shift in light of the death, resurrection, and exaltation of Jesus, but not an abandonment of his message, because Jesus both linked his message to himself and embodied the kingdom he proclaimed.[42]

In surveying the New Testament Winn finds five constants in its *evangelion*. First, it is *good* news—"not a pronouncement of judgment" but a source of great joy.[43] Second, it is good *news*: "Something has happened. There has been a radical, unexpected change . . . in the very structure and fabric of things." Third, the "*evangelion* concerns God's *action*, not human action": it is about "what God has done, is doing, and will do in Christ." Fourth, this action of God involves both "struggle and victory," with unclean spirits, principalities and powers, and death itself. Fifth, this "*evangelion* points beyond itself to still greater victories in the future. It is full of *hope* and *expectation*."[44]

Winn points out that with the emergence of Christendom and into the Protestant Reformation the gospel remained good but it was no longer news.[45] Something of its newness was recovered by Jonathan Edwards in the Great Awakening, who emphasized the nearness of the kingdom

---

38. Coalter and Cruz, *Witness*, 5.
39. Coalter and Cruz, *Witness*, 5.
40. Coalter and Cruz, *Witness*, 5.
41. Coalter and Cruz, *Witness*, 6.
42. Coalter and Cruz, *Witness*, 7.
43. Coalter and Cruz, *Witness*, 10–11.
44. Coalter and Cruz, *Witness*, 11.
45. Coalter and Cruz, *Witness*, 12–14.

Heirs of the Protestant Reformation

and the expectation "of further works of God" to bring it about.[46] In the missionary movement of the nineteenth century the gospel became news, "news announced to peoples and nations that had never heard it before."[47]

Winn believes the collapse of Christendom has created a situation where many Americans have not heard the gospel, so that it can once again become news.[48] This opportunity is enhanced by the rise of Reformed theologies, such as those of Karl Barth and Jürgen Moltmann, "that are more hospitable to the good news of the *evangelion*." It is also aided by "the increase of cross-cultural experiences," in which Americans can become hearers of the good news brought to us by missionaries "from the younger churches."[49] "If," Winn says, "we could see the gospel once again as good news, it would be its own motivation. Good news, by its very nature, has to be shared."[50]

Following the chapter by Winn, Dawn DeVries explores "What is conversion?" She first begins to develop a definition of conversion by examining Scripture and tradition.[51] First of all, in Scripture conversion is the result of divine initiative: "It is because of God's concern for the world that God calls men and women to turn around, and not because they are seeking a new way of life."[52]

Second, "the biblical concept of conversion entails a series of turning points or a process rather than a single moment." As people turn away from their commitments, "conversion must be repeated." Moreover, "Faithfulness to God's call implies a radical change," both personally and "in the structures of society." These are reorientations that by their nature cannot be achieved all at once.[53]

Third, conversion is not how persons attain life after death or avoid divine wrath, but "is the vehicle for turning individuals previously preoccupied with their own desires toward God and their neighbors."[54] Nor

---

46. Coalter and Cruz, *Witness*, 18.
47. Coalter and Cruz, *Witness*, 19.
48. Coalter and Cruz, *Witness*, 21–22.
49. Coalter and Cruz, *Witness*, 22.
50. Coalter and Cruz, *Witness*, 23.
51. Coalter and Cruz, *Witness*, 28.
52. Coalter and Cruz, *Witness*, 29.
53. Coalter and Cruz, *Witness*, 29.
54. Coalter and Cruz, *Witness*, 29.

Part Five: Learning from Tradition

is conversion solely about human transformation. It is, fourth, cosmic in scope, a conversion of the cosmos itself.[55]

Fifth, another source for a definition of conversion is the stories of persons like Paul, Augustine, and Luther. Unlike the dominant biblical views, these "tend to highlight the suddenness and decisiveness of conversion as an individual experience."[56] Finally, there are theologies of conversion, such as among the Puritans and American revivalism, in which the emphasis is less on the givenness of God's action and more on "personal appropriation of salvation."[57]

Considering all these sources, DeVries defines conversion in this way: "Conversion is the transformation of a person or community that arises from the discovery or deepening of beliefs about God, self, and world." This definition leaves open the relation of divine and human action in deference to the range of views among Christians. It has the advantage of including both individual and communal aspects of conversion, as well as both the gradual and sudden ways it can occur.[58]

Looking at the Reformed tradition in particular, DeVries identifies five elements that characterizes that tradition's understanding of conversion. First, "Conversion is a divine gift," "an act of God." Persons "cannot decide to convert but can only respond to God's work already begun in them."[59]

Second, "Conversion is a continuing process." Uncomfortable with "once-and-for-all conversion" and the idea Christians can be perfect in this life, Reformed Christianity understands "repentance, the call to God and to our covenantal responsibilities" to be repeated again and again, in both the lives of Christians and in the church.[60]

Third, conversion is a communal event occurring in the church. This is implicit in the first two points. As a divine gift conversion should be found where Christ is present, which is the church. If it is an ongoing process, the structures that maintain that process (the preached word and the sacraments) are found in the church.[61]

---

55. Coalter and Cruz, *Witness*, 30.
56. Coalter and Cruz, *Witness*, 30.
57. Coalter and Cruz, *Witness*, 31.
58. Coalter and Cruz, *Witness*, 32.
59. Coalter and Cruz, *Witness*, 38–39.
60. Coalter and Cruz, *Witness*, 39.
61. Coalter and Cruz, *Witness*, 39.

Fourth, "Conversion is experienced and expressed in a variety of ways." Personalities, family backgrounds, education, social contexts, and other factors shape how conversions are experienced and expressed, a variety that should be welcomed and celebrated.[62]

Fifth, conversion "is not an end in itself." It "is a call to mission," and as an ongoing process enables persons to participate in God's mission.[63]

Among the implications of this understanding of conversion is that the primary task of the church is to be faithful in word and sacrament, education and nurture. Also, "it would be misguided for the church to focus all its evangelistic efforts outside its own doors." If conversion is a process, "we ought to look for converts first within our own midst."[64] Finally, DeVries reiterates that conversion is not an end in itself. She reminds us that the "Reformed tradition has always insisted that the chief and highest end of human existence is not personal or institutional survival, but the glory of God."[65]

David C. Hester then examines the relationship between evangelism and education in the Reformed tradition. Education, he says, "is *learning how* to live as *disciples*, evidencing in our lives the confession we have made in response to the word we received."[66] It enables our ongoing conversion. Evangelism is "proclaiming the gospel in word and deed, inviting persons to participate in the grace of God and to join in the mutual care and public ministry of the community of God's covenant people." It is for both those outside and inside the community, and, like education, is an ongoing activity. While evangelism does not encompass all that the church does, it does occur "in a variety of ways," including worship, caring for those who hunger or are lonely or who mourn, and seeking justice for the poor—wherever we "consciously and intentionally" seek to witness to Christ.[67]

The link between evangelism and education is this: "evangelism invites persons into the community of Christ, church education equips us to live together faithfully, as Christ's disciples."[68] Hester identifies "three evangelical roles of educational ministry." First is initiation, in which we learn how to belong to the Christian community, through learning its

62. Coalter and Cruz, *Witness*, 39–40.
63. Coalter and Cruz, *Witness*, 40.
64. Coalter and Cruz, *Witness*, 40.
65. Coalter and Cruz, *Witness*, 41.
66. Coalter and Cruz, *Witness*, 47.
67. Coalter and Cruz, *Witness*, 48.
68. Coalter and Cruz, *Witness*, 48.

shared history, sacred symbols, and beliefs. Second is "education for critical reflection," or "life in the Spirit," which opens us to be led by the Spirit in order "to interpret the contemporary world and our personal situations in light of the gospel of Christ."[69] Third is "education for public transformation" which "teaches us that the gospel proclaims a way of justice and love that is intended to bless all creation and not the disciples of Christ alone."[70]

In his introduction Milton Coalter mentioned that at the conference where these essays were first presented a pastor from Ghana said that they had not said enough about the Holy Spirit. In their defense I do think there was a solid emphasis on the divine initiative, certainly a theological claim at the heart of the Reformed tradition. But in light of that comment Coalter affirms that "Christian witness is ultimately prompted, sustained, and efficacious only with the help of the Holy Spirit." While the "church cannot direct the Spirit's action" it can prayerfully seek the Spirit's guidance, both "in discerning where the Spirit is active" and in finding ways to cooperate with the Spirit's ministry of "birthing new life throughout the creation."[71]

The Divine Initiative

The Lutheran and Reformed traditions share a common emphasis on salvation as a gift of God. Evangelism must therefore be centered on enabling persons to know what God has done and is now doing to forgive, reconcile, and transform people who receive this gift through faith.

Because they understand the primary means of God's present activity is through word and sacrament, they emphasize the church, in contrast to an individualistic approach to evangelism. They also value the life of the community itself as a witness to the grace and love of God. The church is at one and the same time an evangelizing community and the central locus where persons are being evangelized. Evangelism is not a once-only event but a process of continual renewal.

Because of the strong focus on what God does, both traditions have had difficulty speaking about what we do in response, apart from our having faith. Yet they insist discipleship is not an option but the form salvation takes. It is being caught up in the amazing love of God and having profound gratitude for grace that impels persons to join God's mission in the world.

---

69. Coalter and Cruz, *Witness*, 49.
70. Coalter and Cruz, *Witness*, 50.
71. Coalter and Cruz, *Witness*, xx.

CHAPTER 11

Wesleyan Ways of Evangelism

> [Wesley] had discovered . . . that evangelism barely begins with conversion and a profession of faith, that it must always lead beyond to a lifelong mission of witness and service in the world for which Christ died.
>
> —ALBERT C. OUTLER[1]

WHEN WE LOOK AT the past to find insight for evangelism today, John Wesley is an obvious choice. He was a leading figure in a large-scale evangelistic event, the eighteenth-century awakening. He belonged to a church that he believed consisted of largely nominal Christians in need of renewal, echoing how many see many churches in America today. The movement he led was organized for both Christian formation and mission. And, along with his Calvinist contemporary Jonathan Edwards, Wesley provides in-depth reflection on how God works in bringing persons to conversion and enabling their growth as Christians.

One of the key architects of the mid-twentieth-century renaissance in Wesleyan studies was Albert C. Outler. The subsequent generation of Wesley scholars built upon, extended, and at times challenged the foundation he laid. Among his contributions was his remarkably prescient 1971 Denman Lectures on evangelism. We will begin with Outler's presentation of Wesleyan evangelism before moving to more recent proposals for evangelism in the Wesleyan tradition.

1. Outler, *Evangelism*, 25.

Part Five: Learning from Tradition

Albert C. Outler: Evangelism in the Wesleyan Spirit

Outler sees the church that is entering the last half of the twentieth century as in crisis. There "is a widespread and spreading demoralization throughout the churches, at every level and in every sector." There is the beginning "of a wholesale defection of the middle-class and the young" from the church.[2] The larger culture is filled with anxiety but notably absent of a sense of guilt, or more precisely, a sense of guilt before God.[3] If evangelism means "the communication of the gospel and the maturation of Christians in the community of the church and in the human community at large," then how can a "half-hearted" and polarized church bring this message of hope to this current cultural context? Outler believes John Wesley can show us the way forward.[4]

He begins by examining John Wesley the evangelist, highlighting three aspects of his theology and practice. The first was a transformation in Wesley himself, "from passion to *compassion* as his dominate emotion, . . . from a harsh zealot of God's judgment to a winsome witness of God's grace." Outler does not locate this change with Wesley's famous Aldersgate experience of May 1738, but with his "embarrassed descent into field preaching on 2 April, 1739," of which Aldersgate was a necessary precondition.[5] There, says Outler, Wesley let go of the focus on his own soul to truly care for and identify with those who heard his preaching. It was their truly hearing the gospel that finally made Wesley "into an assured believer."[6] That "Wesley became an effective evangelist when he was finally enabled, by grace, to offer himself to his hearers as an importunate herald and servant of God," to be filled with the "grace of compassion—the compassion of Christ's self-giving love," is a lesson relevant for us today.[7]

A second aspect of Wesley's evangelism "was his firm conviction that conversion is never more than the bare threshold of authentic and comprehensive evangelism." "Preaching Christ" could sometimes mean judgment on self-righteousness and sometimes mercy in the face of despair, but in all cases it "was aimed beyond confession and conversion toward the fullness

---

2. Outler, *Evangelism*, 15.
3. Outler, *Evangelism*, 16.
4. Outler, *Evangelism*, 16.
5. Outler, *Evangelism*, 18.
6. Outler, *Evangelism*, 19.
7. Outler, *Evangelism*, 20–21.

of faith and the endless maturing in grace." Sanctification, not justification, was "the goal and end of all valid evangelistic endeavor."[8]

Third, Wesley believed "the essence of faith was personal and inward, but the evidence of faith was public and social." Thus those who responded to preaching were brought into societies where they were committed to both the "sacrament of the church" and "to a process of Christian discipline," becoming "a growing company of lay witnesses."[9] It was these laity that were the heart of Methodism, who took initiative and provided local leadership, living witnesses who made the societies themselves centers of evangelism.[10] What Wesley was doing by bringing persons into societies and a process of Christian nurture was not, says Outler, "a stage *beyond* evangelism. It was, rather, the evangelistic enterprise itself in its natural unfolding."[11]

Outler then moves from considering Wesley the evangelist to Wesley's evangel. He identifies five major motifs of Wesley's message that run "parallel to the first principles in the Christian life as a whole."[12]

First, the "prime *motive* of the Christian life is gratitude" for God's providence and salvation through Jesus Christ. Gratitude is likewise the prime motive for evangelism. Those who evangelize out of a sense of duty will communicate their belief that it is a chore, but those who evangelize "with glad and grateful" hearts "will find liberty in" their "testimony and joy in the fruits thereof."[13]

Second, the "prime *certainty* of the Christian faith and life is that God was—and is—in Christ," who has reconciled the entire creation to himself through the cross of Jesus Christ.[14] "This is also our prime certainty in evangelism. We preach Christ—and ourselves as servants to those for whom Christ died."[15]

Third, the "prime *dynamic* of the Christian life is the vital energy of the Holy Spirit in every human heart, the divine life in Christ's body the church." While "many things are useful," Outler says, the Holy Spirit is the one thing we need in the life of the church. The Holy Spirit is also the chief

---

8. Outler, *Evangelism*, 21.
9. Outler, *Evangelism*, 22.
10. Outler, *Evangelism*, 23.
11. Outler, *Evangelism*, 22.
12. Outler, *Evangelism*, 34.
13. Outler, *Evangelism*, 34.
14. Outler, *Evangelism*, 34.
15. Outler, *Evangelism*, 35.

dynamic of evangelism, in both power and prevenience. We evangelize knowing "that the Holy Spirit is already *there*, awakening faith, preparing the heart and mind and will."[16]

Fourth, the "prime and constant *end* of the Christian life is the actualization in feeling and act of God's righteous rule in the human community—which is to say, 'the kingdom of God.'"[17] The "chief end of evangelism" is the same: the people "should hear—really hear—the good news that God's kingdom . . . is a live option for *them*," in the present. It is a gracious invitation to turn from dependence on ourselves and things created to love and depend on God.

Fifth, "the principle *means* in the Christian life for measuring up to God's *expecting* love is God's grace." Wesley frequently spoke of "means of grace"—such as public worship, preaching, the Lord's Supper, prayer, searching the Scriptures, and fasting—as places we encounter the transforming love of God.[18] This is all grounded, says Outler, in God choosing to become known "in and through physical and historical events," most especially the incarnation.[19] Therefore "all valid evangelism must depend on the grace of God and on the means of grace, or else become distorted." The call is not just for "repentance and conversion, but also to incorporation, to an engrafting into the body of Christ and a lifelong process of nurturing and growth in the sacramental fellowship."[20]

It is here that Outler notes "a scandalous discrepancy": so many of our churches are not healthy settings into which persons can be initiated.[21] What this means for us, as it did for Wesley, is that a necessary part of evangelism is to the church itself. "Give us a church of Spirit-filled people in whose fellowship life speaks to life, love to love, and faith and trust responds to God's grace," says Outler, "and we shall have a church whose witness in the world will not fall and whose service to the world will transform it."[22]

---

16. Outler, *Evangelism*, 35.
17. Outler, *Evangelism*, 35.
18. Outler, *Evangelism*, 30.
19. Outler, *Evangelism*, 30–31.
20. Outler, *Evangelism*, 31.
21. Outler, *Evangelism*, 31.
22. Outler, *Evangelism*, 39.

Henry H. Knight III and F. Douglas Powe Jr.: Transforming Evangelism

For Knight and Powe, John Wesley models an approach to evangelism in sharp contrast to that of conveying information to elicit a decision. They describe the Wesleyan alternative this way:

> We believe evangelism is more relational than confrontational, more communal than solitary, and is more a beginning point than an end. Evangelism involves not only sharing our faith with others, but also welcoming them into a community and enabling them to begin to grow in their faith. Above all evangelism is about love: God's love for us in Jesus, our love for our neighbor, and the invitation to receive and grow in a new life that is characterized by love.[23]

What Wesley proclaimed was God's love for all, and the gracious offer of a new life in Christ that enables persons to love as God loves.[24] Salvation, then, is much more than forgiveness of sins (or justification) and a life after death. It is entering into a new life in the present (sanctification) in which love increasingly shapes and governs our desires and motives, our relationships and commitments, our heart and life.[25]

With this understanding of salvation Knight and Powe can now offer their definition of evangelism.

> Evangelism is our sharing and inviting others to experience the good news that God loves us and invites us into a transforming relationship through which we are forgiven, receive new life, and are restored to the image of God, which is love.[26]

Theologically, "Wesleyan evangelism is firmly grounded on what God has done for our salvation in the life, death, and resurrection of Jesus Christ, and relies completely on the presence and power of the Holy Spirit."[27] Salvation is the remedy for our fallen human condition, in which by turning away from God we have lost the key part of the image of God in which we were created, which is love. Our problem is not only guilt, it is that we *are* sinners. Sin is like a disease that afflicts our entire self and which we are

---

23. Knight and Powe, *Transforming Evangelism*, 9.
24. Knight and Powe, *Transforming Evangelism*, 12.
25. Knight and Powe, *Transforming Evangelism*, 14–16.
26. Knight and Powe, *Transforming Evangelism*, 17.
27. Knight and Powe, *Transforming Evangelism*, 17.

Part Five: Learning from Tradition

unable to cure. God's promise is that through faith in Jesus Christ the Holy Spirit will over time restore us to the image of God, enabling us to love God and others as we are loved by God.

The practices and goals of evangelism are shaped by the nature of evangelism. Knight and Powe identify four areas in which salvation shapes evangelism.

The first is that salvation is "a journey we begin."[28] When persons responded to the preaching or personal faith sharing of Wesley's Methodists, they committed themselves to a set of spiritual disciplines. These included doing no harm to others, doing good to the bodies and souls of others, and regularly doing such practices as attending worship, receiving the Lord's Supper, hearing the preached word, studying Scripture, praying, as well as other means of grace. They also committed to attending a weekly class meeting, a small group that held them accountable to this discipline and enabled discussion of how to live as a disciple of Jesus Christ. These were not persons who believed salvation was complete when they made a decision or had an experience. They understood salvation as a lifelong journey of growing in the knowledge and love of God, being increasingly formed in God's image, and growing in love for others. "When the Christian life is understood this way," Knight and Powe insist, "evangelism cannot mark the end of the journey. Instead, it has to be a means to help people begin the journey."[29]

Second, salvation involves entering into community. John Wesley called this aspect "social holiness," by which he meant a community that both exemplifies holiness and enables its members to grow in holiness. Such a community must maintain the difficult balance of being *inviting* to persons outside so they can begin the journey while *sustaining* those already in the community in their growth in love for God and neighbor.[30] Wesley's societies and classes were designed to do both.

Knight and Powe describe an inviting community as "one that shows compassion and acts justly toward its neighbor," while "always remembering the message of salvation so central to the gospel."[31] A sustaining community is one where persons are able to pray for one another, share their burdens, discuss together how to live out their faith, and hold one another

---

28. Knight and Powe, *Transforming Evangelism*, 19.
29. Knight and Powe, *Transforming Evangelism*, 20; see also 89–90.
30. Knight and Powe, *Transforming Evangelism*, 20.
31. Knight and Powe, *Transforming Evangelism*, 37.

accountable for living out that faith.[32] In a subsequent publication Knight and Powe show how the goal of Wesley's communities "was not only the transformation of persons but the renewal of the church and the wider society in holy love."[33] Christian formation led to mission, and participation in mission in turn aided formation. Wesleyan evangelism invites persons to enter into this kind of community.

Third, "Wesleyan evangelism helps us know God." Salvation is more than knowing about God, as important as that is. What the gospel promises "is that we will know God through entering a relationship, and through that relationship will come to know that we belong to God."[34] To be in relationship with God is transformative: "we begin to love God and others as we have been loved by God."[35] This new life is the work of the Holy Spirit, primarily in and through the means of grace mentioned earlier.[36] With this also comes an assurance, our knowing that we are accepted by God through Jesus Christ.[37]

Finally, evangelism involves proclaiming the good news, which includes not only preaching but a calling for all Christians to testify to God's love in Jesus Christ.[38] Wesley, initially with great reluctance, violated the norms of his day to preach to persons outside the walls of a church building. "As Wesley emphasized field preaching, he began to see the word of God reaching audiences who never attended church."[39] He soon was enlisting lay people to join him and his brother Charles in bringing good news to the people (rather than waiting for them to come into a church building).

The Wesleys made the word of God relevant to the lives of their hearers. One way they did this was through the many hymns written by Charles Wesley, which made the message and teaching of the gospel accessible in a way that could be understood and experienced.[40] A second way was the holistic nature of their ministry, in which they cared about bodies as well as souls. John Wesley was concerned for persons' physical needs for

32. Knight and Powe, *Transforming Evangelism*, 40.
33. Knight and Powe, *Transforming Community*, 11.
34. Knight and Powe, *Transforming Evangelism*, 47.
35. Knight and Powe, *Transforming Evangelism*, 48.
36. Knight and Powe, *Transforming Evangelism*, 48–49.
37. Knight and Powe, *Transforming Evangelism*, 51.
38. Knight and Powe, *Transforming Evangelism*, 56–57.
39. Knight and Powe, *Transforming Evangelism*, 58.
40. Knight and Powe, *Transforming Evangelism*, 60–61.

Part Five: Learning from Tradition

food, shelter, medical care, and education. Key to it all was his relational approach, working with people and bringing them into communities of forgiveness and acceptance.[41]

Knight and Powe also emphasize testimony as a form of proclamation. Early Methodist people regularly gave testimonies. For them, testimony meant more "than just stories about conversions." It "describes the intersection between our story and the gospel story." It "is about what God is doing in our lives and sharing that experience with others."[42]

Knight and Powe insist that loving God and our neighbor is at the heart of salvation. "Thus," they say, "the Wesleyan way of evangelism takes seriously the needs of others, whether those needs are physical or spiritual."[43] But we do so in the manner of God's love as revealed in Jesus Christ. We avoid a "cheap love" in which the only neighbors we love are persons like us. We also avoid a "controlling love" in which "we begin determining who should receive the gospel and how they should receive it," closing ourselves off from new ways of outreach and hospitality to which God is calling us.[44]

The Wesleyan way, then, must keep these challenges in mind in reaching out to others, "while recognizing it is only by loving others that God's love can be expressed in concrete ways. Thus for Wesley, loving God and our neighbor is not a component of evangelism, it is what governs our practice of evangelism."[45]

Jeffrey A. Conklin-Miller: Intercessory Evangelism

Jeffrey Conklin-Miller notes that writings on evangelism often seek a balance between Christian identity and contextualization, between faithfulness and relevance. He cites Scott Jones as one example. But the problem as Conklin-Miller sees it is deeper than finding some sort of in-between approach, for one person's compromise looks to another as a capitulation.[46] The "more fundamental question," he argues, is "how shall we understand the differentiation and relationship between the Church and the world?"[47]

---

41. Knight and Powe, *Transforming Evangelism*, 62–63.
42. Knight and Powe, *Transforming Evangelism*, 69.
43. Knight and Powe, *Transforming Evangelism*, 79.
44. Knight and Powe, *Transforming Evangelism*, 78–79.
45. Knight and Powe, *Transforming Evangelism*, 79.
46. Conklin-Miller, *Leaning Both Ways*, 4–6.
47. Conklin-Miller, *Leaning Both Ways*, 5.

Along with this, he asks, "What kind of community is capable of this discernment?"[48]

These are crucial issues for any theology of evangelism in the Wesleyan tradition given Wesley's central emphasis on holiness of heart and life. That emphasis implies a people distinct from the world yet engaged in the world. The church, then, is "a community engaging both the practices of intra-ecclesial formation and extra-ecclesial engagement," leading to an expanded definition of evangelism. Conklin-Miller endorses the view of Stephen Chapman and Laceye Warner that evangelism should be equated with the mission of God, including not only proclamation and initiation but social justice, peace, and care for creation. Evangelism, then, is intercessory at its core, standing "between formation and mission, between tradition and innovation, between God and the world, always *leaning both ways at once*."[49] Conklin-Miller here is not seeking compromise but is insisting instead that we must inhabit the tension between these polarities, neither eliminating nor reducing the tension. Instead of leaning toward one or the other side of the tension, we should simultaneously be leaning toward both.[50]

In examining the church/world distinction, Conklin-Miller says what is significant is not the fact but the nature of their distinction. While both "are part of creation, and thus, historically located, . . . they are to be differentiated by the trajectories they travel or the aims they seek." The agency of the church is governed by "the Lordship of Christ," the agency of the world is not.[51]

Recognizing this differentiation is crucial for evangelism for three reasons. First, without it we are unable "to speak theologically about the mission of the church"; more particularly for Wesleyans, we are unable to see how holiness makes the church distinct from the world while at the same time fueling its mission of serving the world and being a witness to the divinely intended vocation of the world.[52]

Second, the distinction between church and world prevents distortions in our understanding of both. For the church, it both enables us to avoid reducing the church to a mere instrument of evangelism and at the same time to recognize the sins of the church (such as colonialism and the

---

48. Conklin-Miller, *Leaning Both Ways*, 6.
49. Conklin-Miller, *Leaning Both Ways*, 7.
50. Conklin-Miller, *Leaning Both Ways*, 8.
51. Conklin-Miller, *Leaning Both Ways*, 14.
52. Conklin-Miller, *Leaning Both Ways*, 14.

endorsement of slavery) that contradicts its identity.[53] With regard to the world it reminds us that "the world is not a neutral party" but is bent on serving its own interests, not God's. It counters the tendency in evangelism to describe the world "in neutral terms, as 'culture' or 'context,' from which the Church is able to borrow at will" "to communicate the gospel."[54]

Third, the distinction between church and world enables us to envision evangelistic practice in light of the complexities inherent in doing it faithfully in the world. Ignoring the agency of either church or world often "leads to a privileging of one pole of these tensions over another," thus deflating the tensions and undermining faithful practice.[55]

This is precisely the problem Conklin-Miller finds with many Wesleyan writers on evangelism. He argues that Mortimer Arias recognizes the agency of the world but his focus on the kingdom of God lacks consideration of the role of the church. William Abraham does the reverse, having much reflection on the agency of the church but little on that of the world.[56] Church growth advocate George Hunter is long on strategies but short on theological reflection, understating the identity of the church as well as the agency of the world. Thus his call for the church to adapt to the culture in order to reach people runs a serious risk of the church losing its distinctive identity.[57] In contrast, Conklin-Miller sees Bryan Stone as overstating the distinction between church and world. While rightly recognizing the agency of both, Stone emphasizes their separation to the point that their intersection becomes unclear. The church indeed is a witness to an alternate reality, but for Conklin-Miller as an aspect of that witness it is also engaged in the world.[58]

In order to develop his theology of evangelism Conklin-Miller examines in depth the identity and agency of the world, and then the identity and agency of the church. Central to his consideration of the world is the recognition, as Wesley certainly knew, that creation is both created good and fallen into sin, loved by God and waiting for redemption. This is true of creation in its entirety as well as the human portion of creation.[59] In light of

53. Conklin-Miller, *Leaning Both Ways*, 15.
54. Conklin-Miller, *Leaning Both Ways*, 16.
55. Conklin-Miller, *Leaning Both Ways*, 16.
56. Conklin-Miller, *Leaning Both Ways*, 20.
57. Conklin-Miller, *Leaning Both Ways*, 25–29.
58. Conklin-Miller, *Leaning Both Ways*, 29–34.
59. Conklin-Miller, *Leaning Both Ways*, 42–46.

this Wesley encouraged Methodists "to maintain simultaneously a faithful distance from and missional engagement with" the world.[60]

Conklin-Miller describes the identity and agency of the world using the biblical concept of principalities and powers. As he stated earlier, these powers are not neutral: they actively seek to shape our "imagination, perception, and desire."[61] The primary challenge to evangelism, in Conklin-Miller's estimation, is the power of the market, which reduces Christian symbols, beliefs, and practices to objects of consumption. As such their meaning is altered as they are removed from their Christian context which gives them their meaning and understood instead within the context of consumer culture. Evangelism is then transformed from sharing that Jesus is Lord to meeting consumer demand.[62]

The ability of principalities and powers like the market to shape human imagination and perception underscores the necessity of Christian formation. Without intentional practices of formation such as Wesley devised for his Methodists the church, finding itself within a fallen world, cannot become the holy people necessary for faithful evangelism. Conklin-Miller nicely summarizes the relation of formation and mission this way:

> A concern for formation without evangelism pushes the Church toward sectarianism . . . and an account of mission without formation pushes the Church toward unquestioning, apologetic translation. . . . Concern for both formation and mission is a "leaning both ways" in the life of the Church that nurtures both fidelity to tradition and authentic engagement in context.[63]

Turning to the identity of the church, Conklin-Miller describes it as a distinctive people.[64] Thus it is more than the locus for the means of grace and personal salvation.[65] The "telos of salvation," he says, "is not a collection of 'people called Methodists' but rather a formation of a new community, a 'People called Methodist.'"[66] Evangelism for such a People is not a program but a natural aspect of their life as a community, simultaneously leaning

---

60. Conklin-Miller, *Leaning Both Ways*, 49.
61. Conklin-Miller, *Leaning Both Ways*, 41.
62. Conklin-Miller, *Leaning Both Ways*, 60–66.
63. Conklin-Miller, *Leaning Both Ways*, 40.
64. Conklin-Miller, *Leaning Both Ways*, 68.
65. Conklin-Miller, *Leaning Both Ways*, 71.
66. Conklin-Miller, *Leaning Both Ways*, 75.

Part Five: Learning from Tradition

into the Christian tradition and the needs of the world.[67] Focusing on the formative purpose of Wesley's General Rules (do no harm, do good to the bodies and souls of others, attend the ordinances of God), Conklin-Miller shows how Wesley emphasized "the *Visibility* of the embodied, gathered community; . . . the *Practices* that shape the inner life of the Methodist Societies; and . . . the *Witness* that this community offers to those outside in the world."[68]

How, then, "does this People *engage* the world?" Here Conklin-Miller argues that people called Methodist are not only shaped through practicing the General Rules but also "in the ongoing evangelistic engagement with the world."[69] Drawing on the theology of Rowan Williams, he describes an intersection of the church with the world in which the church not only continually reinterprets the world in light of the biblical text but also discovers itself anew as it is recreated by the Spirit.[70] The church is less "a fixed entity" and more "an event of reconciliation and forgiveness,"[71] a work of the triune God bringing "persons previously separated" into communion.[72] "The Church must be the Church," says Conklin-Miller, "but it can only be the Church as it is engaged in the world."[73]

Conklin-Miller calls such an engagement with the world "Intercessory Evangelism." It is a "constant stance of living between God and the world, . . . articulating the work of God in the world as well as the needs of the world to God." The church not only offers prayer but embodies prayer, participating "in God's ongoing creation and redemption of the world through Jesus Christ in the power of the Holy Spirit." In other words, the "evangelistic mission is to *intercede*."[74]

For the Methodist tradition, formation and mission occurs not only in local churches but in entities both smaller and larger, all in connection with one another. The class meetings, governed by the General Rules, were the original examples of groups smaller than the congregation.[75] Conference

---

67. Conklin-Miller, *Leaning Both Ways*, 75.
68. Conklin-Miller, *Leaning Both Ways*, 83.
69. Conklin-Miller, *Leaning Both Ways*, 97.
70. Conklin-Miller, *Leaning Both Ways*, 102.
71. Conklin-Miller, *Leaning Both Ways*, 104.
72. Conklin-Miller, *Leaning Both Ways*, 106.
73. Conklin-Miller, *Leaning Both Ways*, 113.
74. Conklin-Miller, *Leaning Both Ways*, 111.
75. Conklin-Miller, *Leaning Both Ways*, 114.

is a prime example of a larger ecclesial body. Drawing on Russell Richey, Conklin-Miller shows how conference was much more than a business meeting and "constituted an alternative space and time," an eschatological foretaste of Zion.[76] This sense of conference as something one is "in" as well as something "performed" applies more generally to all Methodist ecclesial entities, including class meetings and local churches.[77]

Today this connectional ecclesiology encompasses not only class meetings, congregations, and conference but nonprofit organizations, church-related schools, and the like. The "Methodist ecclesial heritage in Class, Conference, and Connection constitutes the environment within which we can narrate a wide variety of ecclesial forms through which the People called Methodist can engage the world." While much of this work has been called "outreach, or community service, or social ethics," Conklin-Miller argues that it "is most rightly described as *evangelism*—the intercessory stance of the People of God in the world, always leaning between Church/World, between formation and mission, between tradition and innovation, both ways at once."[78]

Jack Jackson: Practices of Proclamation

Jack Jackson seeks to correct a fundamental misunderstanding of Wesley's evangelistic practice. The root of the problem is late nineteenth-century and early twentieth-century revivalism, through which "evangelism became associated with two particular Christian practices: public preaching and calling persons to an immediate conversion to Christ through faith and repentance."[79] Reading Wesley through this lens, many writers assumed this was what Wesley was doing as well. Wesley's concern for holiness, emphasis on community, and commitment to social reform were recognized but seen as disconnected from evangelism.[80]

In the 1980s there was dissatisfaction with this disconnect, and efforts were made to revision Wesleyan evangelism. Some, like William Abraham and Scott Jones, sought to incorporate proclamation and conversion into a larger set of evangelistic practices seen as a process of initiation. Others,

76. Conklin-Miller, *Leaning Both Ways*, 119.
77. Conklin-Miller, *Leaning Both Ways*, 120.
78. Conklin-Miller, *Leaning Both Ways*, 121.
79. Jackson, *Offering Christ*, xi.
80. Jackson, *Offering Christ*, xii.

Part Five: Learning from Tradition

like Laceye Warner, wanted to expand evangelism to include "social justice, peace, and ecological concern" as well as proclamation. Yet others, like Mortimer Arias and Walter Klaiber, still defined evangelism as proclamation but sought to deepen its message.[81]

Jackson believes that Wesley would find the instincts leading to these proposals to be correct, but their remedies flawed. "Instead of expanding evangelism to include all aspects of the church's ministry," Jackson argues, "Wesley believed we should expand our understanding of how people respond to the story of God in Christ through the power of the Holy Spirit."[82] Jackson wants to define evangelism as proclamation. But in doing so "offers at once a broader and narrower interpretation of proclamation in Wesley's evangelistic vision." He describes Wesley's evangelism as a matrix in which the gospel is proclaimed "in a variety of ways," in multiple forums, seeking differing responses along the way of salvation.[83]

Proclamation, the first element in the matrix, included not only preaching but teaching and exhortation. While Wesley at times would use preaching and teaching as synonyms, for the most part he saw teaching as "instruction in the basics of the Christian faith."[84] Exhortation was similar to preaching, only shorter and not strictly based on a biblical passage. Its goal was encouragement or correction.[85] All three were elements of the "Methodist System," which "was designed to encourage continual proclamation and encounters with the Spirit in order to inspire people to maturity as disciples."[86]

This leads to the "second element of the matrix." Wesley believed people went "through three distinct stages of discipleship": (1) awakening "to the gospel story" and beginning to explore its "relevance for life"; (2) "conversion and justification" through faith and repentance; and (3) "a constant journey of holiness."[87] Jackson argues that Wesleyan evangelism is not just concerned with the second of these stages but all three, and the varied forms of proclamation are utilized throughout the entire process. Thus "the same story that encourages conversion also facilitates awakening

---

81. Jackson, *Offering Christ*, xiii–xiv. On Klaiber, see his *Call and Response*.
82. Jackson, *Offering Christ*, xvii.
83. Jackson, *Offering Christ*, xx.
84. Jackson, *Offering Christ*, 32.
85. Jackson, *Offering Christ*, 32–35.
86. Jackson, *Offering Christ*, xxi.
87. Jackson, *Offering Christ*, xxi.

Wesleyan Ways of Evangelism

and sanctification, as the Spirit works to reveal the power and presence of God in people's lives."[88]

The "third element of the matrix includes the primary forums in which . . . proclamation took place, namely, field preaching, society meetings, and most importantly, class meetings and visitation."[89] We will look at each of these more closely below. What should be emphasized now is that each of these were the locus of evangelistic proclamation, not just, as is often thought, preaching in the fields or from a pulpit.

In summary Jackson describes

> Wesley's evangelistic vision . . . as a continual offering of God's gracious love in Jesus Christ. Through that proclamation, which takes place over the course of a lifetime of discipleship, the Holy Spirit works to facilitate various responses of deeper maturity and faith.[90]

Methodism was structured to enable this multifaceted proclamation through those forums Jackson identified.

The first of these forums was *field preaching*, which referred to proclamation that occurred anywhere outside of a Church of England church building. "Field preaching," Jackson says, "facilitated a repetitive encounter between the word of God and people who rarely if ever attended Christian worship in a parish building" and "who might otherwise have never heard" the good news.[91] The actual practice of field preaching included exhortation as well as preaching,[92] and "was the best way to engage the unawakened with the word of God."[93] While awakening was the primary goal and the most common response, people who were awakened could also be "converted as a result of field preaching."[94] The awakened were brought into the Methodist societies and class meetings; it is there that most came to faith and experienced a new birth.[95]

The second forum for proclamation was the *society meetings*. Proclamation there, Jackson argues, "help cultivate people awakened in field

88. Jackson, *Offering Christ*, xix.
89. Jackson, *Offering Christ*, xxi–xvii.
90. Jackson, *Offering Christ*, xx.
91. Jackson, *Offering Christ*, 72.
92. Jackson, *Offering Christ*, 86.
93. Jackson, *Offering Christ*, 87.
94. Jackson, *Offering Christ*, 89.
95. Jackson, *Offering Christ*, 90.

preaching so they could experience both initial and subsequent times of faith and repentance, resulting in justification and sanctification."[96] The societies were considered so essential by Wesley that he only encouraged field preaching where societies existed or could be started.[97]

Societies were designed for mutual care and to nurture discipleship.[98] Those who joined committed to follow the spiritual discipline outlined in the General Rules: do no harm, do good, and attend the ordinances of God.[99] Society meetings were worship services with "prayers, singing, preaching, testimony, and so on." In addition, there were special gatherings such as love feasts, also involving "times of prayer, praise, thanksgivings, and testimonies."[100]

Proclamation within society meetings included preaching, exhortation, and instruction, all aimed at enabling persons to grow spiritually. The majority of the hearers were those who were awakened and seeking justification; the remainder were on the path of sanctification and were seeking Christian perfection. Proclamation needed to address these various needs, and instruction in particular provided spiritual direction for those at different places along the way of salvation.[101] That said, proclamation in societies was especially important for the awakened (or even partially awakened: "Methodist societies were the place where people encountered the work of the Spirit calling them to faith in Christ and to repent of their sins if they had not done so previously").[102]

The third forum were the small groups of Methodism, most centrally the *class meetings*. From 1743 on all Methodists were required to be members of a class. In addition, there were other small groups, most notably the bands for those who had experienced justification and a new birth and were growing in sanctification. While field preaching and society meetings were public forums for proclamation, class and band meetings and visitation were more private occasions for proclamation.[103]

---

96. Jackson, *Offering Christ*, 94.
97. Jackson, *Offering Christ*, 94.
98. Jackson, *Offering Christ*, 105–10.
99. Jackson, *Offering Christ*, 111.
100. Jackson, *Offering Christ*, 112.
101. Jackson, *Offering Christ*, 114–17.
102. Jackson, *Offering Christ*, 118.
103. Jackson, *Offering Christ*, 124.

Band meetings were "a place of mutual encouragement in the pursuit of a holy life." Preaching was rare in band meetings, although exhortation and instruction were used as needed.[104] Much more frequent were testimonies, in which persons by "sharing their own experience encouraged others in a band to mature in their faith." Because testimonies were centered in personal experience (in contrast to teaching, exhortation, and preaching), Jackson does not consider them proclamation. This does not diminish their importance for early Methodists, however.[105]

Proclamation was central to class meetings, most especially instruction and exhortation. Class meetings met weekly and were structured so that each person was asked to share how they had done in keeping the General Rules since the last meeting, as well as the state of their souls. Thus the "meetings were much more conversational and personal than society meetings or field preaching could ever be."[106] Given the ability to know the class members personally, the leader could then provide advice, instruction, and exhortation tailored to their individual needs.[107] The class meeting was also the place where the leader could reinforce the content of preaching in the fields and at the society meetings.[108]

As a result of proclamation in the class meetings, many persons experienced conversion. Wesley's "Methodists took on average two and a half years to ponder and struggle with their faith before responding to the story of God in Christ with repentance and faith."[109] Class meetings with their personalized instruction and exhortation were critical to that process. In addition, the proclamation and testimonies in the class meetings made the meetings a means of grace for those growing in sanctification as well.[110]

Perhaps the most significant contribution of Jackson to a Wesleyan understanding of evangelism is his recovery of the importance of house-to-house *visitation*, the fourth forum. He argues that for Wesley visitation was the "bedrock" of Methodist ministry.[111] Wesley was certainly an avid advocate of its benefits.

104. Jackson, *Offering Christ*, 133.
105. Jackson, *Offering Christ*, 134.
106. Jackson, *Offering Christ*, 141.
107. Jackson, *Offering Christ*, 147–48.
108. Jackson, *Offering Christ*, 149.
109. Jackson, *Offering Christ*, 152.
110. Jackson, *Offering Christ*, 153–54.
111. Jackson, *Offering Christ*, 158.

Part Five: Learning from Tradition

"The point of visitation," as Jackson describes it, "was for the visitor to converse about a Methodist's deep joys, doubts, and struggles, namely, to have a spiritual conversation that would be difficult, if not impossible, in the larger gatherings." It is through such an examination that a leader could assist a person's growth in spiritual maturity.[112] The personal nature of this conversation was essential to its purpose. Even when a visit began with speaking with a family together, Wesley encouraged the movement to private conversations with each member separately.[113] While the result of these conversations might involve "redirecting those who erred to the right path," Wesley insisted that "the leader was to give directions in love," always encouraging persons in a gentle spirit.[114]

Visitation was suffused with all forms of proclamation, including "exhortation, instruction, teaching, and even preaching."[115] Among the goals of this more personal proclamation was "teaching the basics of the Christian faith,"[116] enabling spiritual growth, and encouraging regular practices of prayer and devotional reading of Scripture for both the family at large and each person in it.[117]

Having examined Wesley's multilayered practices of proclamation, Jackson concludes that, "For Wesley, proclamation is no superficial or optional activity; it is the glue that binds together field preaching, society meetings, and visitation—and as such is integral to any accurate understanding of John Wesley's evangelistic vision." Evangelism as Wesley understood it is "a dynamic partnership between the proclaimer, the word, and the Spirit that is operative throughout every human life whether a person is a Christian or not and whether a person has encountered that grace for the first time or for the thousandth time."[118] It is the "story of God in Christ" that truly changes lives,[119] and Wesley was committed to persons hearing that story from the fields to family gatherings, and all along the way of salvation.

112. Jackson, *Offering Christ*, 169.
113. Jackson, *Offering Christ*, 171.
114. Jackson, *Offering Christ*, 172.
115. Jackson, *Offering Christ*, 174.
116. Jackson, *Offering Christ*, 174.
117. Jackson, *Offering Christ*, 175.
118. Jackson, *Offering Christ*, 184.
119. Jackson, *Offering Christ*, 185.

An Evangelism of Love

Evangelism in the Wesleyan tradition is at its heart about love: God's love for us in Jesus Christ, and God's desire to enable us to love as God loves. The good news is that we are loved and can become persons who, in response to that love, can wholeheartedly love God and our neighbor.

The goal of evangelism, then, is not forgiveness of sins (as important as that is) but to invite us to journey in sanctification. Sanctification itself has a goal, Christian perfection, which does not mean being faultless or without error, but for our motives, desires, and disposition to be fully governed by love. This goal of Christian perfection has not been discussed earlier in this chapter except in passing, but perhaps should have been as it was at the heart of Wesley's understanding of salvation. Evangelism, if Wesleyan, must hold to this vision of perfect love as a promise of God for all persons.

The recipients of the good news were found both outside and inside the church. There were multitudes of persons who were in effect marginalized by the church who would never hear the gospel unless it was brought to them. There were large numbers of persons in the church who were at best nominal Christians. The criteria for needing to hear the gospel was not whether one attended church or was baptized, but whether one was either seeking or growing in the new life in Christ.

Apart from field preaching, the context of evangelism was communal. Most Methodists first belonged to and participated in society and class meetings before coming to faith, and all Methodists participated in community for growth in sanctification. With community came spiritual disciplines, and evangelism involved initiating persons into these practices.

The power of evangelism is the Holy Spirit, who awakens, converts, and transforms human lives, and who inspires and guides those who evangelize. Conversion is wholly a work of God, who is the primary agent in evangelism.

The content of evangelism is the love of God in Jesus Christ. Wesley never tired of proclaiming that love and aiding persons in embodying that love in the present until the reign of God's love comes in fullness.

CHAPTER 12

Evangelism in a Religiously Pluralistic World

> Recognizing the cultural situatedness of all knowledge can foster humility as we dialogue with others.... At the same time, convictions about the truth of Christianity need not be compromised but can be the secure center of the focus and meaning of the church.
>
> —FRANCES S. ADENEY[1]

THE QUESTION OF THE relationship of Christianity to other religions is as old as the New Testament. There the concern was twofold: how is Christianity to be practiced in light of its roots in Judaism, and how does it engage with the assumptions and practices of the religions of the gentiles which pervade the culture?

The missionary movements of the last five centuries have raised the question of other religions as one of method. "The primary issue," says William Abraham, is "how far the evangelist should go to accommodate the beliefs and customs of the evangelized." But beginning in the twentieth century "the issues cut much deeper," now not only "about strategy but fundamental questions about the legitimacy of the ministry of evangelism itself."[2] Paul Rajashekar frames the question more positively: "How can

---
1. Adeney, *Graceful Evangelism*, 144.
2. Abraham, *Logic of Evangelism*, 209.

Christians authentically profess their faith in the midst of other faiths while acknowledging the values of other faiths and beliefs?"[3]

Four of the writers we have examined have sought to provide answers to these questions. Their distinctive approaches provide insight into the theology and practices of evangelism amid religious diversity.

William J. Abraham: The Generosity of a High Christology

In addressing what Abraham calls the "wider ecumenism" he argues for what might seem to be a counterintuitive thesis: "that a classical or high Christology mandates both an openness to other religious traditions and a responsible ministry of evangelism on a worldwide scale." He notes that Christians have consistently "claimed that the only way to God is through Jesus,"[4] a scandalous claim but one "many Christians cling to ferociously."[5] So how can such a high Christology mandate an openness to other religions?

Some Christians have concluded it cannot and have revisionist Christologies that challenge this "internal logic of the classical Christian tradition." It leads to "a reworking of the concept of revelation," a "rejection of divine intervention in the world," and rejection as well of classic Christological and Trinitarian doctrine.[6] For Abraham this is abandoning Christianity itself.

Abraham's examination of the implications of a high Christology begins with noting that "the activity of Christ," though crucially related to the life and death of Jesus, is not limited to that. "Jesus is the incarnate embodiment of the cosmic Christ who is at work enlightening all people (John 1:9)." This recognition of the universal work of Christ means "that it is perfectly consistent to hold both that Jesus is the exclusive path to God and that people may genuinely encounter God outside the Christian church without explicitly knowing about Jesus of Nazareth."[7] Abraham, the patriarch of Israel, for example, was "saved without knowing about Jesus." Yet this does not mean "one is saved apart from the activity of God's Son," for "the eternal Son who is fully manifest in Jesus of Nazareth is actively at work

---

3. Bliese and Van Gelder, *Evangelizing Church*, 96.
4. Abraham, *Logic of Evangelism*, 212.
5. Abraham, *Logic of Evangelism*, 213.
6. Abraham, *Logic of Evangelism*, 217.
7. Abraham, *Logic of Evangelism*, 219.

Part Five: Learning from Tradition

in all creation and history."[8] So if one can be saved without knowing about Jesus, and Christ is active in all creation, "then it is reasonable to infer that people outside the biblical traditions may also be saved and acquitted." In this way "a high Christology creates space for openness and generosity to other religious traditions."[9]

One further comment by Abraham needs additional nuance. He says, as a result of this Christology, "the church should be seen not so much as the ark of salvation but as the locus of witness to and experience of the fullness of the work of Christ, which is made manifest in Jesus of Nazareth."[10] If by salvation he means forgiveness of sins and eternal life with God, which seems to be his meaning, then what Abraham says here makes sense. But if salvation is defined as a new life in Christ, having the mind that was in Christ, becoming new creations, then it is hard to see salvation understood in that way occurring outside the church. This understanding of salvation as new life seems to be what Abraham means by "the fullness of the work of Christ."[11]

The promise of new life is why evangelism remains necessary even if persons can respond to Christ without knowing Christ. Abraham argues "that it is vitally important that everyone know of the fullness of what God has done in Christ," through whom "God has acted not exclusively but uniquely." In addition, he believes those who have "responded to the light of God that they have received outside the gospel should know of the true source of that light." Finally, "they should also have access of the full measure of God's grace and power" in Jesus Christ and be fully initiated into the kingdom.[12]

Abraham strongly emphasizes the finality of Jesus Christ, that is, Jesus as the unique revelation of God. Does such a position necessarily lead to intolerance?[13] Abraham addresses this by examining the nature of interreligious dialogue. That Christians "will disagree with adherents of other religions" is simply logical.[14] But that is the nature of dialogue. True "dialogue requires a frank exchange of convictions, and mature believers of

8. Abraham, *Logic of Evangelism*, 220.
9. Abraham, *Logic of Evangelism*, 220.
10. Abraham, *Logic of Evangelism*, 220.
11. Abraham, *Logic of Evangelism*, 220.
12. Abraham, *Logic of Evangelism*, 221.
13. Abraham, *Logic of Evangelism*, 225–26.
14. Abraham, *Logic of Evangelism*, 226.

incompatible traditions will take deep disagreement on fundamental issues in their stride." What is essential is for those engaged in dialogue "to respect the religious beliefs and practices of others."[15] Abraham rejects the attempts of some proponents of dialogue "to play down as secondary or insignificant those beliefs that are at the core of the great religious traditions." This Abraham sees as itself "a form of intolerance."[16]

Dialogue is distinct from evangelism in its intention and is really just another word for conversation. As such, it is also different "from debate and negotiation."[17] Dialogue cannot be genuine if it is "used as a covert form of evangelism," but at the same time there is no reason persons committed to evangelism cannot "engage in dialogue with integrity."[18] Their understanding of their faith is an asset in presenting it, and their passionate commitment to that faith should enable them to understand "the same in others."[19]

Paul Rajashekar: *Simuls* and *Solas*

Paul Rajashekar is part of the Lutheran consortium of theologians whose proposals for evangelism we examined in chapter 10. In the chapter of their book in which he is the primary author Rajashekar offers a distinctly Lutheran perspective on evangelism amid a plurality of religions.

"Christian evangelizing," he says, "presupposes a fundamental commitment to Jesus Christ as Lord and Savior of the world." But given the religious plurality we now experience, this "has become a contested claim," indeed often seen as "arrogant" or "fanatical."[20] While some seek to keep their faith to themselves for fear of offending others, we do not all live in religious silos. The religious pluralism we experience is "dynamic" in that "we encounter continual interaction between people of different faiths. In this context of *dynamic plurality*, each faith is now forced to articulate its distinctiveness and rationale within the same public sphere it shares with others."[21] How, then, can we do this while still respecting the faith of others?

---

15. Abraham, *Logic of Evangelism*, 227.
16. Abraham, *Logic of Evangelism*, 227.
17. Abraham, *Logic of Evangelism*, 227–28.
18. Abraham, *Logic of Evangelism*, 228.
19. Abraham, *Logic of Evangelism*, 229.
20. Bliese and Van Gelder, *Evangelizing Church*, 95.
21. Bliese and Van Gelder, *Evangelizing Church*, 96.

Part Five: Learning from Tradition

Rajashekar notes that Christians find in Scripture a mandate to evangelize the world. These texts, when combined with the exclusive claims made for Jesus in John 14:6 and Acts 4:12, have led Christians "to draw negative conclusions about the faith of another." Rajashekar challenges the common interpretation of these verses. He argues the verse in John is a call for Jesus' disciples to follow the way of the cross and "is not intended as a universal statement denouncing any other way to God the Father."[22] The verse in Acts, he says, is better interpreted as saying there is no other name but that of Jesus by which we may be healed. These are not texts of "comparative religion" but when "read in their context offer a profound testimony and *positive witness* to the reality of Jesus Christ."[23]

With this scriptural interpretation as background, Rajashekar then proposes his understanding of evangelism and other religions through two central elements of Lutheran theology: the *solas* and the *simuls*. The *solas* underscore the exclusivism of Christianity: Christ alone, grace alone, faith alone, Scripture alone.[24] It was these claims that Lutherans made over against Roman Catholicism and are by their very nature exclusive. "Christ alone," for example, does not refer to a "Cosmic Christ" or "universal logos" but to the very particular Jesus Christ of Scripture who reveals God. This "Lutheran way of interpreting Christ is invariably tied to *faith* in Christ, which in turn comes by hearing the word (*ex auditu*)." That word is not simply "the words of Scripture, but a word of promise that points to *grace alone*," which "refer back to what God has done in and through *Christ alone*." This use of the "*solas* appears to draw a rigid boundary between believers and outsiders."[25]

But this exclusivism is balanced by an inclusivism found in the Lutheran "dialectic of law and gospel." Because God has created the world, "all people have some knowledge of God and God's law." Christians can therefore interact with and appreciate the "social and moral contributions" of others.[26] While the realm of creation has moral values, it does not for Lutherans have "*salvific values*." These come only through "the redemptive work of God in Jesus Christ." Lutherans then can say "yes" on one hand to other religions, but must also on the other say "no" due to their lack of

22. Bliese and Van Gelder, *Evangelizing Church*, 97.
23. Bliese and Van Gelder, *Evangelizing Church*, 98.
24. Bliese and Van Gelder, *Evangelizing Church*, 98.
25. Bliese and Van Gelder, *Evangelizing Church*, 99.
26. Bliese and Van Gelder, *Evangelizing Church*, 99–100.

the gospel.[27] Even given this inclusivism, it seems as if dialogue with other religions is limited at best.

This is where Rajashekar lifts up the importance of the *simul* (meaning "simultaneously") in Lutheran theology. We see the *simuls* at work in such affirmations as God is both "hidden and revealed," Christ is both "human and divine," God saves through both "law and gospel," and a Christian is both "saint and sinner." The *simuls*, he argues, "free us to affirm the reality of God's grace and truth in the world, wherever they may be found." They "recognize God is at work in both the law mode and the gospel mode." Because God acts in love throughout creation, "God's love finds expression also among people of other faiths." At the same time, the *solas* remain critical for dialogue, for otherwise "our conversations with people would become ambiguous and lack any particular religious commitment."[28]

This account of the *solas* and *simuls* reflects an unresolvable tension in Scripture. The *simuls* affirm "God's love is *universal* and embraces all people, whether they acknowledge it or not." Thus, it is incorrect to speak of "unreached" people. Yet God is committed "to humanity through the *particular love* demonstrated in the cross and resurrection of Jesus Christ." Christians are called to make a "positive witness" to that particular love while at the same time remaining respectful of the faith of others.[29] Conversion of others is the work of the Holy Spirit, not us; we are to share the gospel we have received as we listen and learn from what others believe.[30]

Scott J. Jones: God's Universal Love

Scott Jones develops a more Wesleyan approach to addressing the role of evangelism within a plurality of religions. As we have seen, God's love is at the heart of his theology of evangelism, governing its "motivation, goal, and method."[31] He agrees with Abraham that commitment to the finality of Christ does not necessarily lead to intolerance, and then strengthens Abraham's argument with his theology of evangelistic love: "If evangelism

---

27. Bliese and Van Gelder, *Evangelizing Church*, 100.
28. Bliese and Van Gelder, *Evangelizing Church*, 101.
29. Bliese and Van Gelder, *Evangelizing Church*, 102.
30. Bliese and Van Gelder, *Evangelizing Church*, 103.
31. Jones, *Evangelistic Love*, 162.

is based primarily on God's universal love for all humanity, it surely follows that such love includes respect for others' beliefs and practices."[32]

Jones identifies a tension within Scripture between God's universal love and the affirmation of Jesus Christ as the way of salvation. On one hand, he notes, verses like John 1:19 and Col 1:19–20 point to universal prevenient grace. This is reinforced by other passages in Acts 14 and 17 that clearly proclaim "that God has reached out to other nations with a measure of knowledge about God."[33] On the other hand John 14:6 and Acts 4:12 both state that salvation is only through Jesus Christ. (Here Jones endorses the traditional interpretation of these verses, in contrast to what we saw in Rajashekar.)

In his reflection on this tension, Jones offers five theses, which I have condensed into two. First, God loves and "is at work among non-Christians," such that "Non-Christians may be saved by Christ without explicitly confessing Christ as Savior."[34] Prevenient grace is saving grace, and the eternal destiny of a person who has not heard the gospel "will presumably be judged on the basis of how God's grace came to that person and the degree of faith with which he or she responded." With regard to other religions, from the Christian perspective "they cannot be judged as completely true," but neither are they completely false.[35] Some aspects of other religions, along with secular culture, "are either neutral with respect to the gospel or are ways in which God has prepared the way for the gospel to be heard." In fact, Jones argues, "other religions are sometimes means of God's grace."[36]

Second, Christians should love non-Christians, and that love entails among other things evangelizing them. Loving others "is a complex task that includes getting to know them and coming to understand their culture, their history, and their needs." It may involve concrete actions to meet human needs or to join with them in the pursuit of justice.[37] "But," says Jones, "the doctrine of the finality of Christ means that all persons would also benefit from an explicit relationship with Jesus Christ as Lord and Savior." While we cannot judge the "condition before God" of persons in other religions we can be confident that for most "their relationship to God will be

---

32. Jones, *Evangelistic Love*, 163.
33. Jones, *Evangelistic Love*, 165.
34. Jones, *Evangelistic Love*, 166–67.
35. Jones, *Evangelistic Love*, 167.
36. Jones, *Evangelistic Love*, 168.
37. Jones, *Evangelistic Love*, 169–70.

improved by entering into Christian discipleship."[38] Jones summarizes his view in this way:

> The reason for evangelizing persons from other religions is that Christianity offers the grace of God in ways that Christians should understand to be more true, more complete, more helpful than the ways that grace is made available in any other religion. Thus, all other things being equal, for a person to believe in Christ as Lord and Savior is an advantage for their salvation.[39]

Jones acknowledges that Christianity's relation to Judaism is distinct from its relations to other religions because of Christianity's dependence on Judaism. Drawing on the work of Ellen Charry, Jones notes that, unlike the baptism of gentiles which brings them into "the household of God," Jews already belong to that household. A baptized Jew enters the body of Christ but still worships the same God. Yet along with this continuity there is a dramatic change, for now the Jew who has become a Christian knows God not only as coming to us but becoming one of us, and the depth of God's love in the cross of Jesus Christ.[40] That said, organized evangelism aimed at Jews is inappropriate due to the damaged relations caused by centuries of Christian persecution of Jews.[41] But Jones also insists, with Paul in the New Testament, that the good news of Jesus Christ is for Jews as well as non-Jews, and "when loving and sensitive conversations and actions with individuals result in genuine evangelistic opportunities" with Jews, Christians should pursue them.[42]

Jones argues that persons of other non-Jewish religions also need to hear the good news of Jesus Christ. Consistent with what he has already said, he affirms that

> all human beings are also God's creatures, made in the image of God, and persons for whom Christ died. They are recipients of divine grace and in some measure enlightened by Christ before the first human evangelist ever approaches them.[43]

---

38. Jones, *Evangelistic Love*, 170.
39. Jones, *Evangelistic Love*, 173.
40. Jones, *Evangelistic Love*, 173–74.
41. Jones, *Evangelistic Love*, 176.
42. Jones, *Evangelistic Love*, 177.
43. Jones, *Evangelistic Love*, 178.

Part Five: Learning from Tradition

Given this, we are called to love adherents of other religions, and to engage with evangelism in relationships "of mutual trust and concern."[44] We need to also be aware that there has often been a history of negative Christian perceptions against other religions in addition to cultural differences that calls for awareness and sensitivity.[45]

One way we learn about other religions is through interreligious dialogue. To enter into dialogue with respect and a desire to learn is itself a manifestation of love for others. "Dialogue," says Jones, "enables Christians to discover what God has done in other cultures." At the same time it provides Christians the opportunity to share their faith in-depth.[46] For this reason, Jones, unlike Abraham, considers dialogue as itself evangelistic in that all partners in an interreligious dialogue are sharing their faith with others, seeking greater understanding but also hoping for the conversion of others. Yet it is also the case "that encounters with other religions can cause Christians to understand their own faith more deeply and to rediscover aspects of their tradition that have been forgotten."[47]

Bryan Stone: Grace and Deep Pluralism

For Bryan Stone, the concept of "pluralism" is problematic. There are many pluralities, including religious plurality. But "pluralism is *the story we tell about plurality*—the way we construct its meaning, evaluate it, and habituate our practices, institutions, and social patterns within plurality."[48] In other words, pluralism is a construct that attempts to unify disparate phenomena.

This is especially the case with the word *religion*. The assumption is that the various "religions" are all "examples of the same kind of thing."[49] Religious pluralists "claim that all religions are oriented in some way or another toward the same religious object or end."[50] Although they claim a neutral stance, Stone argues that what the religious pluralists are doing is

44. Jones, *Evangelistic Love*, 178.
45. Jones, *Evangelistic Love*, 178–79.
46. Jones, *Evangelistic Love*, 180–81.
47. Jones, *Evangelistic Love*, 182.
48. Stone, *Evangelism After Pluralism*, 10; see also his discussion in *Evangelism After Christendom*, 156–62.
49. Stone, *Evangelism After Pluralism*, 11.
50. Stone, *Evangelism After Pluralism*, 107.

actually a form of Western colonialism, imposing commonalities on the various religions while minimizing their distinctiveness.[51]

In contrast to this is what Stone calls "deep pluralism," which holds that the various religions actually aim at different "salvations," and therefore "in important ways it is wrong to treat religions as all doing essentially the same thing. . . . Because of the unique cultural, linguistic, and practical contexts in which they have developed and in which they are imbedded," religions "are in many respects incommensurable with each other."[52]

The understanding of evangelism which Stone advocates is compatible with this deep pluralism. In contrast to both religious pluralists and the absolutism of exclusivist forms of evangelism, Stone promotes an evangelism that results in "the kind of mutual transformation for which those practicing Christian evangelism rightly seek as they share their faith and hope with others and as they also seek forgiveness and open themselves to judgment and correction."[53] His is an evangelism that combines sharing and listening, and confidence in the gospel with humility as we stand "in the presence of other religious traditions."[54]

Stone draws heavily from John Wesley's teaching on universal prevenient grace to argue that God is at work in all persons and cultures, and in other religions. While the universality of this grace "does indeed project a unity onto pluralism," it does so in a way that "embraces difference; and accepts plurality without seeking to conquer it by a prior epistemological unity and the evangelistic apologetics that flow from it."[55]

That God's grace is universally at work "should lead us to suspect— and to embrace—the plurality that we find in diverse religious traditions." Our first response to another religion should not be to find it deficient but to recognize that it is different.[56] Thus Stone believes that

> Christians have every reason to stand humbly in the presence of other faith traditions, encountering them on their own terms as much as possible and engaging their adherents in an ad hoc manner that presupposes the historicity, particularity, and distinctiveness of each tradition. . . . Christians offering the good news to

---

51. Stone, *Evangelism After Pluralism*, 108.
52. Stone, *Evangelism After Pluralism*, 111.
53. Stone, *Evangelism After Pluralism*, 112.
54. Stone, *Evangelism After Pluralism*, 114.
55. Stone, *Evangelism After Pluralism*, 112.
56. Stone, *Evangelism After Pluralism*, 114.

> others possess no indubitable foundations in human experience or grand metaphysical schemes on the basis of which they can clinch the universal superiority of that news as good, saving, or true. They have only the particular story they have been given, the particular savior to whom that story points, and the particular community that attempts to embody and enact his good news.[57]

That God is "at work in the lives of non-Christians" does not mean other religions are essentially the same as Christianity. They may in fact be radically different. What is necessary "is both a willingness to bear faithful witness to Christ and a genuine openness to the non-Christians," even to the point of ourselves being corrected.[58]

Humble Evangelism

For all their differences, these four approaches have in common a deep appreciation of other religions and a commitment to honor the distinctiveness of each. They resist attempts to minimize or relativize their central beliefs and practices in a misguided attempt to reduce the differences between them. Instead, they view sharing the distinctiveness of each as necessary for genuine interreligious dialogue and are convinced Christians can learn much from other religions.

Underlying this is the conviction that God is at work among all persons, cultures, and religions. This not only means we can discover aspects of God's activity in other religions but the final destiny of many of their adherents will be with God.

This does not, however, negate the necessity of evangelism. The finality and uniqueness of Jesus Christ that is central to Christian belief and practice is fully affirmed, and salvation understood as the new life promised by the gospel can only be attained in this life through encountering the good news of Jesus Christ. The good news that hearts and lives can be transformed and we can in the present enter into the reign of God must be shared with all, with confidence but also with humility.

---

57. Stone, *Evangelism After Pluralism*, 114–15.
58. Stone, *Evangelism After Pluralism*, 115.

Conclusion

> We do not draw people to Christ by loudly discrediting what
> they believe, by telling them how wrong they are and how
> right we are, but by showing them a light that is so lovely that
> they want with all their hearts to know the source of it.
>
> —MADELINE L'ENGLE[1]

WE ARE NOW AT the end of our survey of theologies of evangelism, both explicit and implicit. They represent a wide array of approaches and often disagree with one another in their definitions of evangelism. Yet for all of their diversity these newer theologies of evangelism share many common themes. These are not all found in every one of them, nor are they emphasized to the same degree in each. But taken together they show the theological concerns that distinguish their understandings of evangelism from what was widely assumed in the nineteenth century and all but the closing decades of the twentieth.

Perhaps their most notable theological commitment is their confidence in the work of God in the world. We see this in their emphasis on the mission of God and in the varied ways they link evangelism to that mission. God is at work, and we are called to be the Spirit-enabled participants with God in the *missio Dei*. This means God is the primary evangelist and that the Holy Spirit guides and empowers those who do evangelism. The Holy Spirit is also the one who converts people—our role is to share good news through words and actions. As a result of this commitment to divine

---

1. L'Engle, *Walking*, 172.

Conclusion

initiative these new approaches to evangelism de-emphasize technique and place a heavy emphasis on prayer.

This underscores the importance of relationality, both with God and with others. Our very ability to evangelize wisely and well is dependent on our relationship with and reliance upon God. In sharing the good news with others there is an aversion to memorized formulas for what to say and greater sensitivity to particular people and their contexts. Evangelism is as much about listening as speaking; it is about what we do as much as what we say.

The confidence that God is already at work reduces the evangelistic urgency that if we do not reach people with the good news and elicit an immediate response, they are necessarily doomed to an eternity apart from God. It opens the possibility of evangelism conceived as occurring within a caring relationship over time, which for some of our authors occurs one on one or within groups and for others within the Christian community in which belonging leads to belief.

What this belief that God is already at work does not do is reduce their commitment to the radical particularity of the good news. That God's acts of redemption are centered on Israel as a particular people and ultimately on the incarnation in a particular person, Jesus of Nazareth, and that this Jesus who was crucified and risen is Lord and Savior of all, is the nonnegotiable core of the good news for all of them. The God at work in the world and every human life is the triune God, and therefore everyone, knowingly or unknowingly, is encountering Jesus Christ. What the good news brings is the story of what God has done in the life, death, and resurrection of Jesus, identifying who this God is.

This good news brings the promise of new life in Jesus Christ. It is not only about life after death but life in the present; it is not only about forgiveness of sins (as crucial as that is) but a transformation of the heart and life. It is the promise of new meaning and purpose, healed relationships, and a life governed by faith, hope, and love. One cannot have this new life apart from encountering the good news of Jesus Christ.

This is why so many of these authors link evangelism to Christian formation. Making a decision ("accepting Christ") is not enough; the Christian life is something that is entered into, a journey more than a destination. The danger they seek to avoid is a nominal Christianity, and the recognition that nominal Christianity is common if not prevalent leads many of our authors to speak of evangelizing the church.

Conclusion

Although central, for most of these authors the good news is not solely about human salvation. It is after all the good news of the kingdom of God. Evangelism is announcing and for many demonstrating the reign of God, as well as inviting persons to enter into the kingdom. In contrast to forms of evangelism that ask people if they are ready for the return of Jesus, the view of these theologies of evangelism is that the life of the age to come is already being manifested in the present through the Holy Spirit, and both persons and Christian communities can become embodiments of the reign of God.

The emphasis on Christian formation and the presence of the kingdom is inextricably linked to the importance of the church. Evangelism in these approaches is not individualistic in its practice but communal. Persons are seen as always embedded in communities and shaped by the stories and practices of those communities. The church as the Christian community is the locus of both evangelism and Christian formation, and in its own life and outreach is itself a witness to the gospel.

Evangelism is shaped by God's love. Love is the motive of evangelism, and its goal is for persons to encounter God's love in Jesus Christ, to be transformed by that love, and then to live it out both within and outside the Christian community. The focus of evangelism is not on escaping eternal damnation but on the promise of a new life that enables us to mirror God's love in the world. The good news is good because it announces the victory of God's love in Jesus Christ.

Bibliography

Abraham, William J. *The Logic of Evangelism*. Nashville: Abingdon, 1989.
Adeney, Frances S. *Graceful Evangelism: Christian Witness in a Complex World*. Grand Rapids: Baker, 2010.
Arias, Mortimer. *Announcing the Reign of God: Evangelization and the Subversive Memory of Jesus*. Philadelphia: Fortress, 1984.
Arias, Mortimer, and Alan Johnson. *The Great Commission: Biblical Models for Evangelism*. Nashville: Abingdon, 1992.
Arn, W. Charles. "Evangelism or Disciple Making?" In *Church Growth: State of the Art*, edited by C. Peter Wagner, 57–67. Wheaton, IL: Tyndale, 1989.
Barrett, David B. *Evangelize! A Historical Survey of the Concept*. Birmingham, AL: New Hope, 1987.
Barth, Karl. *Church Dogmatics*. II/2: *The Doctrine of God*. Edited by G. W. Bromiley and T. F. Torrance. Translated by G. W. Bromiley et al. Edinburgh: T&T Clark, 1957.
Bell, Skip. "What Is Wrong with the Homogeneous Unit Principle? The HUP in the 21st Century Church." *Journal of the American Society for Church Growth* 14:3 (2003) 3–17.
Benedict, Daniel T., Jr. *Come to the Waters: Baptism and Our Ministry of Welcoming Seekers and Making Disciples*. Nashville: Discipleship Resources, 1996.
Bliese, Richard H., and Craig Van Gelder, eds. *The Evangelizing Church: A Lutheran Contribution*. Minneapolis: Augsburg Fortress, 2005.
Bosch, David J. *Transforming Mission: Paradigm Shifts in Theology of Mission*. Maryknoll, NY: Orbis, 1991.
Coalter, Milton J., and Virgil Cruz, eds. *How Shall We Witness? Faithful Evangelism in a Reformed Tradition*. Louisville: Westminster John Knox, 1995.
Conklin-Miller, Jeffrey A. *Leaning Both Ways at Once: Methodist Evangelistic Mission at the Intersection of Church and World*. Eugene, OR: Pickwick, 2020.
Costas, Orlando E. *Liberating News: A Theology of Contextual Evangelization*. Grand Rapids: Eerdmans, 1989.
Dean, Kenda Creasy. *Almost Christian: What the Faith of Our Teenagers Is Telling the American Church*. New York: Oxford University Press, 2010.
Escobar, Samuel. "Evangelism and Man's Search for Freedom, Justice and Fulfillment." *World Vision* (September 1974) 16–18.

Bibliography

Fong, Bruce W. *Racial Equality in the Church: A Critique of the Homogeneous Unit Principle in Light of a Practical Theology Perspective*. Lanham, MD: University Press of America, 1996.
Fox, H. Eddie, and George E. Morris. *Faith-Sharing: Dynamic Christian Witnessing by Invitation*. Revised and expanded. Nashville: Discipleship Resources, 1996.
———. *Let the Redeemed of the Lord Say So!* Rev. ed. Franklin, TN: Providence, 1999.
Gehring, Michael J., et al. *The Logic of Evangelism Revisited*. Eugene, OR: Pickwick, 2019.
Green, Michael. *Evangelism Through the Local Church*. Nashville: Oliver-Nelson, 1992.
Guder, Darrell L. *The Continuing Conversion of the Church*. Grand Rapids: Eerdmans, 2000.
Gustafson, David M. *Gospel Witness: Evangelism in Word and Deed*. Grand Rapids: Eerdmans, 2019.
Hardy, Daniel W., and David F. Ford. *Jubilate: Theology in Praise*. London: Darton, Longman, and Todd, 1984.
Hartt, Julian N. *Toward a Theology of Evangelism*. Nashville: Abingdon, 1955.
Heath, Elaine A. *The Mystic Way of Evangelism: A Contemplative Vision for Christian Outreach*. Grand Rapids: Baker, 2008.
Hunter, George G., III. *The Apostolic Congregation: Church Growth Reconceived for a New Generation*. Nashville: Abingdon, 2009.
———. *The Celtic Way of Evangelism: How Christianity Can Reach the West . . . Again*. Nashville: Abingdon, 2000.
———. *Radical Outreach: The Recovery of Apostolic Ministry and Evangelism*. Nashville: Abingdon, 2003.
Jackson, Jack. *Offering Christ: John Wesley's Evangelistic Vision*. Nashville: Kingswood, 2017.
Jones, E. Stanley. *The Unshakable Kingdom and the Unchanging Person*. Potomac, MD: E. Stanley Jones Foundation, 2017.
Jones, Scott J. *The Evangelistic Love of God and Neighbor*. Nashville: Abingdon, 2003.
Kallenberg, Brad J. *Live to Tell: Evangelism for a Postmodern Age*. Grand Rapids: Brazos, 2002.
Keifert, Patrick R. *Welcoming the Stranger: A Public Theology of Worship and Evangelism*. Minneapolis: Fortress, 1992.
Kelley, Dean M. *Why Conservative Churches Are Growing*. New York: Harper and Row, 1972.
Kinsey, Andrew. "Evangelism as Initiation." In *The Logic of Evangelism Revisited*, edited by Michael J. Gehring et al., 44–54. Eugene, OR: Pickwick, 2019.
Klaiber, Walter. *Call and Response: Biblical Foundations of a Theology of Evangelism*. Nashville: Abingdon, 1997.
Knight, Henry H., III. *A Future for Truth: Evangelical Theology in a Postmodern Age*. Nashville: Abingdon, 1997.
Knight, Henry H., III, and F. Douglas Powe Jr. *Transforming Community: The Wesleyan Way to Missional Congregations*. Nashville: Discipleship Resources, 2016.
———. *Transforming Evangelism: The Wesleyan Way of Sharing Faith*. Nashville: Discipleship Resources, 2006.
"The Lausanne Covenant." In *New Directions in Mission and Evangelization*, vol. 1: *Basic Statements*, edited by James A. Scherer and Stephen B. Bevans, 276–80. Maryknoll, NY: Orbis, 1992.

L'Engle, Madeleine. *Walking on Water: Reflections on Faith and Art*. New York: Convergent, 2016.
Lewis, Edwin. *Theology and Evangelism*. Nashville: Tidings, 1952.
Logan, James C. "The Evangelical Imperative: A Wesleyan Perspective." In *Theology and Evangelism in the Wesleyan Heritage*, edited by James C. Logan, 15–33. Nashville: Kingswood, 1994.
McGavran, Donald A., and Winfield C. Arn. *Ten Steps to Church Growth*. New York: Harper and Row, 1977.
McGavran, Donald A., and George G. Hunter III. *Church Growth: Strategies That Work*. Nashville: Abingdon, 1980.
McGavran, Donald A., and C. Peter Wagner. *Understanding Church Growth*. 3rd ed. Grand Rapids: Eerdmans, 1970.
McIntosh, Gary L., ed. *Evaluating the Church Growth Movement: 5 Views*. Grand Rapids: Zondervan, 2004.
McNeil, Brenda Salter. *Becoming Brave: Finding the Courage to Pursue Racial Justice Now*. Grand Rapids: Brazos, 2020.
———. *A Credible Witness: Reflections on Power, Evangelism and Race*. Downers Grove, IL: InterVarsity, 2008.
Murphy, Nancey. *Beyond Liberalism and Fundamentalism: How Modern and Postmodern Philosophy Set the Theological Agenda*. Valley Forge, PA: Trinity, 1996.
Newbigin, Lesslie. *The Gospel in a Pluralist Society*. Grand Rapids: Eerdmans, 1989.
Niles, D. T. *That They May Have Life*. New York: Harper, 1951.
Oden, Amy. "God's Household of Grace: Hospitality in the Early Church." In *Ancient and Postmodern Christianity: Paleo-Orthodoxy in the 21st Century*, edited by Kenneth Tanner and Christopher Hall, 38–48. Downers Grove, IL: InterVarsity, 2002.
Outler, Albert C. *Evangelism and Theology in the Wesleyan Spirit*. Nashville: Discipleship Resources, 1996.
Packer, J. I. *Evangelism and the Sovereignty of God*. Downers Grove: InterVarsity, 1961.
Padilla, C. René. *Mission Between the Times: Essays on the Kingdom*. Grand Rapids: Eerdmans, 1985.
———. "The Unity of the Church and the Homogeneous Unit Principle." *International Bulletin of Missional Research* 6:1 (January 1982) 23–30.
Pannell, William. *Evangelism from the Bottom Up*. Grand Rapids: Zondervan, 1992.
Pickard, Stephen K. *Liberating Evangelism: Gospel Theology and the Dynamics of Communication*. Harrisburg, PA: Trinity, 1999.
Pippert, Rebecca Manley. *Out of the Saltshaker and into the World: Evangelism as a Way of Life*. 20th anniversary ed. Downers Grove, IL: InterVarsity, 1999.
Pope-Levison, Priscilla. "Evangelism in the WCC." In *New Directions in Mission and Evangelization*, vol. 2: *Theological Foundations*, edited by James A. Scherer and Stephen B. Bevans, 126–40. Maryknoll, NY: Orbis, 1994.
———. *Models of Evangelism*. Grand Rapids: Baker, 2020.
Reese, Martha Grace. *Unbinding the Gospel: Real Life Evangelism*. 2nd ed. St. Louis: Chalice, 2008.
Robert, Dana L. *Evangelism as the Heart of Mission*. Nashville: General Board of Global Ministries, 1997.
Salter, Darius. *American Evangelism: Its Theology and Practice*. Grand Rapids: Baker, 1996.
Scherer, James A. *Gospel, Church and Kingdom: Comparative Studies in Mission Theology*. Minneapolis: Augsburg, 1987.

Bibliography

Schreiter, Robert J. "Changes in Roman Catholic Attitudes Toward Proselytism and Mission." In *New Directions in Mission and Evangelization*, vol. 2: *Theological Foundations*, edited by James A. Scherer and Stephen B. Bevans, 113–25. Maryknoll, NY: Orbis, 1994.

Sider, Ronald J. *Good News and Good Works: A Theology for the Whole Gospel*. Grand Rapids: Baker, 1993.

Snyder, Howard A. *Salvation Means Creation Healed: The Ecology of Sin and Grace*. With Joel Scandrett. Eugene, OR: Cascade, 2011.

Stallings, James O. *Telling the Story: Evangelism in Black Churches*. Valley Forge, PA: Judson, 1988.

Stone, Bryan. *Evangelism After Christendom: The Theology and Practice of Christian Witness*. Grand Rapids: Brazos, 2007.

———. *Evangelism After Pluralism: The Ethics of Christian Witness*. Grand Rapids: Baker, 2018.

Teasdale, Mark R. "Extending the Metaphor: Evangelism as the Heart of Mission Twenty-Five Years Later." *Methodist Review* 14 (2022) 49–67.

———. *Participating in Abundant Life: Holistic Salvation for a Secular Age*. Downers Grove, IL: InterVarsity, 2022.

Tyra, Gary. *The Holy Spirit in Mission*. Downers Grove, IL: InterVarsity, 2011.

Vickers, Jason E. *Minding the Good Ground*. Waco, TX: Baylor University Press, 2011.

Wagner, C. Peter. "Donald A. McGavran: A Tribute to the Founder." In *Church Growth: State of the Art*, edited by C. Peter Wagner, 15–19. Wheaton, IL: Tyndale, 1989.

Warner, Laceye C. *Saving Women: Retrieving Evangelistic Theology and Practice*. Waco, TX: Baylor University Press, 2007.

Watson, David. *I Believe in Evangelism*. Grand Raids: Eerdmans, 1976.

Webber, Robert E. *Ancient-Future Evangelism: Making Your Church a Faith-Forming Community*. Grand Rapids: Baker, 2003.

———. *Celebrating Our Faith: Evangelism Through Worship*. New York: Harper and Row, 1986.

———. *Journey to Jesus: The Worship, Evangelism, and Nurture Mission of the Church*. Nashville: Abingdon, 2001.

———. *Liturgical Evangelism*. Fayetteville, NC: Morehouse, 1992.

Wesley, John. *The Appeals to Men of Reason and Religion and Certain Related Letters*. Edited by Gerald B. Cragg. Vol. 11 of *The Works of John Wesley*. Bicentennial ed. Nashville: Abingdon, 1987.

———. *A Collection of Hymns for the Use of the People Called Methodist*. Edited by Franz Hildebrandt and Oliver S. Beckerlegge. Vol. 7 of *The Works of John Wesley*. Bicentennial ed. Nashville: Abingdon, 1983.

———. *Journals and Diaries II (1738–1743)*. Edited by H. Reginald Ward and Richard P. Heitzenrater. Vol. 19 of *The Works of John Wesley*. Bicentennial ed. Nashville: Abingdon, 1990.

———. *Letters II (1740–1755)*. Edited by Frank Baker. Vol. 26 of *The Works of John Wesley*. Bicentennial ed. Nashville: Abingdon, 1982.

———. *The Works of John Wesley, M. A.* Edited by Thomas Jackson. 14 vols. London: Wesleyan Book Room, 1829–31. Reprint, Grand Rapids: Baker, 1978.

Whitworth, David Martin. *Missio Dei and the Means of Grace: A Theology of Participation*. Eugene, OR: Pickwick, 2019.

Willard, Dallas. *The Divine Conspiracy: Rediscovering Our Hidden Life in God.* San Francisco: Harper Collins, 1998.
Wimber, John. *Power Evangelism.* With Kevin Springer. New York: Harper and Row, 1986.
———. *Power Healing.* With Kevin Springer. New York: Harper and Row, 1987.
Wright, N. T. *Simply Good News: Why the Gospel Is News and What Makes It Good.* New York: HarperOne, 2015.
Yung, Hwa. "A 21st Century Reformation: Recover the Supernatural." *Christianity Today* 54:9 (September 2, 2010) 32–33.

www.ingramcontent.com/pod-product-compliance
Lightning Source LLC
Chambersburg PA
CBHW052214240426
43670CB00037B/579